THE BIG 50

SAN FRANCISCO GIANTS

The Men and Moments that Made
the San Francisco Giants

Daniel Brown

TRIUMPH
B O O K S

Library of Congress Cataloging-in-Publication Data

Names: Brown, Daniel, 1969–
Title: The big 50, San Francisco Giants : the men and moments that made the San Francisco Giants / Daniel Brown.
Description: Chicago, Illinois : Triumph Books, 2016.
Identifiers: LCCN 2015043516 | ISBN 9781629372020 (paperback)
Subjects: LCSH: San Francisco Giants (Baseball team)—History. | BISAC: SPORTS & RECREATION / Baseball / General. | TRAVEL / United States / West / Pacific (AK, CA, HI, NV, OR, WA).
Classification: LCC GV875.S34 B76 2016 | DDC 796.357/640979461—dc23 LC record available at http://lccn.loc.gov/2015043516

This book is available in quantity at special discounts for your group or organization. For further information, contact:

Triumph Books LLC
814 North Franklin Street
Chicago, Illinois 60610
(312) 939-3330
www.triumphbooks.com

Printed in U.S.A.
ISBN: 978-1-62937-202-0

Design by Andy Hansen
All photos are courtesy of AP Images.

To my beloved grandmother, Berniece,
who taught me the meaning of Willie McCovey

[Contents]

[Foreword]

by Orlando Cepeda

I love the Bay Area. I love the Giants. I love the people here.

I came up through the organization and played for the Giants from 1958 to 1966. Whenever people ask me, I tell them that the biggest thrill of my life was my first game in the big leagues: April 15, 1958.

Because that's when my dream came true.

I was so proud to be part of the Giants' first game in San Francisco, playing alongside guys like Willie Mays, Jimmy Davenport, Willie Kirkland, and Johnny Antonelli. It meant a lot to me.

We beat the Los Angeles Dodgers 8–0 at Seals Stadium that day. I hit a home run in the fifth inning off Don Bessent. The feeling was amazing. I remember when I rounded second base, Pee Wee Reese—who was my childhood idol—told me, "Orlando, nice going. Congratulations." And that blew my mind. Duke Snider said "Hi" to me before the game. It was incredible.

This book is all about memories like that.

I wanted to be a baseball player because my father, Perucho Cepeda, was a baseball player. He was a legend in Puerto Rico. I saw him play when I was a boy and they said I couldn't compare to him.

Father used to work during the day and play at night. The first pro game that I ever saw was in 1945. My father played with Josh Gibson. He played with Satchel Paige. In fact, Satchel Paige used to come to my house. He was a good friend of my father and my mother. I met Larry Doby and Roy Campanella the same year. I saw so many great Negro League ballplayers.

We had so many great ballplayers in San Francisco, too. And we almost won the 1962 World Series. In Game 7 against the New York Yankees at Candlestick Park, it was 1–0 in the bottom of the ninth inning.

Matty Alou was at third base. Willie Mays was at second. Willie McCovey was coming up and I was on deck.

Felipe Alou was standing right behind me, and I told Felipe, "They're going to walk him." I thought they were going to pitch to me, and I was ready.

How many times in your career are you going to have a chance to go to the plate with three men on base in Game 7 of the World Series against the New York Yankees? How many times does that happen?

So I thought, *I'd better do something.*

When the Yankees decided to let Ralph Terry pitch to McCovey, wow, it blew my mind. And when McCovey hit that ball, I was getting ready to tell Mays to slide when he came to home plate. When I saw the ball leave Willie's bat, I thought it was going to be a base hit.

But Bobby Richardson, their second baseman, caught the ball.

It took a long time, but San Francisco finally got to experience what it feels like to win a World Series. Three parades in five years? It's amazing. It's incredible. Bruce Bochy is a great man and a great manager. He's helped so many ballplayers. He lets everybody play.

San Francisco deserves this. It's a great town. It's a great organization. And Larry Baer, the chief executive officer, is doing a hell of a job.

I love working for the Giants as a community ambassador. So I'd like to say thank you to former owner Bob Lurie and former executive Pat Gallagher, because they're the ones who made it possible for me to work for the Giants.

And Peter Magowan, when he took over as owner, he told me right from the start: "We're going to do everything possible to get you into the Hall of Fame." Bob Lurie, Pat Gallagher, and Peter Magowan all helped me so much.

I remember in my first year back at spring training, they put me out to coach first base for a couple of innings. And the fans gave me a standing ovation. Wherever I go now, today, people come to me and let me know how they feel about me. And that makes me feel wonderful.

Even though I played for the Cardinals and was an MVP there, and even though I had some good years with the Atlanta Braves and Boston Red Sox, this is where I want to be right now.

I am a Giant at heart.

If you're reading this book, that means you're a Giant at heart, too.

—Orlando Cepeda

September 24, 2015

[Acknowledgments]

My grandmother, Berniece Leehan, was born nowhere near Major League Baseball, in Malta, Montana, on March 22, 1920.

She moved to Northern California in 1953, a few years before the Giants did.

A longtime grocery clerk who would often have different games (and different sports!) tuned to radio dials around the house, my grandma was listening to the Giants game on KSFO on July 30, 1959.

That's when Willie McCovey, a shy and strapping Giants rookie from Mobile, Alabama, went 4 for 4 against Robin Roberts—single, triple, single, triple.

I was eight years old when she told me the story for the first time. And with the way she beamed, it was the closest I could get to seeing my grandmother as a young woman. She was delighted all over again.

Like so many other early Giants fans, Berniece Leehan adopted McCovey as her favorite because she was part of it now, there from the very first swing.

I loved the story in part because I could not believe that *her* Willie McCovey from 1959 was the same as *my* Willie McCovey in 1978. (Stretch, who retired in 1980, remains among the handful of players to appear in four decades.)

A baseball bond was formed, between my grandmother and me, not unlike those you can see happening every day among the different generations at AT&T Park. Fans enter the park by walking past statues of McCovey and Willie Mays and walk out with memories of Madison Bumgarner and Buster Posey.

My grandmother died in 1994, 16 years before San Francisco won its first World Series and one year before I began working in the sports department of the *San Jose Mercury News*.

I never got to tell her about interviewing McCovey. Or Juan Marichal. Or Orlando Cepeda. Or any of the other magical names she introduced me to back when I was a little kid in need of a baseball education.

This book, in a way, is trying to do for readers what my grandmother did for me: These are the Giants stories that need to be passed on.

The only outright lie in this book is on the cover: "By Daniel Brown." Writing a book like this takes a village, and I'm forever grateful to those who helped me with everything from the rankings to the editing to keeping me sane(ish).

Above all, a big thanks to the writers past and present who cover the team.

Baseball beat writing is the toughest job in sports journalism. The great joy of doing this book was re-reading the incredible work you produce over 162 ridiculous deadlines a year.

A tip of the cap to some scribes past and present, whose talent makes me jealous every day: Nick Peters, Ron Bergman, Andrew Baggarly, Alex Pavolvic, Chris Haft, Henry Schulman, John Shea, Glenn Schwarz, Joan Ryan, Tim Kawakami, Bud Geracie, Mark Purdy, Carl Steward, Janie McCauley, Larry Stone, Tyler Kepner, Ann Killion, Bruce Jenkins, Scott Ostler, Josh Suchon, Marcos Breton, Chris Shuttlesworth, Mark Gonzalez, Jayson Stark, Grant Brisbee, Steve Bitker, Monte Poole, Tim Brown, Lowell Cohn, Mike Wagaman, Matt Kawahara, Bill Arnold, Steve Kroner, Steve Berman, and Dave Newhouse.

Thank you to Jesse Jordan and Tom Bast, my editors at Triumph Books, for getting this whole thing off the ground in the first place.

Thank you to the wondrous Betsy Towner Levine, my friend and unofficial editor, whose insights and intellect rescued some first drafts from drifting foul. It's a relief as a writer to know I can signal to Towner in the bullpen for the save.

Thank you to Crystal Gariano, a great Giants fan from a family of great Giants fans, who ensured that the book had not just information but heart.

If a chapter fell flat, she let me borrow from her McCovey Cove–sized well of energy.

The Giants' media relations staff does a marvelous job of securing interviews, unearthing statistical gold mines, and being polite to annoying reporters: Thanks to all of you, past and present: Jim Moorehead, Blake Rhodes, Matt Hodson, Maria Jacinto, Bertha Fajardo, Robin Carr, Erwin Higueros, Matt Chisholm, Liam Connolly, and Staci Slaughter.

My panel of Giants experts helped me with the rankings, and would have known exactly where to put Larry Herndon and Mike Benjamin if I'd decided to make a longer list: Brian Murphy, Matt Maiocco, Kevin O'Connor, Steve Pletkin, and Robert Rubino.

To my fellow *San Jose Mercury News* staffers who helped me research stuff from the Giants way-back machine: Leigh Poitinger, Mark Smith, and Darryl Matsuda.

Thank you to Brad Horn and Craig Muder at the Baseball Hall of Fame for unearthing transcripts of old induction speeches, a treasure trove for getting to the heart of what matters in Cooperstown.

As any sports scribe knows, writing about baseball means trying to be like Susan Slusser, the luminous A's beat writer for the *San Francisco Chronicle*. Her professionalism and reputation are tops in the business. I'm so glad I married you, Sluss.

My parents, Dean and Sherrie Brown, took me to my first Giants game, at Candlestick Park, on August 29, 1979. The Cardinals won 5–1 that day before a crowd of 6,099. McCovey went 1 for 4.

Thanks, Mom and Dad. For that, for everything. To this day, when I call home after a memorable Giants assignment, one of us will ask the inevitable question.

"What would Grandma think?"

1

WILLIE MAYS

As a jittery and insecure rookie in 1951, Willie Mays went 0 for 12 before breaking through with a home run against Warren Spahn of the Boston Braves.

"I'll never forgive myself," Spahn later joked. "We might have gotten rid of Willie forever if I'd only struck him out."

Nice try. Mays stuck around to torment pitchers and delight Giants fans for nearly another quarter century.

In fact, he's *still* here, his potent swing forever captured in bronze outside AT&T Park.

The statue in Willie Mays Plaza remains the top meeting spot for fans. So the man himself will serve as our gathering place for this book: meet us at Willie Mays, the portal to all things Giants.

The Say Hey Kid, like the franchise itself, began in New York and moved to San Francisco in 1958. He won a World Series at the Polo Grounds in 1954 and helped them win another one 60 years later by giving hitting tips to outfielder Michael Morse.

"Willie Mays was actually writing something down on

a piece of paper, and all I could think about was saving the piece of paper," Morse said a few days after his pinch-hit homer helped propel San Francisco into the 2014 Fall Classic. "He doesn't miss many games. He'll break down your swing. He'll break down the way you're playing defense.

"It's so amazing how the Giants greats are always around the clubhouse and they always interact with the team now. It's the kind of organization where it's just in the blood. It's in the core."

Here are the things to know about Mays' statistics: he hit 660 home runs, batted .302, stole 338 bases, won 12 Gold Gloves and two MVP awards, and made 24 All-Star teams.

Here is the thing to know about Mays' style:

"He always wore his cap size a little bit larger so it would fly off when he was running," the late Giants pitcher Stu Miller said. "But that's what his idea was—to please the crowd."

The most exhilarating show in baseball history ran from 1951 through 1973. The incandescent center fielder was known as a five-tool player because he could hit for average, hit for power, run, catch, and throw.

But the "five-tool" label actually sells him short. Willie Howard Mays could fill a hardware store.

Another tool: Mays played with boundless joy, as if he were merely playing stickball on the streets of Harlem (which he often did after games at the Polo Grounds). Rival executive Branch Rickey once described Mays' zest as "the frivolity in his bloodstream [that] doubles his strength with laughter."

"I'm not sure what the hell 'charisma' is," Cincinnati Reds first baseman Ted Kluszewski once said, "but I get the feeling it's Willie Mays."

Another tool: smarts.

The Say Hey Kid in spring training 1962, the same year Mays would hit 49 homers while taking the Giants all the way to the World Series.

"Willie Mays was not the fastest guy in baseball, but he was the quickest to react," the late broadcaster Lon Simmons once told me. "Go to a game now and watch how long it takes a runner to react on a wild pitch—there are times when it's practically to the backstop. Willie was gone before that ball passed home plate."

Carl Boles, a backup outfielder for the 1962 Giants, recalled a game at Forbes Field in Pittsburgh when Mays scored on a passed ball that had rolled only a few feet from catcher Don Leppert. No one else would have dared to break home on a ball like that, but Mays bolted as though he knew what was coming.

Boles later approached Mays like a young magician trying to figure out a master's trick.

"Willie, how did you do that?"

"Well, their catcher is a boxer: he doesn't catch anything low, he just knocks it down," Mays replied. "So if you watch the flight of the ball, and it's going to be low, you know he's going to box it." That's why, when Al McBean fired a low pitch into the dirt, Mays needed just a nanosecond to dash for home.

Another tool: trickery.

Tim McCarver, the longtime catcher, said Mays used to intentionally swing and miss at a pitch early in the game because he was already thinking several innings ahead. In his book *Baseball for Brain Surgeons,* McCarver wrote that Mays would make a point of flailing on a pitcher's curveball as a way of enticing the pitcher to throw him another one later in a key situation.

Born on May 6, 1931, in Westfield, Alabama, Mays showed rare athletic gifts almost from the crib. His father, Willie Howard Mays Sr., worked as a railroad porter and also swept floors at the local steel mill, where he was a star on the company baseball team. Willie's mother, Annie Satterwhite, was a standout in both track and basketball.

By the time he was five, Mays would play catch with his father on the farmland near their home. Willie Sr. taught his son each position, starting with catcher, and told him that he could boost his value by honing every skill available to a ballplayer. (Mays' childhood is exquisitely detailed in *Willie Mays: The Life, The Legend*, the 2010 book by James S. Hirsch.)

Mays signed to play for the Birmingham Black Barons of the Negro Leagues in 1948, when he was 17. By June of 1950, scouts

"I'm not sure what the hell 'charisma' is, but I get the feeling it's Willie Mays."

were lining up, none more enthusiastic than Eddie Montague of the New York Giants.

"They got this kid playing center field that's practically barefooted that's the best ballplayer I ever looked at," Montague reported, according to Leo Durocher's book *Nice Guys Finish Last*. "You better send somebody down here with a barrelful of money and grab this kid."

It didn't take a barrelful. Mays got a $4,000 signing bonus and a salary of $250 a month.

The multidimensional outfielder made short work of the minor leagues, starting the 1951 season by batting .477 over 35 games for the Minneapolis Millers of the Triple-A American Association.

Mays was in a movie theater in Sioux City, Iowa, when he learned he was being called up to the big leagues. As Hirsch recounted in his book, between features the house lights went on and the manager shouted into the crowd.

"If Willie Mays is in the audience, would he immediately report to his manager at the hotel?"

Is there a more fitting way for the most theatrical player of all time to get the news?

Mays made his debut on May 25, 1951. He bumbled out of the gate, feeling nervous and overmatched, aside from his home run against Spahn. Herman Franks, one of the Giants coaches at the time, noticed the kid crying in front of his locker after a game and alerted Durocher.

Durocher plopped down next to Mays, who was still disconsolate, and wrapped an arm around his shoulder.

Over the course of a 22-year major league career, Mays had 3,283 hits and batted above .300 in 10 seasons.

"As long as I'm the manager of the Giants, you're my center fielder," Durocher assured him. "Tomorrow, next week, next month. You're here to stay. With your talent, you're going to get plenty of hits."

The next day, Mays drilled a single and blasted a 400-foot triple to right-center field. The prodigy had arrived.

Over the course of a 22-year major league career, Mays had 3,283 hits and batted above .300 in 10 seasons. He had 17 seasons with at least 20 home runs and twice topped the 50 mark.

Mays was the first National League player to reach the 30-30 club (homers and stolen bases), leading the league in stolen bases every season from 1956 to '59.

He won 12 consecutive Gold Gloves, tying Roberto Clemente for the most among outfielders; both might have won more had the award existed before 1957.

Mays remains the Giants' all-time leader in runs, hits, doubles, home runs, and total bases—marks threatened but not surpassed by his godson, Barry Bonds.

"I can't believe Babe Ruth was a better player than Willie Mays," Dodgers pitcher Sandy Koufax once said. "I can't believe he could run as well as Mays, and I can't believe he was a better outfielder."

THE CATCH

In 1954, Willie Mays emerged as baseball's supernova. He won the MVP award for hitting a league-leading .345 with 41 home runs and 110 RBI. That served as prelude for Mays' defining moment, his defensive gem in Game 1 of the '54 World Series against heavily favored Cleveland.

With two runners on and the score tied 2-2 in the top of the eighth, Vic Wertz blasted a ball an estimated 460 feet to center field at the Polo Grounds. Turning his back to home plate, Mays ran toward the wall in a dead sprint, caught the ball over his shoulder, and whirled to deliver a powerful throw back to the infield.

It remains known as The Catch.

"I was very cocky. When I say that, I mean that everything that went in the air, I thought I could catch. I was very aware of what was going on," Mays said during a visit to AT&T Park in 2003. "When the ball was hit off Don Liddle, the pitcher, I'm saying to myself, 'Two men are on.' I'm talking to myself as I'm running—I know it's hard to believe that I could do all this in one sequence.

"As the ball is coming, I'm saying to myself, 'I have to get this ball back into the infield.' In my mind, I never thought I would miss the ball. I didn't think that at all.

"When you watch the play, look at the way I catch the ball. It's like a wide receiver catching a pass going down the sideline, which is over the left shoulder, on the right side. I had learned about that while playing in high school."

"As a batter, his only weakness is a wild pitch," Bill Rigney, the first San Francisco manager said.

"You used to think if the score was 5–0, he'd hit a five-run homer," Reggie Jackson said.

Given Mays' love of showmanship, it should be no surprise that he was twice the All-Star Game MVP, in 1963 and '68. He owns or shares the Mid-Summer Classic records for at-bats (75), extra-base hits (eight), hits (23), runs (20), stolen bases (six), triples (three), and total bases (40).

> **"San Francisco is the damnedest city I ever saw in my life. They cheer Khrushchev and boo Mays."**

"They invented the All-Star Game for Willie Mays," fellow Hall of Famer Ted Williams said.

Strange as it seems in retrospect, Bay Area fans were initially cool to the New York import when the team moved west. It didn't help that Mays arrived in San Francisco publicly reminiscing about his New York days. *The Biographical History of Baseball* notes in that initial season of 1958, Mays hit a career-high .347, with 29 homers and 96 RBI—and still heard boos at Seals Stadium.

At the end of that first season in San Francisco, fans voted Orlando Cepeda the team's most valuable player.

"San Francisco is the damnedest city I ever saw in my life. They cheer Khrushchev and boo Mays," writer Frank Conniff of the Hearst newspapers joked after the city once gave a warmer reception to a visit by Soviet leader Nikita Khruschev.

When the Giants traded Mays to the Mets in May 1972, the outfielder was disappointed at leaving the team but happy to see

New York again: "When you come back to New York, you come back to paradise," he wrote in his 1988 autography *Say Hey*, with writer Lou Sahadi.

But as it turns out, his true Eden was by the Bay all along. Mays returned to San Francisco and signed a lifetime contract with the team in 1993. He remains a lively presence at the ballpark, still boyish into his eighties—the Say Hey Octogenarian.

Today he is as interwoven into the Giants fabric as the orange and black.

On November 24, 2015, Mays was honored at the White House with the Presidential Medal of Freedom. It is the nation's highest civilian award.

"The line I always used to describe him is: 'Willie Mays was the happiest guy in the world to be Willie Mays,'" Simmons once said. "That's what he wanted to be: He wanted to be Willie Mays."

THE 2010 CHAMPIONS

2

To explain the sheer absurdity of it, the absolute zany madness of it, it's best to start at the end: at the victory parade for the 2010 World Series champions. There Aubrey Huff stood at a podium in downtown San Francisco, surrounded by an estimated million people, stuck his hand down his pants, and fished around for a while.

As bemused fans looked on, including mayor Gavin Newsom and a live television audience, Huff searched the inside of his jeans for an awkward eternity before holding aloft a skimpy red undergarment.

"I got a little present for you guys in San Francisco," Huff told the crowd gathered at the city's Civic Center that day. "I'm sure all of you have heard about the Rally Thong."

Like a boxer hoisting a heavyweight championship belt, he lifted the skivvies above his head.

"This thing nailed it!" Huff yelled.

The crowd roared with approval.

Want to know what the Giants' 2010 season was like? It was kind of like that.

"This doesn't make sense," right-hander Matt Cain acknowledged on the night they finished off the Texas Rangers with a 3–1 victory in Game 5 for the Giants' first title since 1954. "You don't realize it. It's something that's surreal. But that's what we are: World Series champs."

To long-suffering fans, winning the 2010 title was as fun as it was cathartic. They had never seen a World Series championship at all, let alone one as surreal as this one.

Like a boxer hoisting a heavyweight championship belt, he lifted the skivvies above his head.

The Giants didn't win it when they had Willie Mays, Willie McCovey, Juan Marichal, Orlando Cepeda, and Gaylord Perry. They didn't win it when they had Will Clark, Kevin Mitchell, Matt Williams, and Robby Thompson. They didn't win it when they had Barry Bonds for 15 record-breaking seasons.

Yet they won it this time with...well, what exactly?

Huff, who led the Giants in wins above replacement and almost every other batting category that season, was a 33-year-old journeyman who'd spent much of his career on last-place teams. Cody Ross had been claimed off waivers from the Florida Marlins on August 22, a back-page transaction for the future National League Championship Series MVP.

When the Giants signed Edgar Renteria, the eventual World Series MVP, before the 2009 season, it looked like desperation. An anonymous NL executive told Henry Schulman of the *San Francisco Chronicle* that Renteria "looked 100 years old."

Ladies and gentlemen, the most important team in San Francisco history!

Of course, they also had a shaggy-haired ace (Tim "The Freak" Lincecum), a closer with a beard like Abraham Lincoln (Brian Wilson), and a baby-faced rookie catcher (Buster Posey).

"This buried a lot of bones—'62, '89, 2002," Giants general manager Brian Sabean said, referring to the team's previous World Series heartbreaks. "This group deserved it, faithful from the beginning. We're proud and humbled by the achievement."

The theme of the remarkable 2010 Giants began with an early season loss: On April 19, David Eckstein hit a walk-off homer against reliever Jeremy Affeldt, giving the San Diego Padres a 3–2 victory in 10 innings.

It was the only home run the 5'7", 170-pound Eckstein hit all season. Broadcaster Duane Kuiper, in summing up the proceedings for the audience said, "Giants baseball.... Torture."

That planted the seed. A few weeks later, on May 15, the Giants carried a 2–1 lead into the ninth inning at AT&T Park. The Houston Astros loaded the bases before it took Brian Wilson a total of 15 agonizing pitches to finish off Kaz Matsui for the final out.

Kuiper said it again.

"Giants baseball." Pause. "Torture."

This time, it stuck. Fans embraced the phrase as the unofficial brand of Giants baseball. It applied to the season. It applied to a half-a-century wait for a World Series victory in San Francisco. Torture signs and torture T-shirts popped up at AT&T Park, as a salute to the team's maddening methods. Of the Giants' 162 regular-season games that season, 115—the most by any team in five years—were decided by three runs or fewer.

"At times it felt like this season lasted five years with all the close games," Affeldt told the *New York Times* that October.

The Giants won the NL West by going 92–70, but they never led by more than 3.0 games, and they trailed by as many as 7.5 (on July 4, no less).

But they rallied back, with a little help from the Rally Thong. Such was the power of Huff's fashion statement, a bright red thong with a black waistband and rhinestone-like studs that spelled out "PAPI" across the front. Writer Andrew Baggarly recounted its emergence as if describing King

Ladies and gentlemen, the most important team in San Francisco history!

Arthur pulling the Excalibur from the stone. In his book *A Band of Misfits*, Baggarly wrote that Huff needed inspiration, "and he found it—in his underwear drawer."

"Guys, we've got 30 games left," he announced. "Here's 20 wins right here."

Huff was adamant: this was no personal slumpbuster.

"It's the Rally Thong," he said, four days after slapping it on for the first time. "It's not a slump thong. If I was wearing it to break a slump, I would've burned it a long time ago."

Helping the BVDs was the team's ERA. Matt Cain (13–11, 3.14 ERA) and Tim Lincecum (16–10, 3.43) led the staff, while a 20-year-old named Madison Bumgarner went 7–6 with a 3.00 ERA over 18 starts.

In all, that Giants pitching staff compiled a 1.78 ERA for September, the lowest in one month since the start of divisional play in 1969.

"I've had good staffs, but nothing like this," Bruce Bochy said late that season. "I've got seven guys in the bullpen I'm comfortable putting in any situation."

Posey, promoted in late May, hit .305 with 18 home runs, 67 RBI, and an .862 OPS to win NL Rookie of the Year honors.

At the end of the regular season, the Giants entered a three-game series against the Padres needing just one win to clinch a playoff spot. True to their tortuous nature, they lost the first game 6–4 and the second 4–2.

Of course they did.

On the final day of regular-season play, Giants left-hander Jonathan Sanchez led a 3–0 victory over the Padres and ace Mat Latos.

"I believed in the team, you know?" a Champagne-soaked Sanchez said that day. "We're always together. Look at our team. Look at everybody. We have everything we need to win."

The Giants knocked out the Atlanta Braves in a four-game NLDS. All three victories were by one run, of course, and their triumph ended the career of Hall of Fame manager Bobby Cox. (Bumgarner delivered the victory in the clincher, something the Giants would get used to.)

Ross was the unlikely hero against the Philadelphia Phillies in the NLCS, hitting a pair of home runs off Roy Halladay in Game 1. He hit another off mighty Roy Oswalt in Game 2. He hit an RBI single in Game 3 to break a scoreless tie.

THE ELITE EIGHT

Eight players have been on all three San Francisco World Series champion teams:
P Jeremy Affeldt
P Madison Bumgarner
P Santiago Casilla
P Tim Lincecum
P Javier Lopez
C Buster Posey
P Sergio Romo
3B Pablo Sandoval

For the series, the Giants' late-season scrapheap pickup hit .350 with six extra-base hits. Ross had the highest slugging percentage (.950) over a six-game series in NLCS history.

And to think. The Giants claimed Ross largely to keep him away from the Padres, their chief rivals in the NL West.

"This is the most unbelievable experience I've been a part of," Ross said shortly after accepting the NLCS MVP trophy. "Two months ago I thought I was going home to sit on the couch and watch people celebrate on the field, [while] thinking about my next round of golf. It's crazy how this game works."

It would only get crazier.

In the World Series against the Rangers, Renteria—the shortstop who looked 100 years old—went 7 for 17 (.412) with a Series-leading six RBI. In the Game 5 clincher, Lincecum outdueled Cliff Lee in a matchup that was scoreless until Renteria smashed a three-run homer with two out in the seventh inning.

In a rare break on fans' blood pressure, the only torture during the Series itself was administered to Rangers hitters: Lincecum went 2–0 with a 3.29 ERA. Bumgarner and Cain won a game apiece while combining for 15.2 scoreless innings. In all, Texas hit just .190 in the five games and was outscored 29–12.

"They beat us soundly," manager Ron Washington said, according to the Associated Press. "They deserve it."

It was fitting when one last burst of dominant pitching finished it in Game 5 at Texas: Brian Wilson, at precisely 7:30 PDT on November 2, 2010, pumped a fastball past Nelson Cruz for a swing and a miss. Then he crossed his wrists in front of his chest as Posey and others raced to the mound to start the party all of San Francisco had waited for.

"All the experts out there picked us last," Huff said, tearing up.

Only the Chicago Cubs and Cleveland Indians had waited longer to pop the Champagne.

Among the first fan letters to the new champions came from a man who knew better than anyone just how hard it was to climb the mountain.

"There is no city that deserves this championship more," Barry Bonds said in a statement released after the final out. "I grew up watching my dad and godfather as Giants, lived out my dream playing in the same uniform in front of the best fans in the

And to think. The Giants claimed Ross largely to keep him away from the Padres, their chief rivals in the NL West.

world and I just witnessed the Giants winning the World Series. I am ecstatic for the team, the city and all the fans—you truly deserve it."

The fans felt the same, packing Civic Center Plaza on November 4, 2010, for a parade that doubled as the largest group hug in San Francisco history.

"You guys started this," Wilson told the crowd. "Starting with spring training, you guys had our backs from Day One."

Then Wilson stepped back and handed the microphone to the closer for the day.

"Let's get back to work," Posey said, "and make another run at it."

3

BARRY BONDS

ate in 2001, with Barry Bonds one homer shy of tying the single-season home run record, Mike Krukow checked in with Harry Spilman, the broadcaster's Giants teammate from the mid-1980s.

Krukow wanted to know if the Astros were going to give Bonds any pitches to hit during the three-game series in Houston. Spilman, the Astros batting coach at the time, acknowledged that the answer was a hard no.

"If we do pitch to him," Spilman added, with an air of mystery, "we've got something for his [backside]."

The Astros' secret weapon stayed under wraps until the ninth inning of the final game of the series. Bonds had already been walked a preposterous eight times in 15 plate appearances, prompting his 10-year-old daughter, Shikari, to hold up signs like, "Please pitch to our Daddy" and "Give our Daddy a chance."

That's when the alleged Bonds kryptonite burst from the bullpen.

Rookie Wilfredo Rodriguez took the

mound, firing rockets out of his wild left arm. The 22-year-old, who'd started the season at Double-A, came at the left-handed hitting Bonds as if on a double-dog dare.

The first pitch was a 95-mph fastball that caused Bonds to swing and miss. The next pitch was 97 mph near Bonds' chin.

The next pitch...Bonds hit that one as hard as anything he'd crushed all season. The 454-foot bullet to right-center field tied Mark McGwire's record at home run No. 70.

Such was the nature of the action during Bonds' late-career power surge. They weren't at-bats, they were showdowns at the No-K Corral.

"That's a bunch of history right there," shortstop Rich Aurilia marveled after the game. "It's amazing. You watch the guy stand there for three days without getting a single pitch to hit, then he crushes a 95-mph fastball out of the park. It's unbelievable."

Such was the nature of the action during Bonds' late-career power surge. They weren't at-bats, they were showdowns at the No-K Corral. And when you had a pitcher willing to go after him, to stare down the barrel of those maple bats, the only thing missing were holsters and tumbleweeds.

"It's a personal challenge with him to compete against the pitcher, to figure the pitcher out. It's just the whole persona," Giants general manager Brian Sabean once said.

"I don't know of anyone else in baseball who literally stands in the batter's box and doesn't move between pitches. It tells you how much he respects the art and how much he's into it."

While Giants fans generally viewed Bonds as the good guy in these duels, opponents saw him as the guy in the black and orange hat.

Bonds had a famously difficult personality. A Google search for "Barry Bonds" and "churlish" yields more than 24,000 hits. He played a role in baseball's steroid era that made him a touchy subject at cocktail parties, right up there with politics and religion.

And debating his lagging Hall of Fame candidacy? That could set off a riot in most sports bars.

But for the better part of 15 seasons in San Francisco, nobody made a beer run when Bonds was at the plate. You thought he might do something. And then he did.

"I don't shake my head and say, 'How did he do that?' He's done it about a hundred thousand times," former manager Dusty Baker said of Bonds. "It's the fact he keeps doing it, the fact that everybody in the ballpark expects it.

"But everybody knows Michael Jordan is going to take the last shot of the game. You know Mario Lemieux is going to shoot the puck. Joe Montana is going to go to Jerry Rice. Everybody knows it. That's what true greatness is all about."

By the time he was done with 22 seasons in the majors—the first seven with the Pittsburgh Pirates—Bonds was at or near the top of several significant batting categories.

In addition to setting the single-season mark with 73 home runs, he hit 762 career homers to top Hank Aaron's old mark of 755. He walked 2,558 times, breaking Rickey Henderson's mark of 2,190. His career WAR trailed only Babe Ruth among position players. His career slugging percentage (.607) trails only Ruth, Ted Williams, Lou Gehrig, and Jimmie Foxx.

In each case, it wasn't the numbers that mattered to Bonds. It was the company.

Bonds knew his baseball history. At a news conference early in 2002, when he was making fast ground on the home-run record, he said of Aaron: "I'm just happy that what he accomplished is finally being noticed. He deserves that respect. Regardless of whether the home run record gets broken or not, I'm just glad you guys are talking about Hank Aaron as the home run king."

Bonds' respect for baseball's past began in his own household. His father, Bobby Bonds, played for the Giants from 1968 to 1974. (See Chapter 47.)

Born July 24, 1964, little Barry sometimes went to work with Daddy. Naturally, he gravitated toward the ball-of-energy outfielder with the high-pitched voice. Barry called him his godfather. Everybody else called him the Say Hey Kid.

"He used to come to my locker, eat all my chewing gum, and play with my glove," Willie Mays told sportswriter Nick Peters years later. "I would take him out in center field and play catch with him all the time. This went on daily when we were home."

Bonds told Peters: "I'll never forget it as long as I live. I used to climb to the top of the lockers and hide Willie's glove from him—a great experience."

According to Bonds, he became a ballplayer in part because he dreamed of playing in the same outfield as his idols, with his father in right field and Mays in center. He didn't get that exact scenario, but by playing in a San Francisco uniform starting in 1993, he got as close as possible.

For the duration of Bonds' career, the milestones that meant the most to him were the ones that connected him to his youth in San Carlos, California. After he stole his 263rd career base for the Giants, tying dad Bobby for the team record, he never stole another one.

On tying Mays with career home run No. 660 in 2004, he said: "I felt a sense of accomplishment in baseball. It's a relief now to be able to stand next to my godfather and finally feel like I've accomplished something in the game of baseball. It was a big way of getting his approval that I've finally done something."

Of course, Bonds wasn't always as respectful of his current teammates, even veterans. When asked about the protection he would get in the lineup from newly acquired slugger Andres Galarraga in 2001, Bonds scoffed. "Ain't nobody going to protect Barry but Barry. There ain't no other Barry.

Barry called him his godfather. Everybody else called him the Say Hey Kid.

"He'll help Jeff."

Bonds meant Jeff Kent, his teammate-slash-nemesis, with whom he once tangled in the visiting dugout at San Diego's Qualcomm Stadium. So tumultuous was the relationship of the Giants' potent power duo that Baker once compared them to Sidney Poitier and Tony Curtis in the 1958 movie *The Defiant Ones*.

"Both are handcuffed. The one guy wants to throw the other guy off the cliff. And he realizes, 'Oh man, if he goes, I go too,'" Baker said. "I will urge everybody to get that movie. They end up being cool and being partners at the end. This has been a while, quite a transformation for both of them, actually. They're both great ballplayers, and they're both better together than apart."

Bonds was always that explosive blend—he was great, he was grating—from the moment the Giants signed him to a deal in 1993. In fact, he was the first major player acquisition by the Peter Magowan ownership group, which was in such a rush they signed him before the ownership deal was complete, rankling some feathers.

Bonds paid off immediately. He batted .336 and led the National League in home runs (46), RBI (123), on-base percentage (.458), and slugging percentage (.667) in that '93 season.

He won his third MVP trophy, to go with the two he'd earned in Pittsburgh. Showing his sentimental side again, Bonds said: "This one ranks the best. I get to bring it back home with good people and with my family."

Overall, Bonds won seven MVPs in his career—nobody else in baseball history has more than three. He also won eight Gold Glove Awards and reached the 30-30 Club (homers, stolen bases) five times to tie his father for the record.

He was still putting up big numbers for the Giants in 2007, with 28 home runs and an NL best in 132 walks. But with legal trouble mounting in the wake of his connection to the BALCO steroid scandal, the Giants told Bonds he would not be coming back for another season.

"There is more baseball in me and I plan on continuing my career," Bonds wrote on his website. "My quest for a World Series ring continues."

Bonds was legally cleared of perjury charges in 2015, after more than 11 years in court. But he never played again.

4

WILLIE McCOVEY

Some of the balls Willie McCovey hit in the 1960s should be coming down right...about...now.

(Sound of glass shattering, car alarm going off.)

The first baseman's gracefully potent swing launched 521 career home runs and made him a formidable tag-team partner with Willie Mays in the heart of the Giants order. His majestic drives are such a part of Giants lore that they inspired the name of the water beyond the right-field fence. Hit a long one at AT&T Park and you might dent one of the kayaks floating in McCovey Cove.

"If you pitch to him, he'll ruin a baseball. He'd hit 80 home runs," rival manager Sparky Anderson once said. "There's no comparison between McCovey and anybody else in the league."

Beloved by everyone but opposing pitchers, the slugger nicknamed "Stretch" ranks among the most popular players in franchise history. He was adopted by Giants fans the instant he made his debut against future Hall of Famer Robin Roberts on July 30, 1959.

McCovey introduced himself by going 4 for 4—two singles, two triples—at Seals Stadium. More impressive is how he got there: McCovey played a double-header a night earlier for Triple-A Phoenix before getting word of his promotion.

"Well, I was up all night packing and I flew up the next morning," McCovey recalled, years later. "Horace Stoneham [the

Willie McCovey presents the 2006 Willie Mac Award to Omar Vizquel. The award is given each year to the Giants' most inspirational player.
(Eric Risberg)

Giants owner] sent someone to the airport to pick me up and we drove right to Seals Stadium.

"I requested uniform No. 44 because I've always admired Hank Aaron and I was getting dressed when [manager] Bill Rigney came to me and said, 'How do you feel?' I said fine, not wanting to tell him I had been up all night.

"He said, 'Good, because you're in there and you're hitting third. You know whose spot that is: I'm moving Willie Mays up to second today so you know what we're expecting of you.'"

McCovey kept the hits coming during that '59 season, batting .354 with 13 home runs, 38 RBI, and a .656 slugging percentage. Though he played only one-third of the season, he was the National League Rookie of the Year, giving the Giants another homegrown star to adopt. Orlando Cepeda had won the award a year earlier.

While Mays was viewed as an import from New York, the fans claimed McCovey as one of their own.

"I've always been welcome. And like the Golden Gate Bridge and the cable cars, I've been made to feel like a landmark too," McCovey said in Cooperstown.

Was watching McCovey fun? It was often a blast. He once socked a baseball over the upper deck beyond the right-field fence at Crosley Field in Cincinnati, the only player ever to do so. Long before there was a cove to aim for in San Francisco, at Jarry Park in Montreal, McCovey drowned a few balls in the community pool beyond the outfield fences.

The 6'4", 200-pounder is credited with hitting the longest home run in the history of Candlestick Park—a shot that traveled an estimated 500 feet on September 16, 1966. Nobody, in fact, hit more home runs in that wind-blown home park. McCovey hit 231 long balls there, followed by Mays with 203.

No. 44's power was so prodigious that in a pregame planning meeting, New York Mets manager Casey Stengel joked to his pitcher: "Where would you like me to position the right fielder—in the upper deck or the lower deck?"

Jim Bouton put it most hilariously in his seminal *Ball Four* in 1970. Describing a scene from the previous season, the pitcher wrote:

The 6'4", 200-pounder is credited with hitting the longest home run in the history of Candlestick Park

"A group of terrorized pitchers stood around the batting cage watching Willie McCovey belt some tremendous line drives over the right-field fence. Every time a ball bounced into the seats, we'd make little whimpering animal sounds. 'Hey, Willie,' I said. 'Can you do that whenever you want to?' He didn't crack a smile. 'Just about,' he said. And then he hit another one. More animal sounds."

Willie Lee McCovey, born January 10, 1938, in Mobile, Alabama, was the seventh of Frank and Ester McCovey's 10 children. His upbringing was modest, but no one went hungry and the kids went to church on Sundays.

In a quote that explains much about his own leadership style, McCovey once said of his parents: "Mother did all the yelling, but sometimes we didn't listen to Mother. Father was quiet, like I am. He didn't say much, but when he spoke, we listened."

McCovey was a multisport star growing up—in basketball games, Stretch played center—and his athleticism caught the attention of Jesse Thomas, a local playground director.

Thomas arranged for Willie to get a tryout in front of Giants scouts Alex Pompez and Jack Schwarz, who promptly signed him to a contract.

One of McCovey's first minor league managers, Salty Parker, encouraged the kid to stay true to the quiet, dignified nature that would make him a fan favorite.

"He said, 'You're tall and because you're tall you'll always be respected and you'll always stand out in a crowd,'" McCovey recalled during his Cooperstown induction speech. "He said, 'You are not a very outgoing person and you have an easy-going manner and people may interpret that as though you're not caring.

THAT SECOND NIGHT

By going 4 for 4 against Robin Roberts on July 30, 1959, Willie McCovey made one of the best debuts in baseball history.

Often forgotten is that McCovey had a big second night, too. The score was tied in the bottom of the eighth at Candlestick Park when Harvey Haddix of the Pittsburgh Pirates, another excellent pitcher, issued a two-out walk to Willie Mays.

"Bill [Rigney, the manager] comes storming out of the dugout waving his hands, so I stepped out of the batter's box and said to myself, 'Now, I know he's not crazy enough to take me out for a pinch-hitter, is he?'" McCovey recalled during his Hall of Fame induction speech.

"He came up to me and said, 'If you're patient and take a couple of pitches, that guy on first base will steal second for you and you can win the game for us.'

"So I take the first pitch, strike one. Being somewhat of a good two-strike hitter, I decide to take the next pitch and Mays steals second. The next pitch, I singled to right, Mays scores the go-ahead game and we win the game. Made Bill look like a genius."

"'But whatever people say, stay the way you are.... Don't ever change or let somebody try to make you something you're not.'"

Starting with that sizzling rookie season in 1959, McCovey emerged as the ideal counterbalance to Mays.

Mays was right-handed; McCovey was left-handed.

Mays was theatrical; McCovey was reserved.

But they shared at least one common trait: they could hit the living daylights out of the ball. Mays and McCovey homered in the same game 68 times. The only teammates to do so more often were the Braves' Hank Aaron and Eddie Mathews (75 times) and the Yankees' Lou Gehrig and Babe Ruth (73).

Though he was known for his graceful demeanor, it wasn't always a smooth ride. McCovey and Cepeda emerged as young superstars at the same time, which was great for the batting order but bad for the field—only one of them could play first base.

Managers from Rigney to Alvin Dark to Herman Franks struggled to find an equation that would keep both sluggers in the lineup without costing the Giants on defense. The logical move of shifting one of them to the outfield did not go well. Cepeda, after a brief but disastrous stint at third base, was reluctant to play anywhere but first and rebelled when sent to left field.

"I wasn't ready mentally," Cepeda later explained. "I know I could have played left field if I put my mind to it, but I was 21 and very sensitive. It was all pride with me—and ignorance."

McCovey was more open to making the sacrifice, but he was a mess out there. The resulting lineup shuffling cost him three years as a regular at the start of his career. At times, one of the most feared hitters of his generation was relegated to platoon duty and pinch-hitting. Writer Mark Armour, in a terrific overview of McCovey's career for the SABR Baseball Biography Project, noted that Dark started McCovey just once against left-handers during the 1962 season.

Moreover, Dark pinch-hit for McCovey nearly any time a lefty was brought in.

That '62 season ended with one of the most famous swings of McCovey's career. With the potential winning runs on base, McCovey hit a searing liner that New York Yankees second baseman Bobby Richardson snagged for the final out of Game 7 of the World Series. It haunted McCovey, and San Francisco fans, for years.

"But that out is what many people remember about me," McCovey told the *San Francisco Chronicle*, years later. "I would rather be remembered as the guy who hit the ball six inches over Bobby Richardson's head."

Things got better after that. McCovey went on to lead the NL in home runs three times, including in '68–69 when he became just the fifth player in baseball history to capture back-to-back home run and RBI titles. He helped endear himself to Giants fans by tormenting Don Drysdale, a star pitcher for the rival Los Angeles Dodgers, with 12 career home runs. "He doesn't hit batting-practice pitchers that well," columnist Jim Murray cracked in the *Los Angeles Times*. "If it were a bullfight, he'd get Don's ears."

The Giants traded McCovey to the San Diego Padres on October 25, 1973. He was released on waivers twice in 1976, first by the Padres and then by the Oakland A's.

But McCovey didn't think he was through. He persuaded the Giants to give him a tryout in the spring of 1977, saying: "I can still hit homers, and if I wasn't 100 percent sure that I could make this club I wouldn't be here."

The Giants figured McCovey, even at age 39, would give them a little left-handed pop off the bench, so they brought Stretch back.

McCovey thanked them by hitting .280 with 28 home runs and 86 RBI to win NL Comeback Player of the Year honors.

"I'd like to think that when people think of San Francisco, they also think of Willie McCovey," he told Ron Fimrite of *Sports Illustrated* that season. "It's where I want to be, where I belong. I hope the people there love me a little in return."

He stuck around for a few more years before retiring midway through the 1980 season. Fittingly, McCovey played his last game against the Dodgers. In his final plate appearance, he hit a go-ahead sacrifice fly against Rick Sutcliffe to give the Giants a 4–3 lead.

The crowd—the *Dodger Stadium* crowd, no less—gave him a standing ovation. "One of the greatest moments of my career," McCovey said.

One of only 29 major leaguers to play over four decades, McCovey hit 18 career grand slams. At the time of his retirement, only Gehrig had more, at 23.

McCovey could be reclusive after his playing days, making it only to a game or two a year. But by the time the new ballpark was built in 2000, he was clearly part of the family again. A regular at home games, McCovey can be found some nights shooting the breeze in the office of equipment manager Mike Murphy. Sometimes Mays is there. Sometimes Cepeda. Sometimes all of them.

Not everyone is brave enough to say hello. Plenty of players get that nervous look in their eye, the same one pitchers had a generation ago.

"I still have a hard time walking up to him," said Giants pitching coach Dave Righetti, who idolized McCovey as a youngster. "I'm still in awe."

5

JUAN MARICHAL

In the coolest act of insubordination in Giants history, Juan Marichal told Alvin Dark to get lost.

The manager had made the mistake of trying to pull Marichal late in a game at Candlestick Park on July 2, 1963. Instead, the 25-year-old pitcher pointed in the direction of Warren Spahn, the Milwaukee Braves veteran hurler, across the diamond.

"I told Alvin Dark, 'See that other man over there? He's 42 years old. Nobody's going to take me out as long as that old man is still pitching,'" Marichal recalled.

Marichal won 238 games for the Giants, but his victory over the Milwaukee Braves that night tells you all you need to know: He was San Francisco's answer to every ace of that era, willing to go toe to toe—or in Spahn's case, kick for kick—even if it took all night.

Marichal didn't win every pitcher's duel—this was the era of Bob Gibson and Sandy Koufax—but on that chilly night in 1963, he won the greatest pitching duel of all time. The Giants triumphed 1–0 when Willie Mays smacked a home run in the bottom of the 16th inning,

Juan Marichal smiles after his historic, four-hour-10-minute duel with Milwaukee's Warren Spahn, thanking Willie Mays for ending the game with his walk-off home run in the 16th inning.

finally allowing a weary Marichal, and an increasingly exasperated Dark, to call it a night.

"When I saw that ball leave the park, I was the happiest guy on Earth," Marichal told me in 2013, in advance of the game's 50th anniversary.

Marichal threw an astounding 227 pitches against the Braves that night, a total that would no doubt result in the instant firing of both the manager and the pitching coach if it were to happen today.

But during the arm-rich era of the 1960s, Marichal stood up to the grind of facing off against the other team's star. He ranked among the National League top 10 for complete games 10 times, including NL-bests in 1964 and '68.

Marichal is the best pitcher never to win a Cy Young Award (created in 1956). But he didn't need the hardware to prove his worth.

"He didn't give me the most trouble—Sandy Koufax did—but as far as being a pitcher, I think Juan Marichal was the best I ever faced," Pete Rose once said.

"Sandy Koufax was the best left-hander I ever saw. Marichal was the best right-hander," Orlando Cepeda, who played for the Giants from 1958 to 1966, told me. "Hank Aaron said the same thing. Stan Musial told me that. Duke Snider told me that. Ernie Banks. Frank Robinson. They all told me that Juan Marichal is the best right-handed pitcher they ever faced."

The Dominican Dandy belonged in such elite company. He went 243–142 with a 2.89 ERA over 16 major league seasons, from 1960 to 1975, finishing his career with cameos for the Boston Red Sox (11 games) and Los Angeles Dodgers (two).

But it was with the Giants that Marichal earned his trip to Cooperstown. He won at least 20 games six times while in San Francisco and in 1969 led the National League in ERA (2.10).

As Spahn could attest, Marichal found a little extra motivation against elite competition. The 6′, 180-pounder was the best All-Star Game pitcher in history, going 2–0 and yielding one earned run in 18 innings (a 0.50 ERA) against the American League elite.

Marichal did it all with an astonishing delivery, swinging his left leg up in the direction of the clouds before using the exaggerated kick to propel his pitches toward the plate. Roger Angell of the *New Yorker* once wrote that Marichal "throws like some enormous and dangerous farm instrument."

Bob Stevens of the *San Francisco Chronicle* wrote of the distinctive delivery: "If you placed all the pitchers in the history of the game behind a transparent curtain, where only a silhouette was visible, Juan's motion would be the easiest to identify. He brought to the mound beauty, individuality, and class."

For an idea of what his delivery looked like, check out the Marichal statue outside of AT&T Park, where his left foot soars forever toward the sky.

"The foot is up in your face, and then he comes through like a charging fullback," Hank Aaron told sportswriter Nick Peters. "He lunges right off the hill, and with all that confusion of motions, it's a problem seeing the ball. But his control is the biggest thing. He can throw all day within a two-inch space—in, out, up, or down. I've never seen anyone as good as that."

Despite the wild theatrics of his delivery, however, Marichal showcased pinpoint control. His career WHIP—walks and hits per nine innings—was 1.101, which ranks 19th all-time.

Born on October 20, 1937, in Monte Cristi, Dominican Republic, Marichal grew up on a farm where his house had no running water or electricity. Juan's father, Francisco, died when he was three.

His mother, Natividad, insisted that her youngest boy do his chores—at one point, the Marichals had nearly 500 goats—and wasn't too keen on baseball. She really objected when Juan announced it was his career choice.

"She would say, 'How are you going to support your family when you get married?'" Marichal wrote in his autobiography, with Lew Freeman. "I told her, 'Mother, you're going to be so proud when you hear my name on the radio.'"

By then, Marichal was a teenage sensation as a ballplayer. Major league scouts, who were just starting to realize the talent in the Latin American countries, circled quickly when Marichal was old enough to sign.

Gilbert told Marichal to kick even higher with his front leg because the force of his body would be coming down harder when he released the ball.

Acting on a tip from Alex Pompez—who had also discovered Felipe Alou and Orlando Cepeda—Giants scout Horatio Martinez helped secure Marichal for $500 in 1958.

The pitcher's next big step, in more ways than one, was learning the high leg kick. Marichal was in his second season as a pro, at Class-A Springfield (Mass.) in 1959, when manager Andy Gilbert made a suggestion. Gilbert told the pitcher that he was too young to be throwing the ball sidearm and encouraged Marichal to come with the more traditional overhand delivery.

But when the pitcher tried that, his pitches came in high. So Gilbert told Marichal to kick even higher with his front leg because the force of his body would be coming down harder when he released the ball.

It turned out to be pretty sound advice.

About a year later Marichal nearly threw a perfect game in a scintillating major league debut. He retired the first 19 Philadelphia Phillies on July 19, 1960, at Candlestick Park. With one out in the seventh inning, an error by shortstop Eddie Broussard ruined the perfect game. And with two out in the eighth, pinch-hitter Clay Dalrymple singled to break up the no-hitter.

But the debut signaled the greatness that would follow Marichal.

It wasn't just that he threw with a big windup. It was that he did so from angles they don't even teach in high school geometry. In

THE CLASSIC THAT ALMOST WASN'T

Willie Mays gets credit for playing a hero's role in the greatest pitching duel of all-time. He ended the Juan Marichal-Warren Spahn showdown with a home run in the bottom of the 16th inning on June 2, 1963.

It took more than four hours.

Willie McCovey still insists he could have saved them a lot of trouble.

On the 50th anniversary of the game, he swore that he'd already hit a walk-off home run that night. The trouble is that first-base umpire Chris Pelekoudas ruled it foul.

"He didn't make the call right away. I hit it so high and so far, he waited until it landed...which was in Oakland," McCovey said, chuckling at the memory. "He was the only person in the ballpark who thought it was foul."

(At least one other person agreed with the umpire. Braves catcher Del Crandall still thinks the umpire got it right. "Of course, I might have been a little biased," he added.)

McCovey looks back knowing that wound up being part of something special. The Marichal-Spahn duel remains one for the ages.

"I don't think any of us realized at the time how special it was," McCovey said. "It was just a game we were trying to win."

their exhaustive *Neyer/James Guide to Pitchers* writers Bill James and Rob Neyer conclude that Marichal threw five pitches: slider, fastball, changeup, curveball, and screwball. But they also cite a *Time* magazine story in which an anonymous hitter claims to have counted 10 different speed variations off the fastball.

"Those are kind words, but I cannot claim to have a fastball that travels at 10 different speeds" Marichal later wrote in *A Pitcher's Story*, with author Charles Einstein. "When my fastball is really working, I believe it travels at two different speeds: fast and not-quite-so fast."

Whatever the speed, Marichal went places. In his prime from 1963 to '69 he turned in a record of 154–65. He got his no-hitter, too, blanking the Houston Colt .45s on June 15, 1963, at Candlestick Park. It was the first no-hitter by a Giants pitcher since Carl Hubbell in 1929.

But his true masterpiece was that showdown with Spahn at Candlestick Park. It was four hours and 10 minutes of waiting for the other guy to blink first.

After working out of the 16th inning, which required getting Hank Aaron (0 for 6!) one last time, Marichal avoided returning to the dugout right away. Instead, the pitcher waited by first base for Mays to jog in from center field.

"When he got there, I put my arm on his shoulder and I told him, 'Alvin Dark is mad at me. He's not going to let me pitch any longer," Marichal recalled.

"So [Mays] touched my back and said, 'Don't worry. I'm going to win this game for you.'"

Mays blasted the first pitch he saw that inning into the left-field stands. He had broken the tape, ending the marathon.

As it turned out, Marichal would eventually endure another long wait. Improbably, he fell short of Hall of Fame selection in his first two appearances on the ballot.

Some voters were turned off by Marichal's role in one of the most violent brawls in baseball history. Marichal was batting against Koufax when he grew angry at Dodgers catcher John Roseboro. Marichal believed that Roseboro was whizzing the return throws to Koufax dangerously close to Marichal's ear as retaliation for a knockdown pitch.

Marichal attacked Roseboro with his bat, leaving a bloody gash and igniting a free-for-all between the two benches. The pitcher was fined $1,750 and suspended two starts; San Francisco finished precisely two games behind the pennant-winning Dodgers.

The lingering distaste from the incident is the only way to explain why Marichal fell far short of induction in his first appearance on the Hall of Fame ballot, in 1981. He was named on only 58.1 percent of the ballots. Marichal was up to 73.5 percent the next year, but still short of enshrinement.

That's when an unlikely ally emerged: Roseboro.

The incredible saga is documented in *The Fight of Our Lives: How Juan Marichal and John Roseboro Turned Baseball's Ugliest Brawl into a Story of Forgiveness and Redemption.* Marichal, recognizing that the fight was blocking his path to the Hall of Fame, reached out to Roseboro.

Marichal invited Roseboro and his family to visit the Dominican Republic, where Marichal hosted a charity golf tournament. The two men held a news conference together. Marichal apologized to Roseboro. Roseboro forgave Marichal.

Marichal was elected to the Hall of Fame comfortably in his next try, in 1983, and the two former combatants became the dearest of friends.

Roseboro died in 2002. Marichal delivered the eulogy.

6

BUSTER POSEY

Because Buster Posey was a natural leader at a young age, his coach at Florida State University switched him from shortstop to catcher. Mike Martin wanted Posey to play where he could better influence the action.

Still, Martin figured the transition would take time. A long weekend at least.

"After three pitches, I said, 'You got to be kidding me.' He looked as if he'd been catching all his life," Martin told writer Joan Ryan of the Giants media staff. "The way he could frame a pitch. The way his mitt looked like a pillow. The fact that he didn't snatch at the ball. He looked very polished."

Giants fans know the feeling. From the moment the preternaturally calm prospect arrived in San Francisco, he fit like a glove. Gerald Dempsey Posey III walked through the doors and suddenly three World Series rings followed.

When the Giants won their first title, in 2010, Posey was the National League Rookie of the Year.

When the Giants won their second title, in 2012, Posey was the NL MVP.

When the Giants won their third title, in 2014, Posey looked to be on his way to the Hall of Fame.

"I can't think of a player more valuable to a ballclub than what Buster is to us," manager Bruce Bochy once said. "It's really amazing what he's done.

"Being at a premium position, handling the staff, and hitting cleanup.... Guys feed off him."

In winning their trio of titles, the Giants employed three different second basemen, three left fielders, and three center fielders. They had two different starters at first base, third base, shortstop, and right field.

And they had one catcher. Posey played 46 out of 48 playoff games.

"You hear people say they're blown away, say it's incredible what the Giants achieved," right-hander Jake Peavy told writer Andrew Baggarly of the *San Jose Mercury News*. "Is it really incredible when you have Buster Posey, one of the best players in the league, running the game?"

It sure seems incredible to those who know the history of the franchise. In the 46 years B.P. (Before Posey), the Giants won zero World Series. In the five years A.P., they won three.

Posey became the first player ever to win a Rookie of the Year, an MVP, and three World Series titles before his 28th birthday.

Posey, Yogi Berra, and Roy Campanella are the only catchers to win a World Series and an MVP Award the same season.

He didn't change the franchise's fortunes single-handedly—Posey came up as part of a wave of drafted-and-developed talent that also included Matt Cain, Tim Lincecum, and Madison Bumgarner—but the catcher was the key to the most dominant stretch by an NL team since the Big Red Machine.

"Any time you have a catcher that throws like Buster and hits in the heart of the order," Bochy said, "you think of Johnny Bench."

Posey was the first catcher to win the NL MVP award since Bench did it for the Cincinnati Reds in 1972. He and Bench are also the only two catchers to win both an NL MVP and Rookie of the Year award in their careers.

When Posey batted .336 with 24 home runs, 103 RBI, and a .549 slugging percentage in 2012, he became the first player since Frank Robinson in 1966 to win a league MVP award, a batting title, and a World Series in the same season. The others, according to the Elias Sports Bureau: Joe DiMaggio (1939 Yankees), Stan Musial (1946 Cardinals), Willie Mays (1954 Giants), Mickey Mantle (1956 Yankees), and Dick Groat (1960 Pirates).

And they had one catcher. Posey played 46 out of 48 playoff games.

That's about as elite a dinner party as you can get. And, as the Giants know, Posey might as well pull up a chair.

"This guy is different," pitching coach Dave Righetti said. "He's special."

That much was easy to spot. The son of Demp and Traci Posey grew up on a 50-acre plot of land in Leesburg, Georgia. Demp erected a backstop in the front yard—the makeshift ball field was good enough that Little League teams sometimes used it for practice.

Buster married Kristen, his Lee County High School sweetheart, in January 2009. Their recessional music was "Take Me Out to the Ballgame."

In his final season at Florida State, he led the NCAA in average (.463), slugging percentage (.879), and on-base percentage (.568), while still learning the nuances of catching.

Posey also demonstrated the quiet determination that would characterize his Giants career. On a bus ride back to Tallahassee after a tough loss, a couple of freshmen were joking and laughing. Posey stood, turned, and said: "I don't know about any of you, but I'm not really happy right now and I don't want to hear any laughing."

(This conversation would be the opposite of Posey's trademark victory celebration in San Francisco, the Buster Hug.)

The Giants selected Posey with the fifth overall pick of the 2008 draft.

"Hopefully, I'll be an impact player for the San Francisco Giants for a long time," Posey said that day.

Posey was not, however, an instant hit upon his call-up to the majors on September 2, 2009. That was mostly because he didn't get an instant at-bat. As a third-string catcher, Posey didn't make his first plate appearance until September 11. It took him 22 games before he got his first start, as the Giants made an awkward transition from veteran Bengie Molina to the hot-shot rookie.

The Posey era began in earnest midway through the following season, when the Giants traded Molina to the Texas Rangers on July 1, 2010, to clear the way for the backstop of the very bright future.

Posey responded by launching a career-best 21-game hitting streak starting July 4, batting .440 with six home runs and 23 RBI. It was the second longest hitting streak by a San Francisco rookie, trailing only Willie McCovey's 22-gamer in 1959.

"I had fun with the streak. But I concentrated on winning games as much as possible," Posey said the day it ended. "In a way, it's nice the attention will go back to winning instead of the streak."

The attention went back to winning, all right. Posey's bat stayed hot all the way through the Giants' first World Series victory since 1954. He hit safely in all five games against the Texas Rangers and became the first rookie catcher in major league history to bat cleanup in a postseason game (in Game 1).

That's what life with Buster Posey was like. The Giants got a wretched reminder of life without him the following season when a home-plate collision on May 25, 2011, left the catcher with a fractured fibula and torn ligaments in his left ankle. Scott Cousins of the Florida Marlins came barreling over the catcher to score the tie-breaking run that night.

It was a legal play at the time. Because of what happened to Posey, it's not anymore. Adopted in 2014, Rule 7.13 outlawed two things—catchers blocking the plate when they don't have the ball and runners "deviating from their pathway" to hit the catcher.

"It's a good rule," Posey said after the change was announced. "We shouldn't be going out to injure the catcher. We should be going out to score the run."

The Giants certainly suffered without Posey, finishing 8.0 games out in the season of his injury.

And Posey certainly suffered without the Giants.

"You miss being on the field. You miss the guys. You miss the crowd. You just miss the game in general," he said during his arduous comeback process. "You miss everything about it."

Posey made it back for Opening Day 2012. He went on to become the first NL catcher to win a batting title since Ernie Lombardi in 1942. He also captured a Silver Slugger Award, an All-Star spot, and the Hank Aaron Award as the league's top hitter. (The Georgia native's reaction to that last one: "I'm humbled that Hank Aaron knows who I am.")

In the NL Division Series, Posey propelled a 6–4 victory in the decisive game against the Cincinnati Reds by belting a grand slam off Matt Latos.

Typical Posey, his teammates said.

"Yeah, things like that—he's just an unspoken leader," Cain said that day. "He did a great job of putting an easy swing on in a pressure situation, and he got the job done."

As Posey's final act of that comeback season, he exploded out of his catcher's crouch, sprinted to the mound, and hoisted 185-pound-reliever Sergio Romo over his shoulder to celebrate a four-game sweep of the Detroit Tigers. Apparently, his ankle was feeling just fine.

While his big bat and big hugs get the attention, Giants pitchers swear

"Hopefully, I'll be an impact player for the San Francisco Giants for a long time," Posey said that day.

Posey's most important contribution goes almost unnoticed. His pitch selection and handling of the guys on the mound is the stuff of legend. The former high school shortstop became adept at knowing what fingers to put down behind the plate.

"I've thought about this: I've had catchers who had a tendency to call the pitches they couldn't have hit," pitcher Tim Hudson told Baggarly. "Well, there aren't many pitches that Buster Posey can't hit. He has such a great approach that he understands what the really good hitters are thinking up there at the plate.

"I've learned not to shake him off. There have been times I shake and give up a loud out or a base hit. You look at him sitting back there, and you just see him thinking, *You idiot. You should listen to me more.*"

We're all listening. And it's safe to say there will be echoes of Buster Posey for many years to come.

7

ORLANDO CEPEDA

A day before the Baseball Hall of Fame announced its induction class for 1999, Orlando Cepeda's phone rang. Juan Marichal was on the other line. And he felt good about his friend's chances.

"Orlando, wait until you get to the Hall of Fame," Marichal told Cepeda. "Everything changes."

It was a curious burst of optimism. Cepeda had languished for 15 years on the ballot, at one point getting only 10.1 percent of the vote from the Baseball Writers Association of America. And though his support slowly rose over the years, it peaked in his final season on the BBWAA ballot. In 1994, he got 73.5 percent, still seven votes shy of the 342 needed for election.

But at the time of Marichal's phone call, Cepeda's case was in the hands of the 18-member Veterans Committee, which takes a second look at players no longer eligible in the BBWAA vote.

And this time, San Francisco had Cepeda's back.

A sustained and relentless push from the Giants organization, led by owner Peter Magowan, drove the player known as "Baby Bull" back into the limelight as a player and as a person.

With the fervor of a college pushing a Heisman Trophy candidate, the Giants reminded voters that over the course of 17 seasons, including from 1958 to 1966 with the Giants, Cepeda batted .297 with 379 home runs, drove in 1,365 runs, and made 11 All-Star teams. He won Rookie of the Year for San Francisco in '58 and an MVP for St. Louis in 1967, after one of the worst trades in baseball history.

By the 1999 election year, Cepeda was the only player with more than 300 home runs and at least a .295 batting average who wasn't in the Hall of Fame.

By the 1999 election year, Cepeda was the only player with more than 300 home runs and at least a .295 batting average who wasn't in the Hall of Fame.

The reason: In 1978, he spent 10 months in prison on drug charges, a crime that plunged him into disgrace and depression. Baseball turned on him. So did his native Puerto Rico.

That was the low point.

The high point came with a call from Cooperstown. As it turned out, Marichal's scouting report had been right on the money.

"I lost my mind. I couldn't believe it," Cepeda told me in 2015. "It's hard to explain the feeling that you have when they call and let you know that you're a Hall of Famer. It's incredible.

"When they say, 'Hall of Famer,' that's a huge change in your name. Everything changes completely when they say that. So I'm very proud and I'm very fortunate."

Disgraced and depressed? In retrospect, that's hard to believe. Fans arriving at AT&T Park these days can see Cepeda, cast in bronze, immortalized as a statue at the corner of Second and King Streets.

They might also see Cepeda himself. The engaging, colorful character works as one of the Giants' official community ambassadors.

The love affair between Cepeda and San Francisco bloomed from the start: On April 15, 1958, at Seals Stadium, the Giants played their first game since moving from New York. The powerful 6'2" rookie started at first base.

Just 20, Cepeda introduced himself by belting a homer in the fifth inning off reliever Don Bessent. It was the second home run in San Francisco Giants history—Willie Kirkland had beaten him to the punch an inning earlier, off Don Drysdale.

In all, the Giants beat the Los Angeles Dodgers 8–0 that day—and Cepeda was embraced like a favorite son.

"I had grown up dreaming of becoming a ballplayer and here I was, against the Dodgers. From Day One, I just wanted to say, 'Thank you,'" Cepeda said. "From the night before until after the ballgame, it was like I was dreaming."

Within a month, Cepeda was the toast of the town. The young, handsome rookie was on his way to a remarkable first season in which he would hit .312 with 25 home runs, 96 RBI, and a league-leading 38 doubles.

"He is annoying every pitcher in the league," Mays said during that '58 season. "He is strong, he hits to all fields and he makes all the plays. He's the most relaxed first-year man I ever saw."

Cepeda was a hit off the field, too. The city's lively nightlife suited his tastes. Writing for the *San Jose Mercury News* in 1999, Ron Bergman recounted the night Cepeda walked into a North Beach jazz joint to find Miles Davis, Cannonball Adderly, and John Coltrane playing. When the trio saw the Giants first baseman, they began improvising a musical tribute to the rookie. Thus was born the Latin jazz classic "Viva Cepeda!"

But Cepeda's life wasn't always such a party. Cepeda was born on September 17, 1937, in Ponce, Puerto Rico. His family never had much money, but they did have baseball.

ALVIN DARK

Orlando Cepeda was often all smiles on the field, but behind the scenes there was trouble.

Cepeda clashed with Alvin Dark, the Giants manager from 1961 to '64, over his treatment of Latin players.

Dark prohibited players such as Cepeda, Felipe Alou, and Juan Marichal from speaking Spanish in the clubhouse—even to each other. Cepeda used to love playing Latin music in the clubhouse, but that, too, was banned.

"To be blunt, on many occasions Alvin made my life a living hell. Things got so bad at times that there were days I didn't want to go to the ballpark," Cepeda wrote in his autobiography *Baby Bull: From Hardball to Hard Times and Back*. "I believe that Alvin's racial attitudes were harmful to the best interests of the ballclub in general, and to the Latin players in particular."

It took another 35 years, but the story had a happy ending. The two became friends after Dark wrote a letter of apology around the time Cepeda was selected to the Hall of Fame.

"You deserve it," Dark stated. "And I want you to forgive me for the way I treated you. I was in a different frame of mind."

Cepeda forgave him and opened the lines of communication.

"He really showed me he was a man when he sent that letter," he said.

Cepeda's father, Perucho "Bull" Cepeda, was the Babe Ruth of Puerto Rican baseball and famed for his long-ball prowess. He played with (and befriended) many of the Negro League greats, such as Satchel Paige and Cool Papa Bell, when they played in Latin America.

But Perucho had no interest in leaving Puerto Rico to play in the Negro Leagues. He would play in Venezuela, the Dominican Republic, and Cuba—but not the United States.

"He didn't like me at all as a baseball player. He said I didn't have the tools to be a good player."

"He was afraid of the race thing," Cepeda told me. "He had such a bad temper. He said if somebody called him a [racial slur], he wouldn't know what to do. So he didn't want to come to the States."

Instead, his son—"the Baby Bull"—made the leap. Orlando signed with the Giants in 1955, becoming just the second black Puerto Rican to play in the majors, after Roberto Clemente.

The Giants were pioneers when it came to signing players from Latin America, but the early wave had it rough. Cepeda told author Steve Bitker in *The Original San Francisco Giants* that Giants farm director Jack Schwartz didn't even want the future Hall of Famer.

"He didn't like me at all as a baseball player," Cepeda said. "He said I didn't have the tools to be a good player."

Cepeda grew frustrated with the obstacles of his coaches, the language barrier, and the racism he faced at his minor league stops. During his first year of pro ball, in Salem, Virginia, he had to wait in the car while white teammates went into a restaurant and brought back food for him.

Cepeda considered packing up and heading back to Puerto Rico.

"The reason I stayed with the Giants, when they wanted to release me, was because of Alex Pompez," he said, referring to the scout who mentored that first wave of Latin players. "I loved Alex. He helped me so much."

After being convicted of distributing drugs and sentenced to federal prison, his people turned their backs on him.

Cepeda finally found another ally in Giants manager Bill Rigney. Along with owner Horace Stoneham, Rigney had traveled to Puerto Rico to watch Cepeda play winter ball. "And he told Horace, 'He's going to be my first baseman.' Bill made it very easy for me."

After his unanimous selection as Rookie of the Year in '58, Cepeda kept rolling in 1959 (27 homers, 105 RBI) and 1960 (24 homers, 96 RBI). He blew the doors off in 1961 by leading the National League with 46 home runs.

Never a fan of Candlestick Park, Cepeda told Bitker, "I believe it would have been 65 or 70 home runs in any other ballpark. But I learned not to complain about it. Mays never complained. Willie McCovey never complained. I knew it was hard to play there but I just had to go ahead and do it."

Batting fifth in '61, behind Mays and McCovey, Cepeda also led the led the NL with 142 RBI. He finished second in MVP voting behind Frank Robinson of the Cincinnati Reds.

Cepeda continued to play at an All-Star level, however, helping the Giants to the pennant in 1962 with 35 homers and 114 RBI. But he had knee surgery after the '64 season and barely played in '65, when 27 of his 33 appearances were as a pinch-hitter.

For Giants fans, the most painful part came next: San Francisco traded Cepeda to St. Louis for pitcher Ray Sadecki on May 8, 1966. In fairness, Cepeda had forced the Giants' hand. The Giants had long wanted him in left and McCovey at first base, but Cepeda felt he belonged at first and never embraced the move.

The mistake with the trade was getting so little in return. Magowan once called the deal "the worst mistake this organization has ever made."

In St. Louis, Cepeda immediately won two pennants, a World Series trophy, and the 1967 MVP award. He would eventually make his way back into the Giants family, but it was a treacherous path.

In 1978, a year after his retirement, police arrested Cepeda when he went to the San Juan International Airport to claim a package. Cepeda has said he accommodated a friend by allowing him to include a five-pound bag of marijuana in a box being shipped to Puerto Rico from a baseball clinic they had attended in Colombia.

Before the arrest, Cepeda had been enjoying life in Puerto Rico, where he was treated like a hometown hero. He assumed new importance in the culture after Roberto Clemente was killed in a plane crash on December 31, 1972.

After being convicted of distributing drugs and sentenced to federal prison, his people turned their backs on him.

"I blew it," Cepeda told Bergman in 1999. "I made a huge mistake. When Roberto Clemente died, they said in Puerto Rico, 'At least we have Orlando Cepeda alive.' So when I let everybody down, they got very mad. We are hard on people who mess it up."

Ultimately, Cepeda found peace. He found Buddhism. He met his third wife, Miriam. And he found a personal champion in Magowan. The onetime supermarket tycoon, who became the Giants' managing general partner in 1993, made a point of connecting the franchise to its past.

"Peter Magowan, when he took over, he told me right from the start: 'We're going to do everything possible to get you into the Hall of Fame,'" Cepeda said.

And even when he did, it didn't stop there.

One of the highlights of Cepeda's long and winding baseball journey came when he and Magowan took a lap around the AT&T Park.

They were looking for a place to put that Cepeda statue. Magowan and the Baby Bull decided the best place was at the corner of Second and King.

That's where the man who played in the first game ever played in San Francisco will be part of Giants games for as long as the ballpark stands.

"Believe me, I have a wonderful life. I am a very lucky person."

Cepeda has that right. The quote is a line from his Hall of Fame induction speech.

8

THE FREAK

As early as his minor league days, it was obvious that Tim Lincecum was different from the other boys.

Sometimes, to liven things up during practice at Class-A San Jose, Li'l Timmy would walk around on his hands. One minute he'd just be standing there, the next doing a backflip.

"They come at random," Lincecum said of his acrobatics when I interviewed him in 2006. "I'm kind of a random person."

The pitcher was just as eccentric indoors. Lincecum ate some of his meals from a squatting position. He never iced his arm.

"This guy could be a first-round pick for the circus," marveled San Jose Giants pitching coach Jim Bennett.

Luckily for San Francisco baseball history, the Giants signed him before Barnum & Bailey did. "The Freak" went on to produce some of the most astonishing pitching seasons in franchise history, with feats that would rival the best of Juan Marichal, Carl Hubbell, and Christy Mathewson.

This was a three-ring circus: Lincecum was part of World Series championship teams in 2010, '12, and '14. Along the way, he might have been the most popular Giant since Willie McCovey.

He did it all despite an appearance so boyish and slight that stadium security guards often mistook him for a batboy.

One night in New York in 2009, the 5'11", 170-pound pitcher stepped beyond the gates to say hello to his girlfriend. When he

Lincecum shows off his unique, whirling delivery during his Game 1 victory in the 2010 World Series against the Rangers.

tried to re-enter, the Shea Stadium guard stopped him cold. Never mind that Lincecum already had a Cy Young to his credit, never mind that he had pitched six innings *that night.*

"Yeah, right," the guard told him. "I need to see some ID."

The confusion was understandable. Were this really a circus, you could fit about a dozen Lincecums into a VW Bug.

But on the mound, he was "Big Time Timmy Jim" (or "Seabiscuit" or "The Franchise" or any of the playful nicknames for a pitcher with physics-defying power).

His physique never looked scary, but for about a five-year stretch starting in 2007, the sight of that No. 55 Giants jersey frightened the daylights out of major league hitters.

"He's had some of those spectacular games that just leave your mouth open," pitching coach Dave Righetti said after one such game, a 10-strikeout performance that closed out the Texas Rangers in Game 5 of the 2010 World Series.

With a fastball that in its prime climbed into the upper 90s, Lincecum became the first pitcher in baseball history to win the Cy Young Award in each of his two first full seasons. The right-hander captured the honor both in 2008 and '09, which was double the team's Cy Young haul of the previous 50 years. (Mike McCormick was San Francisco's only previous winner, in 1967.)

Lincecum set the San Francisco strikeout record with 265 in 2008. He struck out 261 more the next year and 231 the year after that. In doing so, he became just the third post–World War II pitcher to lead the National League in strikeouts for three straight years, joining Hall of Famers Randy Johnson and Warren Spahn.

And last Giant to do so? Mathewson, from 1903 to '05.

By holding the San Diego Padres hitless twice—July 13, 2013, and June 25, 2014—Lincecum became just the fourth pitcher with at least two Cy Young Awards and two-no hitters. The others? Sandy Koufax, Randy Johnson, and Roy Halladay.

Such company underscored the lunacy of Lincecum's career. Consider that Johnson was listed at 6'10", 225 pounds, Halladay at a sturdy 6'6", 225.

Lincecum, meanwhile, could walk into a bank early in his career without being noticed as a baseball star. There was the time a teller spotted the Giants logo on his check and asked if he worked at the ballpark. Lincecum said he did.

THE BROKEN TROPHY

Before a supernova named Tim Lincecum came along, the Giants had only one Cy Young Award to their credit.

And that trophy was broken.

Mike McCormick's plaque from the 1967 season toppled during the 1989 Loma Prieta Earthquake. The same jolt that rattled the World Series left a crack in McCormick's historic hardware.

"I thought about getting it fixed," McCormick told me in 2008. "But I just figured the crack just gives it more character."

It was also a reminder of the crack job he did in 1967. The Giants' left-hander went 22–10 with a 2.85 ERA and five shutouts.

McCormick earned 18 of the 20 votes cast that year. The other two were split between Jim Bunning and Fergie Jenkins, a pair of future Hall of Famers.

The pitcher also finished sixth in MVP voting that year.

McCormick, a three-time All-Star, was forever humble about his Cy Young Award, knowing that he timed his career year just right. Juan Marichal, his Giants contemporary, never so much as earned a Cy Young vote in his career because he pitched in the era of Sandy Koufax and Bob Gibson.

"Every time I [was] recognized as the Giants' only Cy Young winner, I made a point of saying that Juan Marichal is the best pitcher I ever saw," McCormick said.

"Oh, that must be fun," the clerk said. Lincecum heartily agreed.

At least he'd beefed up since hgh school, when he was a 4'11", 85-pound freshman at Liberty High in Renton, Washington. He was also a star athlete. During his time at Liberty, Lincecum played quarterback and cornerback on the football team, point guard on the basketball team, and in baseball was Washington's Gatorade Player of the Year.

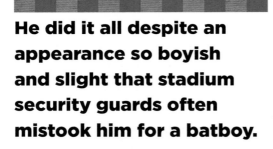

He did it all despite an appearance so boyish and slight that stadium security guards often mistook him for a batboy.

How could the kid throw so hard? His father, Chris Lincecum, always envisioned his youngest son as a baseball star and studied scientific theories in his quest to find the ideal mechanics. Chris mixed a bit of Bob Feller here, a smidgen of Bob Gibson there, and threw in a dash of Satchel Paige for good measure.

The result was a pitcher who looked like a popgun, but fired like a bazooka.

"The way he pitches is a sequence of leverages from toes to fingertips," Chris told *Maxim* magazine in 2010. "He uses all his small muscles, so his body does the work and his arm comes along for the ride."

After Lincecum enjoyed a record-setting pitching career at the University of Washington, the Giants nabbed him with the 10th overall pick in the 2006 amateur draft. (Lincecum's hometown Seattle Mariners famously passed, at No. 9.)

With that pick, the Giants got a pitcher who proved tough to hit and nearly impossible to describe. In addition to his hard fastball, he had a curveball and a slider/changeup that Tyler Kepner of the *New*

York Times described as "virtually indistinguishable for much of its flight, the slider tumbling, the changeup fading, both from a similar trajectory and at a similar speed."

Lincecum also endeared himself to San Francisco fans with his eclectic behavior. He was the rare ferocious competitor with a hippie vibe. I once saw him relaxing in a laundry cart a few hours before a start at AT&T Park. Teammates say that he'd chatter away to them during his no-hitters (a serious bit of baseball taboo).

He celebrated his second no-no by sporting a Team USA soccer jersey and a gladiator helmet in the clubhouse. "It's almost like he's immune to the big moments," outfielder Hunter Pence said that day in 2014. "He's free when it's happening. He doesn't make a bigger deal out of it than it is."

Lincecum became the 32nd pitcher in MLB history to throw multiple no-hitters and the first since Addie Joss in 1910 to throw a second against one team. How would Lincecum celebrate?

"I'm going to go to my house and drink a little bit," he said, smiling. "Can I say that?"

Sure he could, considering the way Giants fans embraced even his transgressions. In 2009, Lincecum was charged with marijuana possession. He apologized for the arrest, paid a $513 fine—and became a bit of a cult hero. Fans wearing "Let Tim Smoke" T-shirts remain easy to spot around AT&T Park today.

Oddly—a common word when discussing the The Freak— Lincecum's no-hitters came not at the peak of his powers but during a prolonged decline.

In 2012, Lincecum's once-electric velocity was clearly down a few volts. His 5.18 ERA that season was the highest among all qualifying pitchers in the NL and the fourth highest in the majors. He also led the league in losses, runs allowed, earned runs, and wild pitches.

Lincecum worked to a slight bounce-back in 2013, highlighted by his suitably nutty first no-hitter. That night he had to bob and weave through 148 pitches, the second-most thrown in a no-hitter since at least 1988. Along the way he was saved by Pence's all-out dive to snag Alexi Amarista's sinking liner with two out in the eighth.

"I thought that was a hit off the bat by Amarista," Lincecum said that night. "But Hunter comes flying out of nowhere and makes the Superman catch. That was awesome."

His second no-hitter was breezy by comparison. To the delight of manager Bruce Bochy, Lincecum needed only 113 pitches and there were no exceptional plays.

"I just want to thank him for making this one a lot less stressful," Bochy said. "This was a lot easier."

Those brief flickers aside, Lincecum was now getting by on guts, not gasoline. His fastball barely cracked 85 mph on some nights. By the time the Giants reached their third World Series, in 2014, the two-time Cy Young winner was an afterthought. Lincecum tossed just 1.2 scoreless innings of relief in Game 2 against the Kansas City Royals before having to leave the game early with a back strain.

Hampered by a bad hip, Lincecum's future was uncertain at the end of the 2015 season, but the Giants will certainly remember him for better days. He and Koufax are the only pitchers to win multiple World Series, win multiple Cy Young Awards, throw multiple no-hitters, and be selected to multiple All-Star Games.

"I love Timmy," Bochy said near the end of the 2015 season. "We all know what Timmy has done for the Giants."

Yes, we do. It's been downright freaky.

9

BRUCE BOCHY

Bruce Bochy, the man responsible for so much Champagne, was born between Cognac and Bordeaux, near an airfield in southwestern France.

His father, Army Sgt. Major Gus Bochy, was stationed in Landes de Bussac in 1955. And while Bruce didn't follow in his dad's bootsteps, the Giants manager grew up understanding what soldiers admire most—discipline, calm, resolve, courage, and loyalty.

Every time the Giants march deep into the baseball playoffs, players point to their unflappable manager as the reason why. They outlast teams with more money, more talent, more buzz—more whatever—and somehow end up with more World Series trophies.

Hunter Pence said it's because of an unshakable October resolve that starts at the top.

"If your leader is a rock as solid as Bochy is, if your leader is as sharp as he is, it leaks into the team," Pence said during the Giants' 2014 title run. "We believe in him and we have faith. And I think a lot can be said for faith."

Before Bochy: zero World Series titles since 1954, when the team was still in New York.

Since Bochy: three parades, with nary enough time to sweep up the confetti in between.

"He seems to always make the right move," said Giants left-hander Madison Bumgarner, who ought to know. "Whether he takes

Tim Lincecum, Bruce Bochy, and Buster Posey hold up the 2010, 2012, and 2014 World Series trophies. (Jeff Chiu)

a gamble and does something or he kind of plays it safe, it always works out."

Bochy is one of 10 managers to win at least three World Series titles. The other nine are in the Hall of Fame. And by leading the Giants to the championship in 2010, '12, and '14, Bochy became just the fifth dugout wizard to lead a team to three titles in a five-year span.

The others? Connie Mack, Joe McCarthy, Casey Stengel, and Joe Torre—all candidates for the Mt. Rushmore of managing.

Over the first eight years of Bochy's tenure in San Francisco, the Giants won all 10 of their playoff series. That's the second-longest streak ever by a skipper, trailing only Torre's 11 straight for the powerhouse Yankees from 1998 to 2001.

"He's very quietly putting together a Hall of Fame career," Los Angeles Angels manager Mike Scioscia, the second-winningest active manager behind Bochy, told the *Los Angeles Times* in 2014. "When you talk about Joe Torre, about Tony La Russa, about Bobby Cox, about guys that have made it, Boch is going to be right there when it's all said and done."

Just don't expect Bochy to engage in such reflection. Asked once if he was comfortable having his name lumped among the great postseason managers, he replied, "Not really, to be honest—I'm not. I'm fortunate that I have a great club here with a lot of character. They just seem to thrive on these types of games."

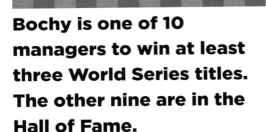

Bochy is one of 10 managers to win at least three World Series titles. The other nine are in the Hall of Fame.

Dave Righetti, the Giants' longtime pitching coach, said Bochy's approach helps explain why young players such as second baseman Joe Panik and reliever Hunter Strickland were able to make significant contributions in the heat of the pennant race.

"We don't have a huge major league–type veteran bench. He's got young kids. But they seem to be playing like they're not tight, right?" Righetti said. "It's got to be him. It's the atmosphere he creates."

The list of Hall of Fame managers is dominated by the colorful and the fiery, with names like Casey Stengel, Sparky Anderson, Earl Weaver, and Tommy Lasorda.

Bochy, in contrast, is almost willfully dull. It's part of what makes him great.

His snooze-fest press conferences during hot streaks sound exactly the same as they do during cold stretches. Bochy keeps a level head the whole time, which is no small feat considering his famously big noggin. (His hat size is 8¾.)

"Bochy's demeanor is extremely important," Pence said. "He has been through these things and has made it as far as he has so many times, and it's not an accident. He knows what he's doing. And we see that and we feel that."

But he has to break sometimes, right? Doesn't Bochy ever lose his cool after a galling loss? "There are a few times," said Will Clark, the former All-Star now on the Giants coaching staff. "But that's the great part about having doors in the clubhouse."

Take 2014, for example: It could have been a year rife with controversy if not for Bochy's knack for preaching calm. Key players such as Matt Cain, Angel Pagan, and Brandon Belt sustained major injuries (and only Belt made it back). Tim Lincecum, the once-dominant starter and fan favorite, was banished to the bullpen. Sergio Romo, a World Series hero in 2012, was stripped of his closer duties.

Soap opera? It wound up about as juicy as C-SPAN. Romo embraced his less glamorous role, posting a sizzling 1.90 ERA after the All-Star break. Yusmeiro Petit, the pitcher who emerged ahead of Lincecum in the pecking order, pitched six scoreless relief innings in the Game 2, series-swinging, 18-inning thriller in Washington.

Loyalty? Brandon Crawford, Panik, and Gregor Blanco went a combined 0 for their past 29 heading into the decisive Game 4 in the Nationals series. Bochy stuck with them all anyway, despite facing tough left-hander Gio Gonzalez. The trio combined to go 5 for 12 with two runs, a walk, and an RBI.

"These are all tough decisions," said Ron Wotus, the Giants bench coach since 1999. "But when you're in a winning situation and the players have your respect... I think it's much easier to check your ego at the door and do the right thing for the club.

"Bochy has created that atmosphere here, where it's the team first. He's been able to make the tough decisions and keep everybody on board."

The only other manager in Giants history to win three World Series championships was John McGraw, who led New York to titles in 1905, 1921, and 1922. McGraw, of course, never had to deal with hurdles like the NL wild-card game or the division series. All three of Bochy's champions, though, teetered on the brink of elimination in the early rounds before his teams found a way to survive. "We're tough to kill," Wotus said. "Like cockroaches."

Bochy never set out to be a manager. As his slow shuffles to the mound suggest, he spent his career as a catcher, serving as a backup in the majors from 1978 to 1987. He hit .239, but had his moments. Bochy hit a home run against future Hall of Famer Steve Carlton in 1985 and, a few weeks later, topped that with a walk-off shot against Nolan Ryan.

The Padres offered him a chance to manage their rookie-league affiliate in Spokane, Washington, in 1989. Bochy promptly won three titles in his first four minor league seasons.

Bochy has said he learned from Bill Virdon, the former Astros manager, to tailor his style to the team rather than the other way around. In 2012, when the Giants had a healthy Pagan, the Giants ranked fourth in the NL with 118 stolen bases. In 2014, they had less than half that (57) to rank last in the league.

Bochy has never worn out his bullpen. Over his first nine seasons in San Francisco, never once did a pitcher rank in the top 10 for appearances. (The Dodgers, in contrast, had three players in the top five in 2013 alone.)

"As a strategist, he knows what he's doing," Clark said. "He knows how he has his bullpen set up. He plays to his strengths and he plays to this ballpark."

Early in the 2014 NLCS against the St. Louis Cardinals, a seldom-used pinch-hitter named Travis Ishikawa tried to explain what it's like to play for such a well-prepared manager. Ishikawa had only 73 at-bats for the Giants during the regular season, but had also served as a role player for Bochy in 2009 and '10.

Not playing much had at least one perk: Ishikawa got to sit next to a manager headed for Cooperstown.

Not playing much had at least one perk: Ishikawa got to sit next to a manager headed for Cooperstown.

"I had the opportunity to actually kind of watch him throughout the game. And as the season went on, I was starting to learn what situations I could possibly be used here. What situations I could see him going other ways," Ishikawa said. "I came to appreciate how very baseball-savvy he is. How much intelligence he has managing a baseball game.

"I had a lot of success pinch-hitting here, and I think a lot of it has to do not only with me preparing for the pinch-hit but also with him getting me in the right situation, the right match-up. Bochy's just proven to me that I have his trust, and my confidence continues to grow each day."

Four nights later, in Game 5 at AT&T Park, Bochy entrusted Ishikawa with another start in left field. Ishikawa delivered by belting a pennant-winning three-run homer, smacking a ball into the dark October sky with one out in the bottom of the ninth.

The Giants were on their way to another World Series.

10

WILL THE THRILL

ecause Nolan Ryan was big and ornery and had the best fastball in the history of baseball, the Giants watching from the bench on Opening Day 1986 figured he'd try to put a little scare into the cocky rookie digging in as the leadoff batter in his major league debut.

Heck, veteran catcher Bob Brenly thought Ryan might even introduce himself to Will Clark by drilling him with a 95-mph heater to the ribs.

Instead, the Houston Astros right-hander threw a curveball for a called strike. That's when Will Clark did the second most impressive thing of his first major league at-bat.

He smiled.

"What are you smiling at," Astros catcher Mark Bailey snapped.

"The Ryan Express is throwing me curveballs," Clark replied, still grinning.

Perhaps sensing that he had the hitter guessing, Ryan followed up with another surprise, floating a high changeup over the middle of the plate. That's when Clark did the *first* most impressive thing of his at-bat: He blasted the ball over the center-field fence.

Unleashing that left-handed swing so pretty it should have been set to harp music, Clark belted a high line drive 420 feet and circled the bases as if he'd done it 100 times before.

One of baseball's reliable pranks is to commemorate a rookie's first homer with a silent act upon his return to the dugout. The Giants did so for Clark, but unwittingly.

"This was a natural silent act. We were dumfounded," former Giants pitcher Mike Krukow recalled for MLB.com. "Our jaws were agape."

Ryan fumed: "It was a high changeup and he hadn't seen enough of me to throw a changeup. It was a bad pitch and a bad pitch selection."

"Will's better than *The Natural.* Because he's for real."

Will Clark would have 7,172 more at-bats in the major leagues, but Giants fans learned all they needed to know with that first swing. Their new first baseman was brash and fearless and funny, with enough talent to leave tongues wagging.

True to form, Clark was *not* silent during the silent act, bounding through the dugout yelling in his excitedly high-pitched drawl: "All right! Let's get some more! Let's get some more!"

And so they did.

Clark's homer proved to be the lightning bolt that reignited the franchise. The listless 1985 Giants had gone 62–100 while their first-round draft pick was still honing his skills at Class-A Fresno. With Clark batting leadoff on Opening Day '86, his hello of a homer set the tone for an 83–79 season and a fresh new era for the franchise.

"Will's better than *The Natural*," manager Roger Craig once said. "Because he's for real."

The New Orleans native promptly emerged as one of the best players of his era, highlighted by binges from 1987 to 1992 in which he finished in the National League's top five for MVP voting four times.

Injuries would eventually derail his path to the Hall of Fame, but Clark finished a solid career with a .303 batting average, 2,176 hits, 284 home runs, and 1,205 RBI over 15 years in the majors.

In his second full season, 1987, he became the first San Francisco player to bat .300 with at least 30 homers since another first baseman—Willie McCovey in 1969.

Clark was also a splendid fielder. He won the Gold Glove Award in 1991 and might have won more had he not played in an era dominated by all-time artists like Keith Hernandez and Mark Grace.

And in case you dig advanced metrics: Clark's WARP3 during the 1989 season was 13.3, a mark topped during the 1980s only by Mike Schmidt's 13.4 in 1981.

And in case you don't: just look at the man's face.

Clark's scrunched-up expressions during the game's tensest moments were so hilarioulsy awesome they had their own nickname: "Nuschler."

Pronounced "NOOSH-ler," it happened to be William Clark Jr.'s middle name. Legendary sportswriter Ron Bergman defined it this way in a 1989 story for the *San Jose Mercury News*: "It's a term used by teammates to describe how his lips tighten into a look of almost hilarious ferocity when he starts to seriously concentrate on the task at hand. His tension level seems like an over-wound watch spring ready to snap."

"It's really strange when I see myself on tape," Clark says. "I didn't know that a jaw could go through that many contortions."

Clark also had a more lyrical nickname of course: "The Thrill."

A 2012 MLB.com documentary on Clark traced the origins of the nickname to Scottsdale, Arizona, in spring training of '86. It goes like this:

He arrived in the desert already hilariously self-confident. And why wouldn't he be? He'd hit for Mississippi State (where he'd won the Golden Spikes Award), for the 1984 U.S. Olympic team (three homers and eight RBI in five games for the gold-medal winners), and for Class-A Fresno (.309 and 10 homers in 65 games).

Looking for a subtle way to knock the kid down a peg, veteran catcher Bob Brenly introduced himself at spring training that year by deadpanning, "We're all *real thrilled* to meet you."

But after a few weeks of watching Clark blast line drives around the Cactus League, Brenly changed his inflection. The way Krukow tells it, Brenly turned to him on the dugout bench one day and said, "You know who we've got? We've got 'Will the F---ing Thrill.'"

The nickname stuck, minus one word.

Clark's arrogance came with a bonus. He was the hitter who yearned to be at the plate when the game was on the line.

"A lot of people fear success more than they fear failure. It's easier to accept mediocrity than it is success. Will Clark never worries about success. He could go 0 for 40 and he wouldn't get down. It's a psychological thing," general manager Al Rosen said then.

"If you went up to Will Clark today and asked him who should be the first baseman on the all-time team, he'd say, 'Will Clark.' If you asked him who should be batting third, he'd say, 'Will Clark.' And there's nothing wrong with that. That's what makes him Will Clark."

Clark was never more at his pressure-punishing best than in the 1989 NL Championship Series against the Chicago Cubs. The series MVP batted .650 (13 for 20) with two home runs and eight RBI.

Along the way, he burned a few terrific pitchers the way he'd once burned Nolan Ryan.

"I've been into games before, but never in my career the way I was against the Cubs," Clark said. "I couldn't believe the concentration level I had in that series. I can't remember ever being that aware."

He arrived in the desert already hilariously self-confident.

In the fourth inning of Game 1, Clark sauntered to the plate with the bases loaded and two out against future Hall of Famer Greg Maddux. The Giants were leading 4–3, and the situation was just tight enough that Cubs manager Don Zimmer walked to the mound to talk things over with Maddux.

They didn't know the Nuschler was watching. Maddux told Zimmer he was going to throw a fastball inside. And because Maddux towered over Zimmer, Clark had a clear line of sight to read the pitcher's lips.

Clark promptly hit that inside fastball like he knew it was coming, for a grand slam that put the Giants ahead 8–4.

If you watch a game now, you'll see pitchers cover their mouths with their gloves while they're talking on the mound—that's because Clark once hit a grand slam off Maddux in Game 1 of the 1989 NLCS.

Another memorable conversation hastened the end of the series. In the decisive Game 5 at Candlestick Park on October 9, the score was tied 1–1 with two out in the eighth.

With Clark due up, Zimmer summoned his best weapon—Mitch "Wild Thing" Williams, a left-hander who fired his fastballs up to 100 mph and only had an approximation as to where the pitch would end up.

Before Clark strode to the plate, on-deck hitter Kevin Mitchell caught his eye.

"Superman has done it again!"

"You have a job to do," Mitchell said.

"It's already done," Clark replied.

The Thrill stepped to the plate, fell behind 0–2 in the count, fought off some helacious sliders, and then hit the sixth pitch, a 95-mph fastball, for a single up the middle to give the Giants a 3–1 lead.

"Superman has done it again!" broadcaster Hank Greenwald yelled.

"You've heard it before," Clark said later. "You get into a situation where the ball looks real big. I've got a lot of confidence—I feel like I'm going to get a hit every time."

Three outs later, the Giants were on their way to their first World Series since 1962. They owed much of that trip to the scrunched-up face of the franchise—the Nuschler.

Improbably, the Giants and Clark parted ways after the 1993 season, in part because an elbow injury was sapping the first baseman's power. He signed a five-year, $30 million contract with the Texas Rangers.

But he eventually found his way home. In 2009, the Giants hired him back as a special assistant and community ambassador, knowing that his enthusiasm, confidence, and baseball savvy would rub off on the next generation of young players.

The Thrill immediately saw parallels between the current Giants and the core of homegrown talent like himself, Robby Thompson, and Matt Williams in the mid-'80s.

"Some of the younger players in the organization came up together for the first time last year and can build on that," Clark said when he was hired. "They can make that part of their rallying cry. Two years after we were called up, we were in the playoffs, and four years later, we were in the World Series."

In the second season after Clark rejoined the organization, the Giants won it all.

11

THE 2014 CHAMPIONS

Fans endured some anxious moments during San Francisco's first two titles, but the fretting was generally finished by World Series time. The Giants needed just five games to knock off the Texas Rangers in 2010 and they swept the Detroit Tigers in 2012.

This time? The seven-game showdown against the Kansas City Royals was such a heart-pounding thriller that it was wise to keep defibrillators next to the peanuts and Crackerjacks.

It ended after 12 breathtaking seconds in Game 7, after the Royals' Alex Gordon whirled around the bases and stopped at third in the bottom of the ninth. That's when Madison Bumgarner, impervious to nerves, put his stamp on San Francisco's third World Series title and one of the most amazing finishes in Fall Classic history.

Only after a crazy bottom of the ninth did the Giants' thrill ride come to a full and complete stop on October 29, 2014. They had already white-knuckled through a wild-card game in Pittsburgh, an 18-inning game in Washington, and a Travis Ishikawa pennant-winning walk-off against St. Louis.

Now, they had to watch Gordon nearly unravel the whole darn championship flag during his mad dash around the bases.

With two out in a 3–2 game—and Bumgarner trying to put the finishing touch on one of the greatest World Series performances ever by a pitcher—Gordon struck a ball toward the left-center field gap.

The ball skipped past him, and appeared to be rolling toward baseball infamy.

Giants left fielder Gregor Blanco approached indecisively, split over whether to attempt a diving catch or to play it safe and hold Gordon to a single. He did neither.

The ball skipped past him, and appeared to be rolling toward baseball infamy.

Center fielder Juan Perez was backing up on the play, but the ball eluded him, too. He reached for it at the wall. He missed. And Gordon's foot just touched the second-base bag.

"I was starting to get a little nervous," Bumgarner said that night. "He can run a little bit and that's a big outfield, so I was just wanting someone to get it and get it in."

Perez finally grabbed the ball and unleashed a relay throw to Brandon Crawford. The shortstop made a sensational pick on a one-hop throw. Or so he was told.

"After the game, guys said, 'Nice pick.' I don't even remember picking that ball," Crawford told Tim Kurkjian of ESPN. "When I did catch the ball, I looked at third. Gordon was just stepping on the bag."

Gordon's legs churned and, like Giants' stomachs, kept churning. And then...nothing.

Royals third base coach Mike Jirschele threw up the stop sign, keeping Gordon at third rather than waving him home. By most accounts—and there were a lot of 'em—Jirschele made the right call. The *Kansas City Star* went so far as to commission college baseball players to recreate the scenario, this time with a "Gordon" heading for home. The experiment suggested overwhelmingly that the real Gordon would have been a dead duck at the plate.

Still, sending Gordon could have been the most exciting ending ever.

"It could have been the weirdest ending," countered Giants catcher Buster Posey.

The actual ending: With the tying run at third, Bumgarner faced Salvador Perez. The batter had homered off Bumgarner in Game 1, the only run allowed by the left-hander in 36 career World Series innings.

Bumgarner fired a series of high fastballs until Perez hit a foul pop in the direction of third baseman Pablo Sandoval.

"At that point you're going, 'Pablo, please catch this thing,'" manager Bruce Bochy said.

Sandoval caught it and fell on his back, and the Giants grabbed their place in history.

San Francisco became the first World Series team to win Game 7 on the road since Willie Stargell's Pittsburgh Pirates beat the Baltimore Orioles in 1979. Visiting teams had been 0–9 since.

They also became the second National League team to win three titles in a five-year span, matching the St. Louis Cardinals of 1942–46.

In 2010, they were misfits and castoffs. By 2014, the Giants looked more like a dynasty.

"I don't know the definition of 'dynasty,' in a sense, when it comes to baseball," Giants reliever Javier Lopez said from somewhere underneath a Champagne shower after Game 7. "I know this is one heck of a team and one heck of an organization. Anybody out there looking for a home, this is always a great place to land. I can speak personally for that."

The 2014 Giants went 88–74 during the regular season, eking into the second wild-card spot with the fifth-best record in the NL.

Noting that the Royals won only 89 games, an ESPN.com headline on October 17 blared: "Welcome to the Worst World Series Ever."

Hardly.

During a low point of the regular season, Bochy reminded his Giants that they had "championship blood" running through their veins from the '10 and '12 title teams.

And when the leaves turned brown, the Giants turned it on.

In the wild-card game, they beat the Pirates 8–0 behind a grand slam by Brandon Crawford and a stellar pitching performance by Bumgarner (get used to that phrase).

Bumgarner tossed a four-hitter with 10 strikeouts, needing just 109 pitches to signal his readiness for the spotlight. "If you don't want to pitch in these games, you probably need to find something else to do," he sniffed.

He celebrated the victory by chugging four beers at once.

The Giants triumphed 3–1 in the best-of-five NL Division Series against the Washington Nationals, but the series was nowhere near as breezy as it appeared.

The turning point was a 2–1 victory in Game 2 in Washington, a sprawling epic that took a postseason record 6 hours, 23 minutes. The Giants forced extra innings by scoring the tying run in the ninth, with help from Nationals manager Matt Williams, who removed Jordan Zimmerman when he was one out away from a complete game shutout.

That night Yusmeiro Petit was the Giants pitching star—not Bumgarner, for once—by entering the game in the 12th inning and delivering six scoreless innings. That bought the Giants time until Brandon Belt, who had been 0 for 6, belted a ball into the second deck for the go-ahead homer in the top of the 18th.

THE ORIGINAL BUMGARNER

In the tense hours before Game 7 of the 2014 World Series, speculation raged over how much Madison Bumgarner would be able to pitch out of the bullpen.

The Giants' rugged left-hander was on only two-days' rest after throwing a complete-game shutout in Game 5. He threw 117 pitches against the Kansas City Royals that night.

So would he be good for two innings? One? At all?

It was around that time that I ran into another October warrior watching batting practice from behind the cage at Kauffman Stadium.

Former pitcher Jack Morris, the MVP of the 1991 World Series, had a feeling what was in store. He called the shot.

"There's no doubt in my mind he could pitch the whole game," Morris said. "I think he wants to and I'm pretty sure he could."

Morris had been in Bumgarner's shoes. He started three times for the Minnesota Twins in the '91 series—Games 1, 4, and 7—and went 2-0 with a 1.17 ERA.

He had a feeling Bumgarner would be there for the end. And indeed the left-hander was, delivering five shutout innings and 68 pitches.

"In a game like this, you want your guy on the mound," Morris said. "You want to win or lose with your guy. You can sleep at night with your guy."

The Giants eked out another win in the decisive Game 5, this time scoring the tying run when Joe Panik came home on reliever Aaron Barrett's bases-loaded wild pitch.

"If it was easy, it wouldn't be as fun," outfielder Hunter Pence explained.

Bumgarner celebrated the victory by chugging five beers at once.

San Francisco became the first World Series team to win Game 7 on the road since Willie Stargell's Pittsburgh Pirates beat the Baltimore Orioles in 1979.

The Giants beat St. Louis 4–1 in the best-of-seven NLCS. Along the way, they took advantage of the Cardinals' sloppy defense. The heroics of Travis Ishikawa and Michael Morse in Game 5 get their own chapter elsewhere, but it's safe to say the Giants' championship blood was pumping again.

"These guys have been through it," Bochy said. "They have been battle-tested and they know how to handle themselves on this type of stage."

The World Series against the Royals, of course, will best be remembered as Bumgarner's show. He became the first pitcher with two wins, a shutout, and a save in a World Series since the save rule became official in 1969.

His Game 5 shutout was just the 16th shutout in World Series history in which no walks were allowed and the first since the Royals' Bret Saberhagen in Game 7 of the '85 World Series.

So dominant was Bumgarner's performance that reliever Jeremy Affeldt joked during their victory parade that players had talked about not putting their own names on the championship rings. Everybody would just put "Mad Bum" instead.

In truth, it took contributions from across the board—familiar names and fresh faces. Affeldt delivered four scoreless outings (and earned the win in relief in Game 7). Pablo Sandoval batted .429 with a .467 on-base percentage and .536 slugging percentage. Hunter Pence batted .444 with a .667 slugging percentage.

And rookie second baseman Joe Panik made the best defensive play of the series at a pivotal moment of Game 7. With speedster Lorenzo Cain at first and the score tied at 2–2, Eric Hosmer bashed a bullet up the middle. Panik made a dive, came up with the ball, and flipped it from his glove to shortstop Brandon Crawford to start a remarkable 4-6-3 double play.

"That was a big deal," Affledt said. "That was the biggest play of the night."

Bumgarner soon sauntered in from the bullpen, like a sheriff coming to quell trouble, and the Giants were on their way to another World Series title. The left-hander cemented himself as an October legend, but at his postgame news conference as the World Series MVP, he had to dispel one lingering myth.

"I don't really drink much of the beer," he clarified. "I just pour it on me. It's pretty difficult to drink six at a time or whatever it was. It started out just for fun in Pittsburgh.

"I just had to keep it going because we kept winning. I didn't want to have anything that could be turned around and blamed on me."

12

BRIAN SABEAN

Before he won three World Series titles, before he pulled off trades that risked grand larceny charges, before he drafted a few potential Hall of Famers, and before he plucked postseason heroes like Cody Ross and Marco Scutaro out of the bargain bin, Brian Sabean had to clear something up.

"I am not an idiot," he declared.

That wasn't so easily believed late in 1996, shortly after Sabean was hired as the Giants' general manager. As his first act he traded beloved third baseman Matt Williams to Cleveland for players so lightly regarded you'd put their baseball cards in your bicycle spokes.

The uproar from fans was immediate, hostile, and intensely personal. Even the Giants flagship radio station piled on Sabean by airing a little ditty: "One little, two little, three little Indians / That's what we got for trading Matt Williams."

The trade backlash was so severe that Sabean arranged an informal press conference to assure people that the pilot light in his brain was flickering.

No, Sabean was not an idiot. He has the Champagne stains to prove it.

There were actually four Indians—second baseman Jeff Kent, pitcher Julian Tavarez, pitcher Joe Roa, and shortstop Jose Vizcaino—and they soon proved invaluable to a team that shot from last place in '96 to NL West champions in '97.

Sabean's dramatic overhaul that season later included the acquisitions of J.T. Snow, Darryl Hamilton, Brian Johnson, and Mark Lewis. Not a bum in the bunch.

No, Sabean was not an idiot. He has the Champagne stains to prove it.

Only 40 years old, Sabean was already the tough, bright, confident executive that someone like Brad Pitt ought to make a movie about. The East Coast–born, Steinbrenner-bred, bare-knuckled savant quietly ranks among the best general managers in baseball history.

In his first 18 seasons as GM, from 1997 to 2014, the Giants won three World Series, four pennants, five NL West flags, two wild-card playoff berths, and forced a wild-card tie-breaker with the Chicago Cubs in '98. San Francisco had a .534 winning percentage during that span, a mark topped by only nine general managers in baseball history.

Sabean won two ways. During the Barry Bonds era, it was by surrounding the perennial MVP with a supporting cast of veteran free agents. After Bonds retired, he infused the franchise with some of the best draft picks of the modern era.

"Maybe because he was a scout, it comes from his history of seeing and evaluating players and not only seeing their physical tools, but their mental side," pitcher Tim Hudson said during the Giants' playoff run in 2014. "Those are the things that general managers can't put a stat on—how tough somebody is, how much guts they have, what kind of chemistry they can bring.

"Too many people nowadays are getting wrapped up in the sabermetrics and the stats. I'm willing to bet almost every one of those people never stepped in a locker room, put on a jock and took the field, and understands those intangibles that help you win."

Sabean grew up in Concord, New Hampshire, and went on to become a scrappy second baseman for tiny Eckerd College in St. Petersburg, Florida. He coached college baseball for a while, most notably as the head coach at the University of Tampa in 1983 and '84, compiling a 61–36 record.

But his baseball education began in earnest as a scout in the New York Yankees organization. Though never a slacker, Sabean found a new gear under George Steinbrenner, the famously demanding owner.

"I can honestly say it was difficult," Sabean once told me. "He gave you the impression that he knew everything about everything. He didn't, but it kept you on your toes. And it kept things from getting political because you focused on your job and only your job—you didn't want to get on the wrong side of any argument.

"The harder you worked, and the lower your profile was, the better chance you had of moving up in the organization."

Sabean pleased The Boss. There was that frigid spring day in 1992 when he traveled to Kalamazoo, Michigan, to watch a high school prospect. It was tough to get much of a read—the kid was playing on a bum ankle—but Sabean liked what he saw from the Central High shortstop. He would later strongly insist that the Yankees indeed draft that kid named Derek Jeter.

"Brian scouted Jeter personally, and it's frightening what a good job he did with that one," said Bob Quinn, the former Yankees GM who later brought Sabean to San Francisco. "Gee whiz, how often do you get a player of his quality and his character?"

Sabean didn't pluck Jeter out of total obscurity; the 17-year-old shortstop was one of the top high school players in the country. Dick Groch, the Yankees' area scout for the Midwest, had already seen the future Hall of Famer. Sabean went to see him at Groch's recommendation.

Sabean's true contribution came later, when he pushed hard for Jeter in the first round. It was a tough sell. Steinbrenner—hardly the patient type—preferred college players who could reach the majors faster. But Sabean made a persuasive case, and the Yankees selected Jeter with the sixth overall choice.

Groch, who worked for the Yankees for 20 years, told me that Sabean's impact on the Yankees dynasty was in creating a winning culture among scouts.

"He was tremendously confident in his staff," Groch said. "That was a special time with special energy. We played off everybody. We fought belly-to-belly with Brian sometimes, but when the time came to make a call, we all supported each other."

Such sentiment followed Sabean to San Francisco, even in those early days.

The GM's inner circle held firm in the face of idiocy charges. Undaunted by the reaction to his first trade, Sabean kept making them, eight major transactions in the span of a year.

Midway through that '97 season he traded six minor leaguers to the Chicago White Sox for pitchers Wilson Alvarez, Roberto Hernandez, and Danny Darwin. The lopsided deal prompted *San Jose Mercury News* columnist Bud Geracie to compare Sabean to Jesse James—"the greatest thief in history."

Of the nine players on the field the day the Giants won the division title in '97, six had joined the team that year.

"He had a plan and he went with it," the late Paul Turco, a longtime scout, said that day. "No matter what anyone else thought, he went with it and it worked. He set this out from Day One. He said, 'We're gonna do it, and we're gonna do it this year.'"

Sabean's ability to make the puzzle pieces fit has kept the Giants an annual contender even in the era of free agency. His lopsided trade coups also include landing Snow, Robb Nen, Livan Hernandez, Andres Galarraga, Kenny Lofton, Hunter Pence, and Jake Peavy for forgettable prospects.

Misfires are rare. He once traded future stars Joe Nathan and Francisco Liriano, as well as Boof Bonser, to the Minnesota Twins for disappointing catcher A.J. Pierzynski. But his track record for someone so bold is astounding.

"The guy that's afraid to trade a prospect because he thinks he's going to

Though never a slacker, Sabean found a new gear under George Steinbrenner, the famously demanding owner.

be a Cy Young winner or an MVP is not going to win as many games as he needs to at the big-league level," Sabean once said. "And he's probably on his way out the door."

Beyond the big names, the GM has a knack for spotting players who have taken their lumps and are all the better for it. Pitcher Yusmeiro Petit had to play in Mexico to keep his dream alive. Ryan Vogelsong, Japan. Travis Ishikawa had to beat the minor league bushes for a number of organizations.

"Most of the guys on our team have been through something that made them tougher," Vogelsong said before the 2014 playoffs. "There's something that makes you tougher when you get released, or have people tell you that the door's closing. It does something to you as a person, and that translates to the baseball field."

"The really neat thing about this organization is that they put the numbers secondary to the player," Michael Morse, a veteran outfielder and first baseman who played a key role in the 2014 playoffs, said. "They look at the personality of the player, whether he fits and belongs to this team. I'm so glad I fit."

So did Peavy, the last piece to the 2014 puzzle, who was so instrumental to the Giants just making the playoffs. While more high-profile pitchers like Jon Lester and David Price were moved at the trade deadline, Sabean zeroed in on a guy who had survived a major shoulder injury, a guy who was having a horrible year, but also a guy the Giants knew had an almost maniacal desire to win.

Peavy in Boston that season: 1–9 with a 4.72 ERA.

Peavy in San Francisco that season: 6-4, 2.17 ERA.

Why did it work? The veteran pitcher fit the room, just like Cody Ross did in 2010. And Marco Scutaro in 2012.

"This game can be very negative," Sabean said. "It's a game of failure. A lot of guys maybe weren't in the right place at the right time or even the right role. There are not enough players to go around, so whether they're your own or somebody from the outside, you want to see, a) where they can help your roster, and b) what they bring to the table.

"One of the things I believe fuels the fire in these players' bellies is that there's a hell of a lot more talent in that clubhouse than is being given credit for. We're the farthest thing from the little engine that could."

Indeed, the Giants manage to blend talent, heart, and toughness. And so far it's made for Sabean's almost unbeatable formula.

13

THE GHOSTS OF GOTHAM

Because the Giants maintain strong ties to their New York ancestors, Bobby Thomson visited AT&T Park in 2001. He was there to celebrate the golden anniversary of his 1951 home run that beat the Brooklyn Dodgers for the National League pennant.

I asked Thomson what happened to the ball he belted into the Polo Grounds' stands for the "Shot Heard 'Round the World."

He smiled ruefully.

Thomson said that a day after his home run, he arrived at Yankee Stadium for Game 1 of the World Series. As he was entering, a fan stopped him, excitedly clutching a baseball. *The baseball.* The man explained that he'd been sitting in the left-field bleachers at the Polo Grounds and managed to make his lucky catch amid the mob scene.

"He said, 'Hey, Bobby, I'll let you have this ball if you get me two tickets to the ballgame today,'" Thomson recalled.

Thomson, already knowing tickets were impossible to get, barely acknowledged the man. There would be 65,673 fans in the stands that day for the opener of the all–New York World Series.

But by the time Thomson got to the clubhouse, he was already feeling nonbuyer's remorse. He should have pulled the trigger. It would be nice to have that special memento, he thought, and he was so close he could have touched it.

The pang worsened, so he tracked down Eddie Logan, the attendant in the visiting clubhouse.

"I said, 'Hey, Eddie, there's a guy up there who has the ball I hit yesterday. He wants two tickets. You've got to get them for me.' I was real serious."

Logan looked at Thomson and laughed.

"I said, 'Eddie, why are you laughing at me?'" Thompson

"The saddest words of all to a pitcher are three— 'Take him out.'"

recalled. "He pointed over to my locker, and there were eight balls already sitting there, all of them supposed to be the ball I'd hit for the home run. That's when I gave up."

Fortunately, not all of New York Giants baseball has been so lost in history. San Francisco makes sure of that. In fact, the coolest place at AT&T Park might be the Gotham Club, a secret lounge for VIPs decked out as a salute to the ghosts of franchise past.

The entrance door features a square with two crossed bats and "GC 1883." That's Giants history: the team was born as the New York Gothams in 1883.

The Gothams became the Giants in 1885 after a staggering win. On that day, Jim Mutrie, who helped found the franchise, cheered: "My big fellows, my Giants!"

The swanky private Gotham Club is hard to find (hint: behind the out-of-town scoreboard), but even those in the cheaper seats can spot links to the team's New York history.

A string of retired numbers hangs from the deck in left field as tribute to all the big fellows, all the Giants. Two of the earliest— Mathewson and McGraw—played in the days before uniform numbers, so they're represented simply by "NY." Here's a look at the men whose legends followed the team from New York to San Francisco.

NY Christy Mathewson

Long before Madison Bumgarner came along, Christy Mathewson set a standard for World Series brilliance. In 1905, the Giants' right-hander shut out the Philadelphia Athletics three times in five days—27 innings, 0 runs, 1 walk, 18 strikeouts—to lift New York to the crown. (Did they call him MatBum?)

In all, Mathewson had a 0.97 ERA in 11 World Series appearances. All but one of those starts was a complete game. He

MATHEWSON, BUMGARNER, AND THE PINCH

Somewhere in a field of dreams, Christy Mathewson and Madison Bumgarner would get along just fine. Both Giants pitchers were fearless in the big moment, which might explain their World Series success. As Mathewson once said: "No man can have a 'yellow streak' and last." Mathewson's career World Series ERA: 0.97. For Bumgarner: 0.25.

Here's from Mathewson's 1912 book, *Pitching in a Pinch*. Somewhere, Bumgarner is nodding along:

"In most Big League ball games, there comes an inning on which hangs victory or defeat. Certain intellectual fans call it the crisis; college professors, interested in the sport, have named it the psychological moment; Big League managers mention it as the 'break,' and pitchers speak of 'the pinch.'

"This is the time when each team is straining every nerve either to win or to prevent defeat. The players and spectators realize that the outcome of the inning is of vital importance. And in most of these pinches, the real burden falls on the pitcher."

once wrote, "The saddest words of all to a pitcher are three—'Take him out.'"

And to think, Mathewson's bosses tried to convert him to a position player. That happened shortly after he was traded by Cincinnati to New York for an aging Amos Rusie in 1900. As *The New Biographical History of Baseball* put it: "Even though the right-hander immediately produced the first [of many] 20-win seasons for the Giants, that wasn't sufficient for Horace Fogel and Henie Smith, the clowns who managed New York over the first half of the 1902 season and who vied with one another in seeking to convert the mound star to first base and shortstop."

Mercifully, new manager John McGraw arrived at the end of the year and put the experiment to an end, returning Mathewson to the mound. The brainy, Bucknell-educated pitcher went 373–188 with a 2.13 ERA in his career and earned a spot in the original Hall of Fame induction class in 1936.

Mathewson did so with an arsenal that included a fadeaway pitch (an antecedent to the screwball).

NY John McGraw

In the midst of the 1921 pennant race, the man known as "Little Napoleon" assessed the chances of his ballclub: "I think we can make it—if my brains hold out."

There was no need to put him on a thought count; John McGraw's brains held up just fine. The New York Giants won it all that season, the second of the manager's three World Series titles.

McGraw did it in his typical pugnacious, insightful, iron-fisted, innovative way. The 5'7", 155-pound scrapper was a pioneer in areas such as making extensive use of relievers and hiring full-time coaches. He was also a master of psychology, pressing the buttons of his own players and opponents. He explained his credo to *Literary Digest* in 1914:

"Learn to know every man under you, get under his skin, know his faults. Then cater to him—with kindness or roughness as his case may demand."

During his three decades at the Giants' helm, 1902–1932, he finished first 10 times and second 11 times.

No. 3 Bill Terry

Ted Williams was the last big-league player to bat .400, going .406 in 1941.

The last National League player to do it was a first baseman who had once been a shaky minor league pitcher.

He jokingly dismissed the Dodgers during the 1934 season, asking, "Is Brooklyn still in the league?"

"I had great control, I never missed hitting the other fellow's bat," Bill Terry quipped in 1934.

Terry converted to first base and became one of the great run producers in team history. In a career that spanned 14 seasons (1923–1936), the left-handed swinger batted .341 and drove in 100 runs six times.

Terry was a starter in each of the first three All-Star Games. He also managed the Giants to a World Series title in 1933, taking over for the retiring McGraw partway through the '32 season and breathing new life into the team.

Moreover, Terry holds an infamous place in the Giants-Dodgers rivalry. He jokingly dismissed the Dodgers during the 1934 season, asking, "Is Brooklyn still in the league?"

Brooklyn reminded him by beating the Giants twice in the final week, allowing the St. Louis Cardinals to eke past New York for the pennant.

No. 4 Mel Ott

Crazy as it sounds now, Vin Scully grew up a Giants fan. Mel Ott was his favorite player.

The future Dodgers broadcaster grew up near the Polo Grounds and would sit in the center-field bleachers watching as Ott blasted home runs at a record rate.

The left-handed slugger finished with 511 of them, the National League mark until another Giants hitter, Willie Mays, came along.

"I absolutely worshiped Mel Ott," Scully told John Shea of the *San Francisco Chronicle* in 2014. "I played a little bit. I hit left-handed, and I always tried to hit like him. I'd raise my leg, I'd start my swing, then something happened. It wasn't the same."

Ott led the NL in home runs six times and drove in 100 runs nine times. He was also the inspiration for Leo Durocher's famous "nice guys finish last" crack.

The line has been clipped by history, but Durocher said it in 1946, when Ott was managing the Giants:

"Look over there. Do you know a nicer guy than Mel Ott? Or any of the other Giants? Why, they're the nicest guys in the world. And where are they? In last place!"

Ott was inducted into the Baseball Hall of Fame in 1951.

No. 11 Carl Hubbell

He threw the best screwball in baseball history, and by the time Carl Hubbell retired he had the arm to prove it. The screwball is, as he himself called it, "an unnatural pitch" because it requires a hurler to twist his wrist violently counterclockwise while releasing the ball.

Sportswriter Jim Murray came across Hubbell long after the pitcher's playing days and found him permanently disfigured. "The only thing eccentric about him is his left arm," Murray wrote. "He looks as if he put it on in the dark."

Hubbell's screwball proved just as unnatural to hitters. Supernatural was more like it. In his 16 seasons—all with the Giants—Hubbell went 253–154 with a 2.98 ERA. He led the league in WHIP (walks + hits/per innings pitched) six times.

Most famously, Hubbell struck out five consecutive batters at the 1934 All-Star Game. The sluggers were Babe Ruth, Lou Gehrig, Jimmie Foxx, Al Simmons, and Joe Cronin—all future Hall of Famers.

After his playing days, Hubbell made another lasting contribution to the Giants in the front office. He worked in player development from 1943 to 1977, helping the team groom homegrown talent such as Willie McCovey, Juan Marichal, Orlando Cepeda, Gaylord Perry, and many others. Then he worked as a scout from 1978 to 1985.

No. 20 Monte Irvin

Jackie Robinson broke baseball's color barrier, but it could have been Monte Irvin. Talented and charismatic, many Negro League owners wanted Irvin to be the man to begin integrating the major leagues.

But in 1947, Brooklyn Dodgers owner Branch Rickey balked at the idea of paying for a player who looked to be on the decline, according to the *New Biographical History of Baseball.* Irvin had missed three years of baseball while in the Army during World War II, and Rickey worried the outfielder/first baseman might be rusty. So he refused when the Newark Eagles of the Negro Leagues demanded $5,000 in exchange for Irvin's contract.

Robinson got the call in 1947. On July 8, 1949, Irvin and infielder Hank Thompson became the first African Americans to play for the Giants.

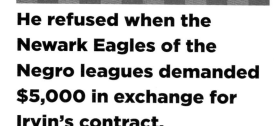

He refused when the Newark Eagles of the Negro leagues demanded $5,000 in exchange for Irvin's contract.

Irvin was 30 by the time he reached the majors, but still had time to post some big seasons. He was instrumental to the Giants' 1951 pennant win, batting .312 with 24 home runs and a league-leading 121 RBI. That season he was also a mentor to a young rookie named Willie Mays.

Irvin was also a key player for the 1954 Giants that won the World Series—but his ring was stolen from his home in the 1960s.

The modern Giants have taken care of that. After each of their three modern titles, they thanked Irvin for his contributions to the franchise by presenting him with a World Series ring. Irvin died on January 11, 2012, at age 96.

"I lost someone I cared about and admired very, very much, someone who was like a second father to me," Mays said. "Monte Irvin was a great man."

14

MADISON BUMGARNER

Because there was no real mystery to it, manager Bruce Bochy announced early in spring training that Madison Bumgarner would be his 2015 Opening Day starter.

"Oh and he's going to pitch the second game, too," Bochy said.

The line got a laugh. But with Bumgarner, is anything really that far-fetched?

This is a guy who has ridden horseback across the AT&T Park warning track to present a World Series championship banner. Who has grumbled, "I'll take care of it" and clambered out of the team bus to repair a stalled engine. Who has wielded an axe next to a blue ox (for a magazine cover shoot) and chopped wood with Khal Drogo of *Game of Thrones* (for a Carhartt clothing ad).

This is a guy who blows his nose on the mound so often and so gloriously that "snot rocket" has become part of the Giants lexicon. Who was once hit by a pitch and made a subtle detour on his way to first base to shout toward the Colorado Rockies dugout, "Y'all better hope that wasn't done on purpose."

Who celebrated his World Series MVP trophy by flying to Vegas—to watch the National Finals Rodeo.

This is a guy who practiced his cow-roping skills while visiting teammate Jeremy Affeldt's house.

"I'd come home and he'd be spinning this rope," the reliever explained. "He's lassoing all my furniture. Then he wants to make me walk this weird, funky walk while he's trying to lasso my foot."

So starting two days in a row? You half-expected Bumgarner to saddle up and ride.

"He's got that hard-nosed, pitcher mentality, and he doesn't let any of the magnificence that's going on around, like the World Series, affect him," outfielder Hunter Pence said. "He's just Madison Bumgarner."

Bumgarner's true legend, of course, has been built on the mound. And his astounding feats there are just as hard to believe.

He really did come out of the bullpen on two days' rest after winning Games 1 and 5 to throw five shutout innings in Game 7 of the 2014 World Series, capping the longest save in Fall Classic history. In all against the Kansas City Royals, he was 2–0 with a 0.43 ERA, with one walk and 17 strikeouts in 21.0 innings.

Bumgarner became the first pitcher with two wins, a sub-0.50 ERA, and at least 20.0 innings in a single World Series since Hall of Famer Sandy Koufax for the 1965 Los Angeles Dodgers.

"What he did was historic," catcher Buster Posey said. "And I think we all appreciate history."

That's the Series that cemented Bumgarner's reputation as an all-time postseason ace, but he is hardly a one-October wonder. In 2010, he became the fourth-youngest starter ever to win a World Series game. He was 21 years, 91 days old when he pitched eight innings of a 4–0 victory over the Texas Rangers in Game 4. The only

Madison Bumgarner and Buster Posey celebrate after Game 7 of the 2014 World Series. (Matt Slocum)

pitchers younger were all 20: Bullet Joe Bush (1913 Athletics), Jim Palmer (1966 Orioles), and Fernando Valenzuela (1981 Dodgers).

In 2012, he delivered 7.0 scoreless innings in Game 2 against the Detroit Tigers as part of the Giants' pitching-dominated four-game sweep.

And in 2014, he shut out the Pittsburgh Pirates (wild-card game), delivered two stifling starts against the St Louis Cardinals (for the NLCS MVP award), and confounded the Royals in the Fall Classic. All told, his 52.2 innings broke the record for heaviest workload in a single postseason, topping the 48.1 innings by the Diamondbacks' Curt Schilling in 2001.

"You know what? I can't lie to you anymore. I'm a little tired now," Bumgarner said after the final out against Kansas City.

This master of the big stage grew up in a small town. Bumgarner was born in Hickory, North Carolina. He went to high school in Hudson, a town about 90 minutes from Charlotte with a population of 2,800 people.

"You wave at everybody you see, pretty much," Bumgarner explained.

He lives now in Lenoir, North Carolina, where farming is the way of life. Around the time he married his high school sweetheart, Ali Sanders, on Valentine's Day 2010, he also bought her a five-day-old bull calf. (Bumgarner says the story of it being a wedding present is exaggerated; Ali wanted a calf and he bought her one.)

The Bumgarners go back 100 years in Caldwell County, which is why an area of the farming community along a stretch of Deal Mill Road came to be known as "Bumtown."

As the Bumgarner bio in the Giants media guide explains, one of the greatest pitchers in team history did not arrive with a smooth delivery: His mother, Debbie, underwent major surgery—5½ hours—just to be able to conceive him, after having an earlier family of three children. Doctors gave her a 38 percent chance of being able to have additional babies. "Mr. Madison is quite a miracle," Debbie said.

Her other children were 18, 16, and 14 when Madison arrived on August 1, 1989. His first word was "ball."

Madison grew up to be a star for South Caldwell High School in Hudson. In the final game of his prep career, Bumgarner hit a walk-off two-run, inside-the-park homer to win the state championship.

"The Giants need injured ace Tim Lincecum down the stretch. His replacement wasn't half bad."

But here's one thing he didn't do as a kid: throw a curveball. Dad Kevin, concerned about his son's long-term future, didn't let Bumgarner throw a breaking ball until he was 16.

"Probably longer than that, actually," Bumgarner told me during 2015 spring training. "It's just what we were taught back then—that breaking balls are bad for your arm. Don't throw them. So I didn't."

Learning to play good ol' country hardball would serve him well. Over time he added a late-breaking slider, a curveball, and a change-up.

The Giants drafted him in the fist round (10th overall) in the 2007 first-year player draft. In fact, they didn't hesitate. Giants scout Pat Portugal told *Sports Illustrated*: "You don't ever think you're looking at a Hall of Famer, but I was thinking that with Madison. I've never done that. But he was that special."

He breezed through the minor league system, compiling a 34–6 record with a 2.00 ERA over 62 starts. In 2008, he was named Minor League Baseball's Most Spectacular Pitcher.

The Giants called up Bumgarner to his major league debut on September 8, 2009. He was there as a last-second fill-in for a starter dealing with a bad back. The opening to the Associated Press game story that night struck a tone that suggested there were bigger things to come: "The Giants need injured ace Tim Lincecum down the stretch. His replacement wasn't half bad."

CHICKS DIG THE LONG BALL

Magnificent Los Angeles Dodgers ace Clayton Kershaw gave up just one home run to an opposing pitcher over his first eight seasons in the majors.

With Madison Bumgarner at the plate, he should have known better.

"Fastball right down the middle," Kershaw lamented on May 21, 2015. "I should have had a little more respect for him, I guess."

Bumgarner has 11 career home runs as of this writing, the most by a Giants pitcher since Johnny Antonelli had 15 from 1954 to 1960.

In 2015, Bumgarner became just the fourth Giants pitcher to hit at least five in a single season. None of the others were likely on your fantasy team: Hal Schumacher (1934), Art Nehf (1924), and Jouett Meekin (1894).

A year earlier he hit four and became the first pitcher to hit two grand slams in a season since Tony Cloninger hit two in the same game in 1966.

Because of Bumgarner's powerful right-handed swing and impressive plate discipline, manager Bruce Bochy has been known to use the pitcher as a pinch-hitter.

So you can imagine the reaction when Washington Nationals pitcher Max Scherzer urged the National League to adopt the designated hitter rule because nobody pays to see a pitcher "swinging a wet newspaper."

"Oh, well, my wet newspaper is 34-½ inches, 33-½ ounces," Bumgarner said. "And I'm waiting on some new ones right now."

No, he wasn't. And at 20 years and 38 days, Bumgarner became the fourth youngest Giants pitcher to make his major league debut. Only Mike McCormick (17 years and 342 days), Nestor Chavez (19 years and 65 days), and Ron Bryant (19 years and 321 days) were younger.

"He showed good poise out there," Bochy said of the future World Series MVP.

Maybe sticking with fastballs as a kid helped nurture his durability. But it didn't hurt that Bumgarner "has a body built for plowing cornfields," in the words of Giants broadcaster Mike Krukow. From the second Bumgarner arrived in the big leagues, the 6'5", 235-pound left-hander looked impervious to the red flags facing other young pitchers. He blows through innings as if they are just another nostril impediment.

In 2014, Bumgarner totaled 270 innings, including the playoffs, for the most by a Giants pitcher since Ron Bryant reached that same total in 1973. Bryant was essentially toast after that—he went 3–16 the remainder of his career and was finished at age 27.

Bumgarner, meanwhile, went back to his "training," which is to say back to North Carolina to work on his 116-acre farm with 20 horses, 60 cattle, and no shortage of chores.

Some athletes worry about their brand. Bumgarner worries about his branding iron.

"What he does in an average workday on his ranch is pretty incredible," said Tony Ambroza, an executive for the Carhartt clothing company, after filming a spot on Bumgarner's property. "People who follow him quickly realize what makes him as strong as he is. Before workouts, there was work."

Bumgarner reported to spring training in 2015 amid a flurry of questions about how his body would hold up to the strain of such a heavy October workload. He answered them by topping 200 innings for the fifth consecutive year and establishing a new career high with 234 strikeouts.

He became the first Giants pitcher to win 18 games or more in consecutive seasons since Gaylord Perry in 1969–70. He became the first Giants left-hander to do it since Carl Hubbell, who did it for six straight seasons (1932–37).

"Unreal," Posey said after Bumgarner's final start of the season. "I mean, for the amount of innings he pitched last year, and the amount he's thrown this year—it's hard for people to understand how taxing that is on your body.... It's something he should be really proud of. I'm proud of him, for what he's done this year."

Part of Bumgarner's rogue charm is that he treats his unthinkable baseball accomplishments as if he is still chopping wood back in Lenoir. When the questions are at their most breathless, he is at his laconic best.

How does your arm feel?

"It feels like an arm. It's the craziest thing."

What about all those high-stress innings?

"High-stress for you?"

How did your World Series MVP award raise expectations?

"Did it? It didn't change mine from what they were."

At some point, Bumgarner's feats of strength might simply have to be believed. This is a guy who really did get challenged to a wrestling match by Nori Aoki shortly after the outfielder signed a free-agent deal with the Giants. Aoki, who played for the Royals in 2014, backed down almost the second he arrived for spring training.

"He was a little bigger than I expected," Aoki said. Through his interpreter, Aoki added that weapons should be allowed in any match against someone Bumgarner's size.

15

GAYLORD PERRY

Gaylord Perry was so cagey about his spitball that his Hall of Fame plaque ought to have immortalized him with a wink.

Oh, he threw a greaseball, all right. There was no denying that. Long after his retirement, Perry said: "I reckon I tried everything on the old apple but salt and pepper and chocolate sauce topping."

Heck, his autobiography was called *Me and the Spitter: An Autobiographical Confession.* Perry wasn't exactly subtle.

But catching him wet-handed was a different matter. He'd tug at his cap, brush a hand against his hip, and tug at his belt, all in an effort to make the batters guess where he was hiding something.

So where was it?

"I'd always have the grease in at least two places, in case the umpires would ask me to wipe off one," Perry wrote. "I never wanted to be caught out there without anything. It wouldn't be professional."

Often, the only thing being applied was psychology. Perry knew the fear of his spitter was enough to get in a batter's head. He once befuddled an overthinking Hank Aaron with a pitch he said was "as dry as a Baptist wedding."

Perry used those expectations—and expectorations—to drive hitters batty over the span of 22 seasons. The big right-hander won 314 games, starting by piling up wins for the Giants from 1962 to 1971.

Over 10 seasons in San Francisco, Perry went 134–109 with a 2.96 ERA. He threw a no-hitter in 1968 and still ranks among the team's all-time leaders in most significant categories. He owns the San Francisco (post NY-move) mark for most innings in a season (328⅔) and ranks second to Juan Marichal for wins (134), ERA (2.96), complete games (125), and shutouts (21).

It was also in San Francisco that Perry learned some of the, ahem, tricks of his trade and set off his opponents' career-long quest to catch him at it. A reporter once asked Perry's

He once befuddled an overthinking Hank Aaron with a pitch he said was "as dry as a Baptist wedding."

daughter, Allison, if her daddy threw a greaseball. "It's a hard slider," she responded.

She was five.

Perry learned the spitball from teammate Bob Shaw in 1964 and took the plunge on May 31, 1964. That's the day he entered as a reliever during the second game of a marathon doubleheader against the Mets at Shea Stadium in New York.

He came in to start the bottom of the 13th, throwing 10 shutout innings as the Giants finally won 8–6 in 23.

Perry called that game the "first spitball victory of his career." He took the mound that day with slippery elm in his mouth to generate extra saliva. Then he applied some to the ball, making it break in confounding ways.

"The juice in my mouth was slicker than an eel," Perry wrote in *Me and The Spitter.* "My mouth was watering like a hungry hound's at eating time. Suddenly, I felt like a pitcher again."

Late in the 1965 season, Giants pitching coach Larry Jansen helped Perry refine one of his legal pitches—his slider—and the right-hander was soon one of the best pitchers in baseball. He went 21–8 with a 2.99 ERA in 1966 and was the winning pitcher in his first All-Star Game.

Publicly, Perry said the refined slider was the key to his career. Hitters weren't swallowing it.

Publicly, Perry said the refined slider was the key to his career. Hitters weren't swallowing it.

"All that slider stuff is a bunch of bunk," said Eddie Mathews of the Milwaukee Braves. "Perry is the pitcher he is today because he learned to control his spitter."

It was the worst-kept secret in baseball. It helped that Perry, a native of Williamston, North Carolina, had a bunch of homespun one-liners to make his rule-breaking seem endearing. Even hitters joined in his comedy routine.

Perry wrote about the time he faced the Cincinnati Reds in 1968. Perry opened the game with a greaseball to Pete Rose that had Charlie Hustle flailing badly. Rose snapped at the home-plate umpire for letting Perry load up by hiding a foreign substance in his cap.

Now that the pitcher knew he was in Rose's head, Perry struck him out with a pair of changeups. Rose, really incensed, screamed at the ump and earned an ejection from the game.

Then Rose turned to the mound.

"Hey, Perry, where do you keep your dipstick?" Rose asked.

"What do you mean?" Perry responded.

"How else will you know when your cap needs an oil change?"

Antics aside, Perry could really pitch. Along with the spitball and the hard slider, the 6'4", 205-pound righty threw a fastball, curveball, forkball, and changeup.

In the waning days of the 1968 season, he used all those pitches to become part of one of the weirder feats in baseball history. Pitching that night only because Juan Marichal had a sprained knee, Perry no-hit the St. Louis Cardinals on September 17 at Candlestick Park; a day later, the Cardinals' Ray Washburn repaid the favor by no-hitting the Giants.

What were the odds? There were only six no-hitters in the history of Candlestick Park, and two of them happened within a 24-hour period. (One mathematician ventured that the odds were 250,000 to 1.)

The late baseball writer Nick Peters noted that what is often forgotten is that Perry was fresh off a near no-hitter against the Chicago Cubs: Just weeks earlier, on August 26 at Candlestick Park, the only hit off Perry was a seventh-inning single by Glenn Beckert.

"When I got to the seventh against the Cardinals, I couldn't help thinking of Beckert," Perry told Peters in *Tales from the San Francisco Giants Dugout*. "I was very excited about it because the Cardinals were the best, and there was nothing close to a hit that day."

Perry would go on to win two Cy Young Awards, becoming the first pitcher to win one in both leagues. But he did so only after one of the worst trades in Giants history. San Francisco traded Perry and shortstop Frank Duffy to the Cleveland Indians for pitcher Sam McDowell on November 29, 1971.

This was a bad idea. McDowell had led the American League in strikeouts five times, but he also led the league in walks five times. The Giants figured that McDowell, four years younger than Perry, had a better future. And McDowell vowed to reward their faith.

DARK TO JUPITER ON
GAYLORD AND THE MOON

Legend has it that Gaylord Perry was taking batting practice one day while Giants manager Alvin Dark stood and watched his raggedy swing.

"They'll put a man on the moon before he hits a home run," Dark sniffed.

Neil Armstrong and Apollo 11 touched down on the lunar surface on July 20, 1969.

Minutes later, Perry blasted his first career home run off Claude Osteen at Candlestick Park.

The story is so cosmically awesome that it has the whiff of urban legend. In fact, it was once featured in *Ripley's Believe it or Not*. I always leaned toward "not," so shortly after Armstrong's death on August 25, 2012, I called Perry at his home in North Carolina to ask, essentially, "C'mon, is that really true?"

Absolutely, Perry said.

He said that Dark made the comment to sportswriter Harry Jupiter while both were behind the batting cage on a day the right-handed-hitting Perry was knocking them out of the park with ease. Jupiter told Dark, "He's going to hit a home run for you someday," prompting Dark's famous retort.

Perry was a lifetime .131 hitter.

"I was always facing Drysdale and Koufax and Gibson and Seaver," the pitcher said. "My teammates didn't do too well against them either."

But his third-inning solo homer off Osteen that July 20 helped the Giants erase an early deficit as they rallied to beat the Dodgers 7–3. Perry pitched a complete game.

He said that for the rest of his life, he felt a kinship with the pioneering astronaut.

"Neil and I both had good days," Perry said. "But he had a better day than I did. I won a game. What he did was awesome."

"I'm going to take them to the pennant," McDowell said after the deal. "San Francisco gave up too much for me. I intend to show them they were right."

Instead, "Sudden Sam" McDowell's alcoholism hastened the end of his career. His addiction was so severe in San Francisco that after the pitcher was arrested for being drunk and disorderly, manager Charlie Fox said: "So what else is new.... We already have our fines set up. We call it the Sam McDowell Fund."

McDowell's career in San Francisco consisted of an 11–10 record with a 4.36 ERA over 46 games.

Perry, in contrast, won the Cy Young Award in 1972, turning in what baseball writer Bill James deemed the best season by an American League pitcher since 1931. Perry went 24–16 with a 1.92 ERA in 342.2 (!!!) innings that season, despite pitching for a lousy Indians team.

He loved pitching in the AL, aside from facing Rod Carew, the seven-time batting champion, of whom he once said: "He's the only player in baseball who consistently hits my grease. He sees the ball so well, I guess he can pick out the dry side."

Perry would go on to win another Cy Young Award with the San Diego Padres in 1978, before retiring after the 1983 season at age 45.

By then it was clearer than ever that the Giants underestimated Perry's staying power. Perry won 239 games after age 30, a figure topped only by Warren Spahn and Cy Young himself. During that time, Perry had five 20-win seasons and eight years of at least 200 strikeouts.

When finally Perry hung up his spikes for good, he did so with his typical humor.

"The league will be a little drier now, folks," he said.

18

THE
2012
CHAMPIONS

Sergio Romo stands about 5'10" and weighs 166 pounds, regardless of what the official listings say.

Underestimate him at your own peril.

"He gives every ounce he has when he pitches," said Orlando Cepeda, the Giants Hall of Famer. "He has a lot of guts."

Romo's strikeout of Miguel Cabrera to end the 2012 World Series provides the perfect example. Let's call it Exhibit K.

It was two out in the bottom of the 10th with the Giants nursing a 4–3 lead when the closer stared down Cabrera, the Detroit Tigers' behemoth Triple Crown winner.

With a 2-2 count, catcher Buster Posey signaled for Romo to throw his best pitch, a slider. Romo shook his head.

"He shook to a fastball there," Posey said after the game, still blown away. "That shows the type of guts he has and faith in what he's got."

Romo threw a fastball. In fact, he threw a fastball *right down the middle*. Never mind that his 89-mph heater is a jalopy in a league of 95-mph Ferraris. Never mind that Cabrera hit

.379 against fastballs in the strike zone that season, according to BaseballAnalytics.org.

The little guy threw it as if he stood 6'6". "If I hadn't believed in myself and my abilities," Romo said later, "I wouldn't be standing where I'm at."

A stunned Cabrera watched the fastball sail by for a called strike three.

Romo threw a fastball. In fact, he threw a fastball right down the middle. Never mind that his 89-mph heater is a jalopy in a league of 95-mph Ferraris.

And the Giants were World Series champions, again.

If you tuned in only for that last pitch, you'd still understand all you needed to know about the 2012 champs: they had no use for odds.

It took Romo's pitching and Hunter Pence's speeches and Posey's grand slam and Marco Scutaro's Mr. October imitation, and Barry Zito's dip into the fountain of youth, but San Francisco had its second title in three years.

The Giants staved off playoff elimination six consecutive times, overcoming improbable deficits against the Cincinnati Reds (trailing 2–0 in the division series) and St. Louis Cardinals (trailing 3–1 in the National League Championship Series).

The World Series? That was the easy part.

"Detroit probably didn't know what it was in for," Giants general manager Brian Sabean said after the four-game sweep. "Our guys had a date with destiny."

Sergio Romo reacts after striking out Omar Infante to end Game 3 of the 2012 World Series. (Matt Slocum)

These Giants were no longer the "misfits and castoffs," as manager Bruce Bochy had described the 2010 champs. By now, Posey, Tim Lincecum, and Matt Cain were established stars.

Still, the 2012 title run was nearly as unlikely. Romo was the closer only because All-Star Brian Wilson had blown out his elbow in April and because Bochy's first choice, Santiago Casilla, had fallen into a mid-summer funk.

Gregor Blanco—who played wondrous defense throughout the postseason—was in the outfield only because July's All-Star MVP Melky Cabrera was suspended for 50 games in August after a positive testosterone test.

Two-time Cy Young Award–winner Lincecum had posted a career-worst 5.18 ERA that season and "led" the National League with 15 losses. The Freak started just one game in the playoffs, and lost.

And all of that was nothing compared to the obstacles the Giants faced in the playoffs.

In a best-of-five NLDS round that matched the Giants against their old manager, Dusty Baker, the Reds won the two opening games at AT&T Park. The series headed back to Cincinnati, where the Reds had to win just one of three games to advance.

The Giants were on the brink of elimination without winning a game—but that sound you hear is Pence clearing his throat.

During a memorable pep talk before Game 3 in Cincinnati, the free-spirited right fielder stood up in the clubhouse and implored teammates to find a way to extend the season.

"Look into each other's eyes! Play for each other! Win each moment! Win each inning!" Pence yelled.

There's a more extensive look at Pence's oration sensation in Chapter 26 but suffice to say the Giants got the message.

"We went out there and we felt like warriors, trying to hunt people," Giants outfielder Angel Pagan said that October. "I don't know how to explain it. There was so much energy."

The Giants captured Games 3, 4, and 5 on the road, winning the clincher 6–4 behind Posey's fifth-inning grand slam (and a Romo save).

Riding the high from that wave, San Francisco headed off to St. Louis...and promptly lost three of the first four games. That meant staring at elimination again in Game 5 in St. Louis, with Zito on the mound.

The Giants were on the brink of elimination without winning a game— but that sound you hear is Pence clearing his throat.

To that point, Zito was best known in San Francisco for not living up to his six-year, $126 million contract. But on this night, he paid off big, like a slot machine that hits after one last quarter.

Zito saved the Giants' season with 7.2 shutout innings and a 5–0 victory, looking at last like the Cy Young Award winner he'd been for Oakland in 2002. Like Romo, Zito did it without much of a fastball. Cardinals third baseman David Freese marveled that Zito beat them with pitches so soft, it looked like the left-hander was "throwing pillows on the couch."

The Giants never lost again.

They finished off the Cardinals when the series shifted back to AT&T Park for Games 6 and 7. That's where Scutaro, inheriting Cody Ross's old role as the unlikely MVP, joined Romo as a little man playing big.

The 5'10", 185-pound second baseman had six multihit games in the series. Like Ross, he was a late-summer acquisition that barely registered a blip at the time of the deal. The Giants got the 36-year-old journeyman infielder from the Colorado Rockies on July 27 by trading Charlie Culberson and cash.

It looked like a ho-hum deal to all but those who knew Scutaro's heart.

"He'll play a huge role; he always does," Scutaro's former A's teammate Mark Ellis told Chris Haft of MLB.com. "Every team he's on, he has a huge impact."

In the final inning of the clincher, on October 22, 2012, he repeatedly looked into the rainy San Francisco sky as if Champagne were falling.

Scutaro hit .362 with a .385 on-base percentage and .473 slugging percentage down the final stretch of the regular season. By the time the Giants reached the playoffs, teammates were calling him "Blockbuster."

Scutaro batted .500 (14 for 28) with six runs scored and four RBI in the NLCS. He also provided the enduring image of the series.

In the final inning of the clincher, on October 22, 2012, he repeatedly looked into the rainy San Francisco sky as if Champagne were falling. Scutaro appeared to put his hands out in wonder, as if to ask, can you believe this?

"The rain never felt so good," he said.

The World Series itself was a mismatch from the start. Pablo Sandoval made that clear in Game 1 at AT&T Park.

Sandoval had been benched for poor play during the Giants' previous World Series triumph, batting just three times against the Texas Rangers in 2010. He made up for lost time in the 2012 opener, going four for four with three homers, including two rockets against Tigers ace Justin Verlander.

"I'm sure he wasn't too happy with how it went there in 2010," Bochy said of Sandoval after the 8–3 victory. "He looks very determined to show not just us, but everybody, what a great talent he is."

The rest of the series was about pitching, which played to the Giants' strengths. San Francisco combined for a 1.42 ERA, outscored the Tigers 1–6, and held them to a .159 batting average.

Scutaro, of course, delivered the go-ahead hit in the clinching Game 4. His single off reliever Phil Coke in the top of the 10th inning drove home Ryan Theriot, breaking a 3–3 tie and setting the stage for Romo vs. Cabrera in the ninth.

So this is how World Series are won—with a 5'10" guy driving in a 5'11" guy so that a 166-pounder can get the save?

These guys—*Giants?*

"In stature, no," Theriot said. "But in will and desire, yeah. I would probably say we are Giants."

17

DUSTY BAKER

The man who grew up to be the relentlessly positive, contagiously energetic manager of the Giants was repeatedly cut from Little League teams for being a sourpuss.

Dusty Baker got the boot the first time at age eight, after striking out and hurling his bat at the backstop.

At nine, he threw down his glove and stomped on it because he missed a ball during tryouts.

At 10, his good friend beaned him in the head with a pitch— just as he'd said he would. And that was going to be it for Dusty's baseball career.

"I quit," Baker told me, years later. "I was going to get a paper route because a quarter a week was all my dad was giving me for all the hard work he had me doing. I said, 'Man, I always wanted to be a businessman.'"

But the coach who kept cutting him was also the man who refused to let him leave: Johnnie B. Baker Sr. sat his boy down for a talking to and, this time, he got through.

"My dad told me that if I could take that bad attitude and put it in a positive direction," Dusty recalled, "I could really be someone one day."

That's how the world was denied a promising young newspaper carrier. But the Giants eventually gained a leader who won 840 regular-season games, three National League Manager of the Year Awards, two division titles, a wild-card spot, and a National League pennant. Baker's resume is famously incomplete—he never won a World Series—but before Bruce Bochy came along, he was the most successful manager in San Francisco history.

Baker also pressed a lot of magic buttons during his decade-long reign, and his players loved him unabashedly.

Baker holds the San Francisco record for most regular-season victories and is third highest in winning percentage (.540).

His Giants career started and ended with a bang. In Baker's first year, 1993, he engineered the greatest one-year turnaround in baseball history by inheriting a 72–90 squad and guiding it to a 103–59 finish. In Baker's last year, he piloted the Giants to the 2002 World Series, just the team's third appearance in the Fall Classic since moving West in 1958.

Along the way, he operated from the dugout in a fashion that a taciturn Connie Mack would have found unrecognizable. Baker wore wristbands, chomped toothpicks, cheered wildly, and hugged often.

"You knew that he was the guy in charge," Darryl Hamilton, the late outfielder, told the *New York Times* in 2000. "Then again, you didn't. He kind of came to you like another player. All the guys who played for him respected him because of that.

"He'd always be talking to the hitters about hitting," Hamilton said. "I'd be like, 'Dusty, come on, man, you can't hit anymore.' He'd grab a bat and go out and hit. Most managers aren't like that. They're not as easy to talk to."

As with most managers, Baker's strategic approach over the years was a mixed bag and some of his big-ticket choices forever rankled. Slumping rookie pitcher Salomon Torres starting the crucial 1993 regular-season finale? Light-hitting Tsuyoshi Shinjo as a World Series designated hitter?

But Baker also pressed a lot of magic buttons during his decade-long reign, and his players loved him unabashedly. Over Baker's final six seasons with the Giants, they won at least 86 games every year.

Barry Bonds once compared him to the future Hall of Fame boss he had with the Pittsburgh Pirates.

"Dusty Baker is like a Jim Leyland–type person," Bonds said. "We would have played for Jim Leyland for nothing. I have the same feeling for Dusty Baker."

Relief pitcher Jeff Brantley said: "There's not one person who doesn't hold Dusty in the highest respect."

Some of Baker's credibility came from his standout playing career. A two-time All-Star outfielder, he batted .278 with a .347 on-base percentage and a .432 slugging percentage over 19 seasons in the majors. He hit 242 home runs, won a Gold Glove in 1981, and was the 1977 NLCS MVP while with the Los Angeles Dodgers.

Baker was just 19 when he broke in as a rookie with the Atlanta Braves. His teammates on that 1968 team included Hank Aaron, who took the youngster from Riverside, California, under his wing. When

Aaron broke Babe Ruth's home run record, with No. 715 in 1974, it was Baker who was on deck.

"It was a cold night in Atlanta—cold as heck," Baker recalled one spring training. "And right before Hank walked to the plate, he told me: 'I'm going to get it over with right here.'"

Baker recounted Aaron stories often throughout his Giants managerial career. He also told stories about the other great players or opponents from those early days, including Roberto Clemente (who would influence how he rested veterans) and Pete Rose (who urged him to raise the bar when setting goals).

But much of Baker's management style came from the lessons he learned while playing for Uncle Sam. He graduated from the U.S. Marine Corps in 1969 and was named the outstanding Marine in his platoon. Baker, a reserve, was there just to pass the time. But his drill instructors identified him as a leadership candidate and had him carry the flag on drill day. His debut did not go well.

"One day our drill instructor said, 'STOP!' I had just gone in a complete circle," Baker said with a laugh. "I didn't know the whole platoon was following me. He said, 'If you don't go straight, they don't go straight.' So he told me to put my eyes on something way out front and follow that. And then I took pride in what I was doing."

Baker also learned something in the military that would forever shape his handling of a major league clubhouse.

"That's where I learned teamwork, the Marines," he said. "Whether you like a guy or don't like a guy, or you don't like his color or religion or whatever, you still have to protect his back in wartime. You need each other for survival. That's what teamwork is. That's teamwork to the max."

Baker finished his playing career in the Bay Area, spending the 1984 season with the Giants and '85–86 with the Oakland A's.

During that time, he made an impression on Giants general manager Al Rosen, who in 1988 hired him as the team's batting coach.

Baker served as a coach under Roger Craig for the final five of Craig's seven seasons as manager. Then Baker replaced him. Baker was 43 at the time of his promotion. And the sunny outlook was clear from the start.

"This is the greatest day of my life, so far," Baker said. "The next greatest day is when we win the pennant and the world championship."

For a while, such a goal looked possible in his first season. Despite zero managerial experience, he guided the team to 103 victories to tie the franchise record set in 1962. (That season gets its whole chapter elsewhere in this book.)

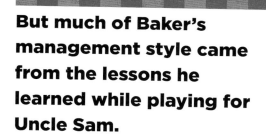

But much of Baker's management style came from the lessons he learned while playing for Uncle Sam.

Baker engineered an NL West title for an otherwise overmatched 1997 team. That squad was actually outscored over the course of a season (793–784) and had a ho-hum pitching staff that finished ninth in the NL with a 4.39 ERA. But it won anyway, racking up one improbable victory after another. After a late-September victory over the San Diego Padres that kept them in the race, reporters went to the clubhouse looking for an explanation.

"It's destiny," Baker said.

"No, I'd say it's Dustiny," countered reliever Rod Beck. "This is Dusty's team, and that's what I call it: Dustiny."

That term—*Dustiny*—followed Baker for the rest of his managing career, evoked whenever his Giants pulled out an unexpected victory. But, privately, he often rankled at the perception that he was nothing but a good luck charm. Baker did lean on mysticism—he'd sometimes crank up some John Lee Hooker in his office to set the proper mojo for a big game—but he felt that people forgot that he had a brain to go along with his heart.

Contrary to his reputation as a gut-instinct guy, Baker carried a lineup card jam-packed with stats he'd personally written in the margin before games. He'd have notes about what a batter hits vs. left-handed hitters,

You don't win Manager of the Year Awards just by pressing "play" on John Lee Hooker CDs.

vs. right-handed hitters, how he hits with runners in scoring position, what counts he likes to run in, how many double plays he'd hit into, etc.

And then he could catch teams off-guard. He was fond of saying, "I'm not a squeeze dude." But in Game 2 of the 2002 NLCS against the St. Louis Cardinals, he pulled the trigger with light-hitting Ramon Martinez at the plate. Martinez dropped an exquisite suicide squeeze bunt for the final run of a 4–1 victory.

You don't win Manager of the Year Awards just by pressing "play" on John Lee Hooker CDs. Bobby Cox and Tony La Russa won the most Manager of the Year Awards, with four each. Baker, Lou Piniella, and Jim Leyland are in the next tier, at three.

"He's very well-prepared," rival manager Bobby Valentine once said. "He's one of the real professional guys in the league."

A voracious reader, Baker also continued to hone his natural leadership skills. He studied the insights of sports leaders like Phil Jackson and Vince Lombardi. He also found strategic help in unlikely places. I was in his office once in 2002 when he reached into his shelf and pulled down *The Leadership Secrets of Attila the Hun.*

"Whether you agree with the sacrifice bunt or not, you have to be obedient," Baker explained. "It's just that I can't cut off your head like Attila the Hun did."

In all, Baker took the Giants to the postseason three times. But Game 7 of the 2002 World Series was his last as Giants manager. Baker's relationship with the team's managing general partner, Peter Magowan, had deteriorated that season because of what the manager considered a lack of respect. General manager Brian Sabean, in announcing the parting, diplomatically described the dispute as "noncompensation issues that [Baker] seemed reluctant to embrace."

So ended one of the most successful managerial tenures in Giants history. Only John McGraw (4,424) managed more games for the franchise than Baker (1,556).

"It's sad for San Francisco, but Joe Montana left, and he was the greatest figure in San Francisco," outfielder Shawon Dunston told the *San Francisco Chronicle* the day Baker left. "The Giants are going to win, and whatever team Dusty's on is going to win, too."

18

ROD
BECK

Rod Beck, an affable fellow with a plush toy for a heart, sported facial hair that could scare a motorcycle gang. And if his sprawling Fu Manchu wasn't fierce enough, it got backup from a shoulder-length mullet that flapped magnificently in the Candlestick Park breeze.

Because he was a closer, it seemed reasonable to assume that Beck's hirsute styling was modeled after fabled intimidators like Goose Gossage, Rollie Fingers, and Al Hrabosky. But he was no hair apparent.

"I admired those guys," Beck explained. "But I grew the mustache my junior year in high school so that I could [look older and] get into places I wasn't supposed to get into."

Beck grew up to lead the Giants in saves, if not shaves, during a career in San Francisco that lasted from 1991 to 1997. Alas, he still got into places he wasn't supposed to get into, and his hard-partying ways led to an early death at age 38.

Beck left behind an incredible legacy in baseball and remains one of the most beloved Giants of modern times. The right-hander's 48 saves in 1993 remain a franchise record, tied by Brian Wilson in 2010.

Beck had a fastball in the low 90-mph range and a split-fingered fastball that dove like a swan. And on days he had neither? Well, he figured out something.

"Because he was a gunslinger, man," recalled Mike Krukow, the broadcaster and former Giants pitcher. "That's the way he approached everything. He had a huge heart, a Hall of Fame heart."

Only Robb Nen, with 206 career saves, ranks ahead of Beck's 199 on the all-time Giants list. But there's a funny story about one of the greatest relievers in team history—he didn't wanna do it.

Rodney Roy Beck was a starter when the A's drafted him out of Grant High School (Van Nuys, CA) in the 1986 amateur draft. The 13th-round pick had two rough seasons in low Class A ball, going 6–11 with a 5.20 ERA. His wife, Stacey Beck, once floated the idea of Rod getting a real job.

"I love you," Rod replied. "But all 28 teams are going to have to tell me that I'm not good enough before I quit doing this, so you can come with me or not."

He lasted only two years in the A's organization, but that was long enough to change his life. During that time a pitching coach named Butch Hughes taught him how to throw a splitter.

"I thought Rod was a fringe guy," Hughes said, years later. "He needed something to get him over the hump. He had good control, and his mechanics were okay. I'm very happy for [his success]."

The A's traded him to the Giants in 1988 for pitcher Charlie Corbell, who never reached the majors. Beck got a cup of coffee in San Francisco, starting in 1991 with the big club, but was sent back to Triple-A Phoenix by May after racking up a 9.00 ERA in five outings.

The Giants wanted him to committ to being a full-time reliever. Beck took the news as an insult.

A 1996 photo of Shooter.

"I'd come home at night going crazy because they wouldn't tell me why," Beck told Mark Gonzalez of the *San Jose Mercury News*. "I thought I had my chance and blew it. They stuck me in the 'pen, and now they're going to forget about me. I'm not on the 40-man roster. I thought they gave up. It made me more mad, and I wanted to bite someone's head off."

But the Giants were right. They'd seen the way Beck's splitter was evolving from decent to devastating now that he'd had a chance to learn from San Francisco manager Roger Craig, the godfather of the pitch.

Beck came out of the bullpen in Phoenix and surrendered only five runs in 32⅓ innings. He was back in San Francisco by the All-Star break.

In retrospect, it's nutty that his journey to closer took so long. Beck had everything a ninth-inning reliever needed, and not just because of the facial hair.

Intimidating? He stood 6'1" and 215 pounds.

Awesome nickname? Teammates called him "Shooter" because he used the word all the time in dugout chatter.

Mound presence? Beck would bend and squint for the catcher's signs like John Wayne searching the horizon for bad guys. Then Beck's right arm would swing like a pendulum, a motion so rhythmic that *Mercury News* columnist Mark Purdy once wrote a poem about it:

Stand up straight. Let your right arm drop.
Swing it back and forth. Never let it stop.
Ticking, ticking, ticking, like the hands on the clock.
Now you're doing it, the Rod Beck Rock.

Beck's hypnotizing arm action was essentially an accident.

"It goes back to the way I used to pitch," Beck said, when asked for the roots of the Rock. "When I looked for the sign, I used to keep the ball in my hand, behind my back. But the coaches made me stop that. Baserunners could see my grip on the ball and signal to the batter what I was throwing."

The solution was obvious.

"They made me put the ball in my glove and grip it there during the windup," Beck said. "But if I do that, I've got to do something with my right arm before the windup."

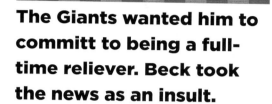

The Giants wanted him to committ to being a full-time reliever. Beck took the news as an insult.

And so it was as simple as that. Beck's arm swayed to stop it from getting bored between pitches. Back and forth. Back and forth. As Purdy put it: "Hey, batter. You're getting drowsy. Verrrry drowsy."

"As a hitter, what would cross my mind is, 'This guy is impatient,'" said Bob Brenly, a coach during Beck's years. "You know, like this guy really wants to throw the ball."

In truth, Beck said the swaying arm act relaxed him. Manager Dusty Baker once compared it to an NBA free-throw shooter making his way through the same routine—dribble dribble, bounce bounce—before taking a big shot.

Whatever the reason, this Shooter got on a roll. In 1992, his first full season in the majors, he posted a 1.76 ERA, the second lowest among National League relievers, and saved 17 games. He would go on to earn three All-Star selections with the Giants and win the Rolaids Relief Man of the Year Award in the strike-shortened 1994 season.

Beck's most memorable outing, however, was the one he almost blew.

On September 18, 1997, with the Giants slugging it out against the Dodgers for the NL West lead, Beck entered a tie game in the 10th and nearly unraveled. Fresh off a wretched blown save against the Atlanta Braves, the right-hander took the mound at Candlestick Park and surrendered three consecutive hits.

Bases loaded. Nobody out. Home fans booing. *Home* fans.

Beck simply focused on the next guy.

"To do this job, you've got to be able to forget yesterday," he said later. "To do this job, you need a short memory and thin skin."

Um...thin skin?

"Right, sorry. Thick skin," Beck said. "Whatever. You need skin."

With all looking lost, manager Dusty Baker came to the mound.

Bases loaded. Nobody out. Home fans booing. Home fans.

A crowd of 52,188 applauded, thinking he was there to take Beck out. Instead, the manager looked into the pitcher's eyes.

"I told him to dig as deep as he could and to use all his bag of tricks," Baker said that day. "I told him, 'You can do it.'"

Beck struck out Todd Zeile, catching the Dodgers' dangerous third baseman looking at a fastball. He greeted the next batter, Eddie Murray, with his best splitter of the day. The left-handed batter hit it weakly to second base, leading to an inning-ending, season-saving double play.

Those fans who wanted Beck out of the game? They were cheering like mad.

"The fans booed him!" Barry Bonds said in the cluhouse later. "We didn't think that was right.... He blew one in Atlanta. So what? He's been the guy for us all year long and we have confidence in him. You're supposed to give him confidence, not knock him down."

Often forgotten is that Beck pitched two more scoreless innings that day, mowing down the Dodgers in the 11th and 12th before Giants catcher Brian Johnson blasted a ball into the left-field seats. (See Chapter 39.)

For Beck, it was a signature moment: the sight of him screaming and pounding his glove after getting out of the 10th-inning jam captures him forever in all his thick-skinned glory.

But he would never save another game in San Francisco. The Giants let him go as a free agent after that season, acquiring Robb Nen from the Florida Marlins to be the closer.

Beck wasn't ready to leave, but he thrived elsewhere. He promptly saved a team-record 51 games for the Chicago Cubs. The last one? A 5–3 victory over the Giants in an extra game to determine the wild-card playoff team.

After his retirement following the 2004 season, Beck struggled with drug addiction. Writer Amy K. Nelson, in a mesmerizing look at his final days, reported for ESPN.com that on the day Beck died— June 23, 2007—there was a ceramic plate in the form of a baseball found in his home. On the plate was a rolled-up dollar bill, a dusting of cocaine, and Beck's 1993 baseball card. (The Maricopa County medical examiner has not publicly disclosed the cause of death.)

Stacey Beck, who had coaxed her husband into rehab more than once, co-founded a non-profit called Pitch 4 Kidz (pitch4kidz.org), which is a program for children affected by a parent's addiction.

"When Rod died, the girls and I vowed to use our experiences to help other families," Stacey Beck wrote in a blog for Shatterproof. org. "We made a family decision to not hide in shame and secrecy, two common characteristics of the family disease. So instead of shame and secrecy, we are using our voices to share with others what we have learned on this journey. Rod will live forever in our hearts, forever."

19

MATT CAIN

Matt Cain was a mere 20 years old when he made his major league debut on August 29, 2005. But by the time he was through with the Colorado Rockies, the kid looked all grown up.

Cain's epic confrontation against slugger Todd Helton that night demonstrated the fearlessness that would define the pitcher's career. Helton, one of the league's established stars, kept fouling off pitches and Cain kept charging at him like a bull after a red cape.

One foul ball...then another...another... another....

In all, the fifth-inning at-bat lasted 14 pitches, including nine consecutive foul balls. Helton ultimately hit a harmless fly ball to left field. And by the time it settled into the glove of Moises Alou, the Giants knew this was no ordinary rookie.

"I think everybody in the stands, on the field, and in the dugout had a lot of respect for how he kept coming after him," Giants catcher Mike Matheny said after the game.

So began the career of a reliably ferocious competitor. Before the arrival of The Freak and

MadBum, the far less colorful Cain was the anchor of the Giants staff. The nickname for the sturdy 6'3", 230 pounder? "The Horse."

While the nickname was workmanlike, The Horse's accomplishments were thrilling. In 2012 alone, Cain threw a perfect game, started the All-Star Game, and won every playoff series-clinching game en route to the Giants' World Series title.

While the nickname was workmanlike, The Horse's accomplishments were thrilling.

As a kid growing up in Alabama and Tennessee, Cain never lived in a town with more than 3,000 people. But he was ready for the big time.

"Cainer's just a big country boy who comes at you with everything he's got," Lincecum told Andrew Baggarly of the *San Jose Mercury News* in 2009. "I love the way he eats up innings and competes and never gives in. I think I've learned a lot from him, watching the way he handles himself out there."

In that memorable debut against the Rockies, Cain was the youngest Giants starter to take the mound since Mark Grant in 1984. The right-hander showed more than poise in that first game. He threw fastballs that touched 95 mph and a darting slider that showed why he was leading the Pacific Coast League in strikeouts at the time of his call-up.

Asked for his reaction to what he saw that night, manager Felipe Alou said: "There's plenty there to win games if we score runs."

Aye, there was the rub. That dastardly phrase—*if we score runs*—tormented Cain for much of his early career. The Giants most certainly didn't when he was pitching: losing close, low-scoring games with Cain on the mound became a phenomenon. There's now a word for it: "Cained."

UrbanDictionary.com defines "Cained" as: *"Having one's good work spoiled by teammates' incompetence, such as when Matt Cain gives up only two runs but nonetheless loses due to a lack of run support. Example: I spent months setting up the experiments, but my labmate Cained me by accidentally deleting all the data."*

The right-hander got Cained a little his first full big-league season, in 2006, when he led all National League rookies with 179 strikeouts. It was the third-highest single-season strikeout total by a Giants rookie. Only Christy Mathewson (221 in 1901) and John Montefusco (215 in 1975) did better. Still, Cain finished only a tick above .500 that season, at 13–12.

He went 7–16 in 2007, despite a 3.65 ERA that ranked among the league leaders. He went 8–14 with a 3.76 ERA a year later, when the Giants gave him the league's worst run support.

So wide was the gap between Cain's record and his performance that ESPN.com once headlined a story: "Matt Cain, Unluckiest Pitcher in History?" In that August 18, 2011, piece, writer David Schoenfield compared Cain's career W–L to pitchers with a similar ERA+ (that is, ERAs adjusted for home ballpark and league ERA) and concluded that getting Cained was no myth.

The right-hander's career mark at the time was 67–71. Pitchers with similar stats, but better support, included Tim Hudson (177–94), Lefty Gomez (189–102), Jim Palmer (268–152), and Bret Saberhagen (126–95).

Considering his plight, Cain could have led the league in complaints. Instead he never allowed himself so much as an eye roll. He'd lose 2–1 or watch his bullpen blow a late lead and then blame himself in postgame interviews. It was his fault for not pitching better.

"If you're sitting there and think you're having your whole career based on luck, that's not going to happen," Cain once said. "You've got to put a lot of it in your own hands."

Later he'd spin it as a positive: "I think ultimately, really, it helped a lot. It built me and a lot of guys into who we're going to be in the future."

In fairness, Cain really did need to refine his game. He made some of his own bad luck because he was a wild and inefficient pitcher. Some of those losses stemmed from him racking up huge pitch counts by the fifth or sixth inning, putting undo stress on the bullpen.

From 2005 to '08, a span of 104 starts, Cain threw only four complete games—precisely one per season.

But things changed in 2009, in part because Randy Johnson took Cain under his very large wing. The Giants signed the Hall of Fame pitcher for the final season of his career, and the 45-year-old dropped a little wisdom on Cain, Lincecum, and other promising young 'uns.

The Big Unit's biggest lessons to Cain revolved around how to pitch deeper into games. Cain responded by going 14–8 in 2009, with a 2.89 ERA, leading the NL with four complete games, and making his first All-Star team.

"He did a great job of picking my brain to figure out what I was thinking on the mound and would add things to them," Cain told writer Chris Haft of MLB.com in 2015. "He did really harp on going deep into games. He prided himself on pitching a ton of innings and wanted the rest of the staff to do the same."

After spending a season with Johnson and honing his craft through so many narrow losses, Cain was ready for the pressure of the playoffs. His brilliant showing in October 2010 included throwing 21.1 innings over three starts without allowing an earned run. He threw 6.2 shutout innings against the Atlanta Braves in the NLDS, 7.0 shutout innings against the Philadelphia Phillies in the NLCS, and 7.2 shutout innings against the Texas Rangers in the World Series.

And, suddenly, Cain's luck didn't seem so bad anymore.

"He's one of the elite pitchers in the game," Giants manager Bruce Bochy said. "You know when he goes out there he's going to give you all he can."

In 2012, during another solid postseason, Cain explained his advice for handling pressure.

"Matt Cain, Unluckiest Pitcher in History?"

The key to big moments was thinking small. "You almost have to revert back to when you were in Little League because the game is about having fun," he said.

No wonder Cain liked to revert back: An entry in the Giants media guide notes that when he was five, Cain pulled off three unassisted triple plays over the course of a seven-game tee-ball season.

By the time Cain was a senior at Houston High School in Germantown, 15 to 20 scouts were at his every game. His pitching coach in those days was former big-leaguer Mauro Gozzo, who taught the kid how to harness his explosive fastball.

"He's pretty much like an older brother to me," Cain told the *San Jose Mercury News* in 2004, while in town as a Class-A player. "But he's also like a best friend. I worked real hard with him since I was 11, on my mechanics, being consistent on my mechanics, and throwing a lot of strikes."

The Giants took Cain in the first round (25th pick overall) of the 2002 amateur draft. And it's possible they'll never let go. In 2012, the Giants signed him to a six-year contract extension with a vesting option for 2018.

"He's such a huge part of what we do every day with his work ethic," Giants catcher Buster Posey said on the day of the signing. "The days he's not pitching, he comes in and is working so hard. That stuff really rubs off on the rest of the guys."

For eight consecutive seasons starting in 2006, Cain made at least 30 starts. But injuries derailed him beginning in 2014, when he racked up just 25 mostly ineffective starts over two seasons.

But Cain always knew it wouldn't be easy. He learned that on his very first night in his marathon duel with Todd Helton.

"You're thinking, *Oh, great, is every lefty hitter going to be like this?*" Cain recalled with a smile years later. "If they are, I'm in for a really tough career."

20

JEFF
KENT

On the surface, it was an alarming sight: Jeff Kent and Barry Bonds, the Giants' two best players, engaged in a dugout scuffle right in the middle of a game. As TV cameras zoomed in on June 25, 2002, the two sluggers shouted and shoved and swore at each other until they were pried apart by cooler heads.

Dissension! Turmoil! Clubhouse poison!

Or, in this case, just another day at the ballpark. Kent was chuckling by the end of the night.

"Add this to the half-dozen times we've done it before," the second baseman shrugged during a postgame interview. Then he noted that the fight actually lit a fire for the Giants offense: Bonds hit a three-run homer not long after the fisticuffs. Kent added a solo homer in the sixth.

Such was life during the Kent-Bonds era. Sure, their personalities made for a combustible mix, but they always saved their biggest blows for opposing pitchers. The irascible left fielder and the aloof second baseman got along just fine between the lines, providing the Giants' best power duo since the days of Willie Mays and Willie McCovey.

"These guys needed each other to do the things that they did together," former Giants shortstop Rich Aurilia once said. "Even if neither one would admit it."

Jeff Kent pumps his fist after hitting a two-run homer during Game 5 of the 2002 World Series. (Amy Sancetta)

Kent had some solid seasons elsewhere during his 17 major league seasons, but never was he more prolific than during his six years paired with Bonds. The right-handed hitter topped 100 RBI in all six of his seasons with the Giants, making five All-Star teams, capturing four Silver Slugger Awards, and winning MVP honors in 2000—the year he eked past Bonds in the balloting.

He hit 560 career doubles—more than players such as Derek Jeter (544), Tony Gwynn (543), and Willie Mays (523).

The 1-2 finish demonstrated how much they helped each other. Pitchers preferred to walk Bonds, even if that meant facing Kent with runners on base. During Kent's MVP year, Bonds led the league with 117 walks and Kent made them pay by hitting .343 with runners in scoring position.

"It's actually funny they would be on the same team," Rich Donnelly, the Los Angeles Dodgers third-base coach, told the *New York Times*. "And how did Dusty Baker handle that? It was probably like Arthur Mercante, the great referee. 'Okay. Break, now box.' And everything was wonderful."

Kent was overshadowed during the Bonds era—wasn't everybody?—but his career numbers demand that Hall of Fame voters at least glance his way. Of his 377 career home runs, 351 came while playing second base. That's a record for major league second basemen. (Hall of Famer Ryne Sandberg held the old mark at 287.)

He hit 560 career doubles—more than players such as Derek Jeter (544), Tony Gwynn (543), and Willie Mays (523).

Kent took an almost perverse pride in how little he knew about the game's history. He once joked that Rogers Hornsby had to be more than one guy.

But as his own numbers mounted he could no longer take the game's tapestry so lightly: he was too much a part of it. When he won the MVP in 2000, he was just the fifth NL second baseman to earn the award. The others were Sandberg, Joe Morgan, Jackie Robinson, and Frankie Frisch.

"It's truly an honor to be mentioned in the same breath as those guys," Kent said that day, sounding genuinely in awe of his company.

Then again, the rest of his MVP celebration spoke volumes about Kent's personality. He got off the phone, casually told a friend that he'd just won the MVP, then hopped back aboard his power mower to finish a job on his ranch in Tilden, Texas. Eventually, he gathered his family and drove into town for the best feast in town— $6.99-a-plate barbecue.

In some ways, his blue-collar vibe was at the heart of his uneasy relationship with Bonds. Kent cast himself as the anti-star, the kind of guy who spent his off-season with 200 cattle while fixing broken water lines and avoiding trips to the big city. Such ruggedness helped Kent years later when he appeared as a contestant on the CBS reality show *Survivor*.

For a guy who could speak with a twang and speckle his phrases with "doggone" and "dang," Kent was a late-blooming cowboy. Born in Orange County, California, and educated in Berkeley, he adopted the "cowboy way" after falling in love with Texas when Cal played in Austin in the 1989 NCAA baseball playoffs.

That's when the Cal boy became a cowboy.

"The 'cowboy way' is a true respect for everything," Kent told me during spring training in 2002. "It's a respect for women. It's a respect for the land. It's a respect for the job. It's a respect for other good folks. The 'cowboy way' is finding honor and integrity in things that you do. It's not a focus on things you have. It's a focus on what you can do and what you can give.

"That's a way this generation is not going, and that's sad. But the respect does exist, more so in south Texas than anywhere else in the country."

Learning how to approach life like John Wayne eventually paid off. Kent's true grit helped him transform from a solid player to the most productive second baseman in Giants history, even if it took a while.

Drafted in the 20th round by Toronto in the 1989 amateur draft, Kent had solid if unspectacular stops with the Blue Jays, Mets, and Indians before the Giants acquired him in a landmark trade on November 13, 1996. Fans hated the deal largely because Kent was the centerpiece of a swap that sent the popular Matt Williams to Cleveland.

Really? A 29-year-old journeyman coming off a 12-homer season is the centerpiece?

To silence the uproar, two things happened. First, general manager Brian Sabean had to declare: "I am not an idiot."

Second, Kent had to prove that was true.

"Brian stuck his neck out for me, and he had that faith in me. It all started with him," Kent said, years later. "But it's funny. I still hear about that trade wherever I go around the country. I even heard about it when I was in Japan."

The trade indeed proved lopsided—in the Giants' favor. Kent batted .250 with 29 home runs and 121 RBI in his first San Francisco season.

So began one of the most prolific stretches by a middle infielder in history. He went on to join Hornsby as the only NL second baseman to drive in 120 runs in multiple seasons. He became the second right-handed hitter with three consecutive 100 RBI seasons for the Giants since Mays (1959–66).

"Nobody knew that Jeff was going to be this kind of player," manager Dusty Baker said.

A modestly built hitter whose physique hardly matched other notable sluggers of his era, Kent's power came from a compact stroke and strong wrists. He could be equally dangerous with a gap-to-gap approach, topping 40 doubles four times in his six seasons with the Giants.

His 49 doubles in 2001 set a Giants franchise record, topping Jack Clark's long-standing record of 46 in 1978.

To silence the uproar, two things happened. First, general manager Brian Sabean had to declare: "I am not an idiot." Second, Kent had to prove that was true.

Overall, Kent batted .297 as a Giant, a mark that trails only Bonds (.312), Orlando Cepeda (.308), Mays (.301), and Will Clark (.299) in San Francisco history.

As a defender, Kent was never going to be mistaken for Bill Mazeroski. He led NL second basemen in errors four times, including a whopping 20 in 1998. But Kent became an expert at turning the double play, perennially ranking in the top five among NL second sackers.

"The best way I can explain Jeff Kent," said broadcaster Duane Kuiper, a slick-fielding second baseman during his career, "is that all players like to go to the ballpark and work on things we do best, because it's the easiest. The hardest thing to do is work on your weaknesses—and that's what Jeff does every day."

His defense is a strike against him when it comes to Cooperstown. So, too, is missing out on a World Series ring. Bonds and Kent, the dysfunctional power duo, helped push the team to the brink in the same season as their famous fight.

The Giants led the Anaheim Angels 5–0 in Game 6 of the 2002 World Series, scoring their last run on Kent's single in the seventh. Kent, in a rare moment of emotion, raised his right fist—this time in celebration.

But it all came crashing down that year. The Angels roared back to win Game 6, then rolled over the emotionally flattened Giants in Game 7. A devastated Kent found a measure of peace only years later, in retirement, when the Giants really did win it all.

"I guarantee you I'd be standing here with a lot more bitterness in my heart if this team and this organization didn't have a World Series trophy," he said while visiting AT&T Park in 2012. "Individually, personally, I am bitter. But I am proud of the organization and grateful that Brian Sabean started something a long time ago.

"They finished it. I just happened to miss the boat."

21

TRAVIS THE HERO

For Travis Ishikawa, hitting the home run was the easy part. He connected on a high fastball. He raised a triumphant right fist. He watched the ball disappear into the moonlit skies.

But getting around the bases? He practically had to call in the National Guard.

Ishikawa's Giants teammates went so bonkers they began mobbing him mid-run. Showing the least patience, pitcher Jake Peavy raced from the dugout to bear-hug Ishikawa between second and third.

"We forgot we had to let him touch home plate for a minute," pitcher Madison Bumgarner explained.

Accompanied by his orange-and-black convoy, Ishikawa finally made it home. He stomped on the plate and he left his footprint on San Francisco history.

That walk-off homer in Game 5 on October 16, 2014, provided a 6–3 victory over the St. Louis Cardinals. It propelled the Giants toward a third World Series title and left Ishikawa feeling like AT&T Park was one hazy dream.

"Yeah," manager Bruce Bochy said. "I'm sure he's going to wake up and realize what just happened."

Not likely.

Ishikawa became just the fourth player to end a league
championship series with a walk-off homer. This pennant-winning
home run was so similar to Bobby Thomson's "Shot Heard 'Round
the World" in 1951 that the Associated Press instantly dubbed it the
"Shot That Shook the Bay."

*Michael Wacha holds his glove up to his face as
Travis Ishikawa celebrates hitting the walk-off
home run that sent the Giants to the 2014 World
Series.* (St. Louis Post-Dispatch/Chris Lee)

"That's baseball history right there," outfielder Hunter Pence said.

It sure was. It was also a fitting ending for a team that prides itself on unlikely heroes from Cody Ross to Marco Scutaro.

Ishikawa, 30, was about as unlikely as it gets. Earlier that year he was languishing in the minors and wondering if his journeyman career would soon be coming to a full and complete stop.

He opened the season as a first baseman for the Pittsburgh Pirates, lasting just 15 games before being cut. Ishikawa then re-signed with the Giants, his original organization, because he remembered the club as the land of opportunity.

He inked a minor league deal and was dispatched to Triple-A Fresno. But even there, the only thing he was hitting was rock bottom.

"Not only are you in the minor leagues, but you're struggling in the minor leagues," Ishikawa said. "Definitely there are times where it crosses your mind and you wonder if God is continuing to put me through this trial or if it's him telling me that it's time to hang 'em up and do something else.

"I just remember calling a buddy of mine, halfway through the year this year, crying. We were in Texas and I was putting every effort I possibly could into the hitting and no matter what, I was 0 for 4 and just didn't look like I could hit a ball on a tee if you put it there."

Ishikawa eventually found his swing, as well as his niche with the big-league club. The Giants summoned him back to the majors on July 29, giving Bochy a useful puzzle piece. The left-handed batter started 11 games at first base, three in left field, and went 7 for 21 as a pinch-hitter.

In the postseason, the team started him out of desperation. The Giants needed an outfielder due to earlier injuries to Michael Morse and Angel Pagan, so they rolled the dice with Ishikawa.

"I'm not surprised he hit a home run," Sabean said the night they won the pennant. "I'm surprised he's our starting left fielder. That's amazing to me. That's the kind of commitment he had to wanting to get on the field."

Putting an inexperienced left fielder in AT&T Park's cavernous expanses almost backfired. In the third inning of Game 5, long before

He opened the season as a first baseman for the Pittsburgh Pirates, lasting just 15 games before being cut.

his heroics, Ishikawa misplayed a liner to left field that cost the Giants a run. Jon Jay's drive skipped by him, allowing Tony Cruz to score for a 1–0 lead against Bumgarner.

"Obviously, I spent the rest of that defensive inning thinking that I might've just cost us the game," Ishikawa said of his blunder. "But Bum did a fantastic job only allowing that one run to score.

"Every single guy on this team, every single coach came up to me, slapped me on the back and said, 'Don't worry, you're going to get 'em. Stick with it."

The pep talks cheered him up. So did one big swing by Morse.

And yes, Morse had his own backstory: The Giants' everyday left fielder had been hampered by an oblique injury for the final weeks of the season, hadn't been particularly good for many weeks before that, and was held out of the Giants' wild-card game against Pittsburgh and the NL Division Series against Washington.

And then, with the Giants down 3–2, Morse stepped in as a pinch-hitter to lead off the eighth inning against tough reliever Pat Neshek.

"I had a feeling he was going to do something good," Bumgarner said. "Nobody—especially no right-handed hitter—likes facing Neshek. So you know it's going to be a tough at-bat. But we had a good feeling with him going up there."

Morse promptly blasted the ball into oblivion (more specifically, the left-field seats). He went berserk in his celebration. He was not alone.

"It was a moment that was absolute chaos, total anarchy," said outfielder Hunter Pence, one of Morse's best friends on the team. "I lost my mind. He lost his mind. He deserved it, because stepping up in that moment, it's special. He battled back from that injury, got healthy for us, and made it count."

Improbably, that was just the warm-up act.

In the bottom of the ninth, with Michael Wacha on the mound and one out, Ishikawa came to the plate. Pablo Sandoval was at second base and Brandon Belt at first.

There was no time to brood about his misplay earlier in the game. It was time to become a legend. Wacha fell behind in the count 2–0.

Let's let Ishikawa himself handle the play-by-play:

"I was looking fastball," he said. "I knew that he didn't want to get behind 3–0, chance of walking the bases loaded. I was just trying to be aggressive.

"I know that they have been pounding me in a lot, so I was just trying to stay short to the ball. Just try to put the barrel on the ball and put a good swing on it.

"Obviously I got a good pitch. When I first hit it, I just thought it was going to be a walk-off hit, so I was throwing my hands up in

LCS WALK-OFF BLASTS

Since the advent of the League Championship format in 1969, four players have ended a series with a home run. Here's the list:

Year	Player	Team	Opponent	Series
2014	Travis Ishikawa	Giants	Cardinals	NLCS
2006	Magglio Ordóñez	Tigers	A's	ALCS
2003	Aaron Boone	Yankees	Red Sox	ALCS
1976	Chris Chambliss	Yankees	Royals	ALCS

the air. I remember hearing the crowd just going crazy, and so my thought was, *Okay, if this gets out, it's going to be fantastic.*

"And I saw it get out and I remember high-fiving Roberto [Kelly, the first-base coach], I don't remember going from first to second. Later, I found out it was Peavy that was jumping at me between second and third. I didn't know who it was. I just knew it was somebody. I didn't know what the rules were.

"I know the base coaches are not allowed to touch runners when they are trying to score, so I didn't know if touching [Peavy] was going to cost me the home run. I was just trying to push him out of the way.

"And I don't remember touching third. I don't remember touching home. The last thing I remember—the next thing I remember—was my being thrown down and having my jersey ripped off. I was just so out of breath from yelling and screaming, and I had to have guys help me stand back up to finish celebrating."

Ishikawa's concern over a rules violation was unfounded: Once the homer reached the seats, it was a dead ball and contact with Peavy and the bases coaches was permissible. Besides, who was going to spoil this party?

San Jose Mercury News columnist Tim Kawakami described the scene this way: "Time stopped. The moment froze. The Cardinals players drooped. That's what happens when history happens in a lightning flash."

"The story of tonight's Ishikawa, man—that was unbelievable," reliever Jeremy Affeldt said. "Him running around the bases—he had to have been floating. He felt so bad on that misplayed fly ball there. So for him to get redemption like that, can't be any greater feeling for him."

A few days later, on the eve of Game 1 of the World Series, I asked Ishikawa how his life had changed. The lifelong journeyman, who played nearly 1,000 career games in the minor leagues, was suddenly being stopped on the street by strangers and posing for pictures.

"Basically, they say, 'Thank you. Thank you for that hit that got the team to the World Series.' And they say how excited they are for me," Ishikawa said. "It's hard because I don't want to take the credit for it.

"I wouldn't have been in that situation without every single guy on our team doing what they were supposed to be doing."

Ishikawa was back to his journeyman ways by the next season. The Giants designated him for assignment twice before he wound up re-signing with the Pittsburgh Pirates.

But he left San Francisco with one heck of a souvenir.

On the night of Ishikawa's pennant-winning home run ball, the man who caught it, Frank Burke, saw no need to drive a hard bargain. After briefly floating the idea of demanding World Series tickets in exchange for the ball, he decided to hand it back for nothing.

"Ishikawa is the guy who hit the ball," the Oakdale, California, resident shrugged. "I'm just the lucky guy who caught it."

22

KRUK & KUIP

Like any classic couple, Giants broadcasters Mike Krukow and Duane Kuiper have a cute story about how it all began.

On March 24, 1983, just before Krukow was getting ready to throw his first pitch as a Giant, his second baseman called time and came to the mound for a visit.

Krukow was mystified. Sure, this was only a spring training game, but nobody ever halted play before the first pitch of the game. The right-hander, who had come over in an unpopular trade with the Philadelphia Phillies, figured Kuiper wanted to go over some signs.

"Instead, he walks up and says, 'Whatever you do, don't let them hit it to me,'" Krukow recalled. "Then he patted me on the back, turned around, and walked back to his position."

Krukow chuckled to himself, thinking it was a wisecrack. Then he spent the next few innings watching ground ball after ground ball zip by an aging second baseman who was struggling with bad knees.

"It turns out he was serious!" Krukow recalled, howling at the memory. "He would take one step, dive, and miss it by 50 feet. I had a rough outing. But I had a place in my heart for this guy already."

The equation that day—inside baseball plus lots of laughs—set the tone for one of the great pairings in Giants history. "Kruk and Kuip," as they are known, began working regularly together on the air as early as 1991, and the baseball lexicon hasn't been the same since.

With their catchphrases, one-liners, and deep-drilling insights, they come across as if they're in your living room, not a broadcast booth. The team found out just how popular the duo was when they made their replica jerseys available in 2003. They sold more than 1,000 in the blink of an eye.

"Instead, he walks up and says, 'Whatever you do, don't let them hit it to me.' Then he patted me on the back, turned around, and walked back to his position."

"The great thing is the interaction between them," said retired broadcaster Hank Greenwald, who tutored the ex-players in their early days as broadcasters. "Here are two guys who were friends and teammates long before they stepped into the booth. And that comes across on the air. From the start, there has been a natural rapport."

Their long careers behind the microphone make it easy to forget that once upon a time they were valuable players. Krukow, a right-hander with a terrific 12-to-6 curveball, went 124–117 with a 3.90 ERA over 14 seasons. He finished in the National League's top 10 for ERA twice (in '82 and '86).

Krukow's best season was with the Giants in 1986, when he went 20–9 with a 3.05 ERA. He finished third in Cy Young Award voting, behind winner Mike Scott and runner-up Fernando Valenzuela.

Kuiper gets a lot of comedy mileage out of his lack of power—he hit one career home run in 3,379 career at-bats—but he had a seriously good career. He was a terrific defensive second baseman for the Cleveland Indians from 1974 to 1981, twice leading the American League in fielding percentage. He even had a claim to fame with the bat: Kuiper three times had the lone hit in a one-hitter, spoiling no-hit bids by Nolan Ryan, Ron Guidry, and Andy Hassler.

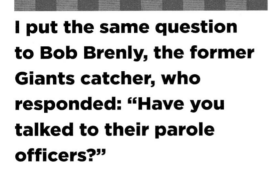

I put the same question to Bob Brenly, the former Giants catcher, who responded: "Have you talked to their parole officers?"

Starting in 1982, Kuiper became a valuable bench player for the Giants. And in 1983, his partner came along in the unpopular trade that had sent Joe Morgan to the Philadelphia Phillies.

I once asked Frank Robinson what it was like to have Krukow and Kuiper in the same dugout.

"Ah, jeez, it was like managing a funny farm," Robinson replied, playfully. The Hall of Famer managed the Giants from 1981 to '84. "They were kooky, goofy people. It was like, 'What are they going to do next?'"

I put the same question to Bob Brenly, the former Giants catcher, who responded: "Have you talked to their parole officers?"

But for all their joking around, Krukow and Kuiper were always serious about the game itself. "On the days Krukow pitched, you couldn't even talk to him. Nothing was funny about anything on those days," Brenly said.

From 1983 to '85, the years Krukow and Kuiper were on the roster together, the Giants went 207–279 and racked up the most defeats over a three-year stretch in franchise history. Still, each credits those years for ultimately making them better broadcasters. You hear them now talking about "Ninety-foot mistakes"—because they spent those lousy Giants days trying to avoid them.

The only chance they had of beating more talented teams was to be smarter, so they soaked in the nuances—the positioning of the cutoff man, the proper way to back up a base—the same attention to detail that now makes for enlightening broadcasts.

"If you did what they did, you were going to play the game right," said Mark Davis, a youngster on the Giants who went on to win the Cy Young Award for the San Diego Padres in 1989. "I really looked up to them."

Kuiper eased into broadcasting in 1983, when he took over Morgan's postgame show on KNBR radio. He realized he was nearing a full-time career change when a heckler let him have it during his final playing season.

"I was standing in the on-deck circle in 1985 when some leather-lunged guy in the stands screams, 'Kuiper! Go to the booth—*now!*'" he said. "I remember thinking, 'I'm going to accept this as a compliment.' A year later, I was in the booth."

Corey Busch, then the team's executive vice president, helped orchestrate Kuiper's second career by pairing him with Morgan when GiantsVision made its debut in 1986.

When Morgan bolted for ESPN after the 1990 season, and with cable interest in the Giants on the rise, Busch persuaded Krukow, who had been Morgan's occasional fill-in, to take broadcasting more seriously. By '91, Krukow was doing about 40 games a year, and his chemistry with Kuiper carried over on the air.

"First and foremost, those guys knew the game, which is what we were trying to build our broadcasts around in those days," Busch recalled. "We wanted them to be entertaining, too, but it was more important to be enlightening. We wanted things explained not just at the macro level but with all the nuances."

Kuiper's transition from player to play-by-play man came effortlessly. Krukow, however, struggled early. His enthusiasm for making a point ran roughshod over the action, and he often yapped right through a pitch.

"It was like trying to break a horse," Greenwald recalled with a laugh. He was always ready to charge ahead with what he was going to say and not always putting a lot of thought into it."

Krukow also tended to baffle listeners. He used the lexicon of the locker room without much consideration for whether the layman would understand what he meant by a "hanging banger" or a "one-hop seed." His partners urged him to tone it down, but hundreds of broadcasts later, fans seem to have met Krukow halfway. The pitcher's verbal curveballs are now part of his charm.

At his best, Krukow can sound like a cross between Mr. Baseball and Dr. Seuss. Consider how he once described it when Jesse Foppert made a mistake and threw an 0-2 pitch down the middle to the Diamondbacks' Dave Dellucci: "Foppert got pretty froggy with that fastball. He put one right in Dellucci's sweet hole."

A diving stop by the Giants first baseman was rendered as, "J.T. Snow goes down to his belly to snuggle up to a line drive."

An inside pitch that breaks a bat is a "shark bite." A long home run by Bonds is a "big potato." The victim of a dugout prank is a "raving yahoolio."

And, of course, there is "meat," the moniker Krukow slaps on any Giants opponent who does something weak or stupid. Krukow heard that term within his first minute in a major league clubhouse, in 1976. The lanky rookie walked in the door, and George Mitterwald, the Chicago Cubs' veteran catcher, alerted his teammates to the arrival of fresh meat.

"When I first started doing broadcasting, I was talking in a vernacular where nobody knew what the hell I was talking about," Krukow said. "But it made sense to me. That's the way we talked about baseball on the bench and in the clubhouse."

Kuiper, meanwhile, carved his niche with a rousing home run call. He started doing

"Foppert got pretty froggy with that fastball. He put one right in Dellucci's sweet hole."

it on television broadcasts in the early 1990s, when Matt Williams was bashing majestic shots across Candlestick Park.

The call comes as a dramatic trilogy—"He hits it high! He hits it deep! He hits it out of here!"—and viewers embraced it from the start. Kuiper fell in love with the call, too, and began using it on the radio. At least until Bob Agnew, his boss at KNBR, phoned him after a broadcast in Denver.

"In his typical warm-and-fuzzy style, Bob says, 'By the way, I understand that Bonds hit it high and hit it deep and hit it out of there. But would you mind telling me where the home run went? Did it go to right or left or center?'" Kuiper recalled. "I was ticked, but he was right. You have to be more descriptive."

No broadcast featuring Kruk and Kuip is complete without a tongue-in-cheek riff on the fans in the crowd. A crooked hat or a dropped foul ball might keep the duo occupied for several innings, especially if the score is lopsided. On other days, they might fixate on a kid eating cotton candy or a ball dude misplaying a shot in foul territory.

"They're unbelievable," said Jim Lynch, who is the longtime director of Giants television broadcasts. "There are some shows that I think are driven by production people, but our show is announcer-driven. We really listen to them and try to complement what they're talking about."

How long will this marriage last? Krukow revealed in 2014 that he was suffering from a degenerative muscle disease called inclusion-body myositis. IBM causes progressive weakness in the muscles of the wrist and fingers, the front of the thigh, and the muscles that lift the front of the foot.

Luckily, Krukow has a broadcast partner who knows how to play to his strengths. In baseball, as in love, diamonds are forever. A *San Francisco Chronicle* story detailed how the two were making the best of it. Writer C.W. Nevius reported that on the road, Kuiper has quietly taken up duties as personal Sherpa, toting Krukow's bags—not that anyone is making a big thing of it.

"Well look, I sat next to him on the plane for 25 years," Kuiper said. "If I'm not going to carry his bag, who is?"

"Kuip says he wants to do this until he is 80," Krukow said. "So do I."

23

PABLO SANDOVAL

Somewhere under the Champagne hurricane swirling through the Giants clubhouse, Bruce Bochy held the World Series trophy aloft. The golden prize glistened and dripped and shimmered under the lights as the manager barked his congratulations to the 2014 champions.

Then Bochy put baseball's ultimate prize into fitting hands. He handed the trophy to Pablo Sandoval.

"We got three! We got three! We got three!" the Giants third baseman shouted, to the delight of his teammates. He splayed the fingers of his hands wide to make sure everyone was counting along.

Fittingly, it was Sandoval's last act in a Giants uniform. One last bit of Panda-monium before he signed a free-agent deal with the Boston Red Sox during the off-season.

It was a difficult goodbye. As exasperating as the roly-poly third baseman could be for most of the year, Sandoval had a way of making sure all was forgiven by autumn. Yes, he ate too much. He swung at pitches in another galaxy. His body broke down often.

Then, in October, the pumpkin-shaped man helped turn the Giants into Cinderella.

Sandoval ranks among the best playoff performers in baseball history, right up there with Reggie "Mr. October" Jackson, Babe Ruth, and other larger-than-life figures. As a fitting farewell to San Francisco, he caught the last out of the Giants' 3–2 victory over

After Michael Morse's single scored Hunter Pence in the fourth inning of Game 1 of the 2014 World Series, Pablo Sandoval let Morse know exactly how he felt about it. (*The Sacramento Bee*, Jose Luis Villegas)

the Kansas City Royals in Game 7, squeezing Salvador Perez's foul popup and then falling on his back and screaming to the skies.

With three championships to choose from, Sandoval picked that one.

"This was a crazy one. Drama? Everything," he said. "This is the one I enjoyed more than anything."

Madison Bumgarner was the 2014 World Series MVP, but only the pitcher's historic brilliance prevented Sandoval from winning the award a second time. The switch-hitter batted .429 against the Royals and tied Hunter Pence for a team high with 12 hits. In the decisive game at Kauffman Stadium, he went 3 for 3 with a double and two runs scored.

Of course he did. The man nicknamed "Kung Fu Panda" was always a bear at playoff time. He had been the World Series MVP in 2012, largely because of his Game 1 performance against the Detroit Tigers.

Sandoval hit three titanic home runs that night, including two off of Justin Verlander, the usually impervious Tigers ace. The 42,855 fans at AT&T Park for that October 24, 2012, game got a show for the ages.

Verlander had given up exactly two homers to the previous 137 hitters he'd faced. Sandoval needed all of the three innings to match the total.

The first one came with two out in the first inning, on a chest-high, 95-mph fastball. (Sandoval belted it back 421 feet to right-center). The second one came with two out in the third, on another 95-mph heater, low and away (Sandoval smacked it into the left-field seats).

"Wow," Verlander said as TV cameras zoomed in for his reaction.

But there was one more to come. In the fifth inning, Sandoval—batting right-handed this time—smacked a slider from Al

Albuquerque 435 feet to center field. With that blast, Sandoval joined Jackson, Ruth, and Albert Pujols as the only players to hit three home runs in a single World Series game. The *San Francisco Chronicle* headline the next day: "Senor October!"

Adding to the cinematic night was an almost-forgotten plot twist. During his third at-bat, Sandoval broke his bat on a foul ball. Wasn't he a little bothered about losing a bat with so much magic in it?

"I'm not too much into superstition. It's not the bat. It's you," he replied. "It's everything you've got inside you. If you have faith, you have to believe in yourself."

Maybe his offensive onslaught that night was just Sandoval's clever way of thanking Barry Zito for coming up with the "Kung Fu Panda" nickname. Zito was the winning pitcher in the 8–3 victory.

Zito came up with the moniker after a game against the Dodgers on September 19, 2008. Sandoval scored on a play at the plate, going airborne over catcher Danny Ardoin. To the pitcher, the agility of Sandoval's large frame called to mind the hero of the 2008 DreamWorks computer-animated hit.

Zito left a stuffed Kung Fu Panda in Sandoval's locker.

And fans promptly went ape.

Panda hats became a staple at the ballpark for the next six seasons, and the nickname joined a Giants pantheon with "The Say Hey Kid," "Will the Thrill," and "The Count."

It helped that Zito's comparison was so apt. Sandoval was incredibly athletic and incredibly large. The one-time catcher finished the 2010 season at 278 pounds—a weight the Giants no longer found so endearing. The team put the 5'11" Sandoval on a strict diet and workout regimen—they called it "Operation Panda"—and the slugger reported for spring training in 2011 at 240 pounds.

The pattern would repeat itself for the remainder of his career, with Sandoval packing on pounds, slimming down, then packing 'em right back on.

But Sandoval was worth the weight: In 2009, he batted .330 with 25 home runs and 90 RBI. Though he never reached those dizzying heights again during the regular season, he was an All-Star in both 2011 and 2012. During his six full seasons with the Giants from 2009 to 2014, Sandoval led National League switch-hitters with 896 hits and 303 extra-base hits.

Sandoval wanted a position of leadership and figured that was the spot that would keep him involved in every play.

And he played a surprisingly acrobatic third base. According to the metric kept at baseball-reference.com, Sandoval led the NL in "range factor" at the position in 2012. At the time he left the Giants, his lifetime .960 fielding percentage at third base ranked third among active players who had at least 750 games at the position.

Panda's versatility emerged early. Born in Puerto Cabello, Venezuela, on August 11, 1986, he grew up working toward the big leagues. A natural lefty, he learned how to throw with his right arm at age nine because he wanted to be a catcher.

Why catcher? Sandoval wanted a position of leadership and figured that was the spot that would keep him involved in every play. By the time he was a teenager, he added switch-hitting to his switch-throwing. He learned how to hit by having his brother, Michael, throw him sharp-breaking wads of tape.

Sandoval added first base and third base to his resume while in the minors, and became skilled enough to play all three in the majors. He spent 14 games behind the plate for the Giants. But he developed bone spurs in his elbow early in the 2009 season and never went behind the dish again.

After a hot career start, Sandoval struggled in his second full big-league season. He batted just .268 with 13 home runs and 63 RBI. The future postseason hero was buried so far in the doghouse that he barely played in the Giants' first World Series run. He went 0 for 3 in his only game of the Fall Classic against the Texas Rangers.

But in '12 and '14, he made up for lost time.

- Among players with at least 40 World Series at-bats, Sandoval's .426 batting average trails only David Ortiz (.455) and Bobby Brown (.439).
- His 26 hits in the 2014 playoffs established a major league record for a single postseason, eclipsing the previous mark of 25 set by Marquis Grissom (1995 Braves), Darin Erstad (2002 Angels), and David Freese (2011 Cardinals).
- Sandoval's 19 career postseason extra-base hits are a Giants franchise record. And his 20 RBI trail only Barry Bonds (21) and Buster Posey (also 21) in the team's postseason record book.

On that October night in 2014, after Bochy handed him the trophy, Sandoval found a relatively quiet space in the corner of the clubhouse. Standing near him was Brad Horn, a representative from the Baseball Hall of Fame. Sandoval joked that he was in no rush to hand over any more of his equipment. After the three titles, he knew the Cooperstown halls were already pretty well stocked with Panda memorabilia.

"I've been giving a lot lately," Sandoval said. "I want to enjoy and take everything that I can."

24

KEVIN MITCHELL

Kevin Mitchell was always unflappable with the game on the line. After growing up in a gang-plagued area, the idea of batting with two out in the bottom of the ninth didn't seem so daunting.

His idea of a pressure situation?

"Being shot at," Mitchell said.

The San Diego native once gave a tour of his scars to a *Sports Illustrated* reporter, who described Mitchell's body as "looking like a relief map of an old battlefield." The thin white line on Mitchell's right thigh? He said it was from a .38 caliber bullet. The welt on his right wrist was from a smaller slug. The crescent on his back was from a shotgun blast of rock salt.

"Of course I packed a gun," he told writer Franz Lidz. "I wasn't going to get shot and have nothing to shoot back with. I only have a certain amount of lives: one."

Despite a career-long struggle to put his past behind him, Mitchell emerged as the good kind of dangerous for the Giants in the late 1980s. Paired with Will Clark in the middle of the lineup, the duo delivered a one-two punch that twice carried the Giants to the playoffs.

When Mitchell won the MVP award in 1989, Clark finished second, making them the first National League teammates to finish 1-2 in the voting since Joe Morgan and George Foster of the 1976 Cincinnati Reds.

They were San Francisco's answer to the "Bash Brothers," Jose Canseco and Mark McGwire, who were going homer-for-homer across the Bay in Oakland. Clark and Mitchell even had their own awesomely cheesy poster—"The Pacific Sock Exchange"—featuring the duo wearing suits and wielding bats amid a crowd of busy brokers.

Mitchell was the cool to Clark's fire, sometimes strolling casually to the plate with the top three buttons of his jersey undone and grinning to show off a gold front tooth.

Mitchell owed his big-league calm to his violent childhood. Far from the beaches of La Jolla, he grew up in a part of San Diego where trouble was a way of life. Mitchell's father, Earl, demanded toughness.

"If I came home beaten-up, Dad would take his strap out and whip my butt," Mitchell told Lidz in that memorable 1989 profile. "Then he'd send my butt back out and say, 'Don't come home till you've whipped the butt that whipped yours.' I started whipping other butts to save my own."

The lesson stuck.

"I didn't mess around," Mitchell said. "If anybody looked at me funny, Pow! I'd knock him out."

As a teenager, Mitchell said he landed with a street gang called Pierules. But he eventually turned his life around because he could play ball better than almost everybody else.

"Everyone sees Kevin's home runs and all," said Dusty Baker, the Giants batting coach in Mitchell's day. "They don't see his determination and desire. His background makes Kevin a natural warrior."

Mitchell would forever be a little rough around the edges, but he showed his affable side during his best times in San Francisco. Long before there was a "Panda" in town, Mitchell was known as "Boogie Bear"—another round body with a knack for round-trippers.

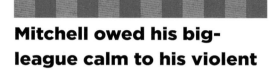

Mitchell owed his big-league calm to his violent childhood.

He began his career in the New York Mets organization, batting .335 for his rookie-league team in 1981. (He also fought with instructional league teammate Darryl Strawberry during a pickup basketball game.)

Mitchell was playing for the Mets' Triple A team in Tidewater, Virginia, in 1984 when learned that his 16-year-old stepbrother, Donald, had been shot and killed by a rival gang. Mitchell figured he knew who did it, and coaches had to intervene to keep him from going to San Diego on a revenge mission. Mitchell stayed in Virginia but barely cared about baseball, living his life with a perpetual scowl.

That's when one of his coaches and mentors told him to snap out of it.

"He felt that the world owed him things," Bill Robinson recalled. "I just politely told him, really, he was not likable, and I first saw his attitude, saw some ability, told him that if things didn't really change, he was going to be out of baseball and would be back on the streets."

By 1986, Mitchell and Strawberry were both key members of the Mets' world championship team. Bill Buckner's infamous error in Game 6 was made possible only because Mitchell kept the inning alive with a pinch-hit, two-out single in the bottom of the 10th.

He was traded twice within the next year, first to San Diego, which proved to be the worst possible destination. Distracted by his past, Mitchell batted .245 and lasted just half a season.

That's when one of his coaches and mentors told him to snap out of it.

The Padres turned around and traded him to the Giants on July 4, 1987, in a blockbuster deal. The Giants got Mitchell and pitchers Craig Lefferts and Dave Dravecky; San Diego got third baseman Chris Brown plus pitchers Mark Davis, Mark Grant, and Keith Comstock.

Mitchell was distraught. He told his grandmother, Josie Whitfield—who doubled as his confidante and batting coach—that he was tired of always moving around.

"Why don't you take out your frustrations on some of them white balls," Whitfield responded.

Mitchell prompty belted a pair of home runs over the Wrigley Field ivy in his Giants debut.

He finished that season with 15 homers and 44 RBI in just 69 games for the Giants, helping them win their first division crown since 1971. Mitchell quietly played all of 1988 on swollen and aching knees that needed fixing in the off-season.

But in 1989 he was healthy again. And that's when opposing pitchers felt the pain.

Roger Craig, the Giants manager from 1986 to 1992, saw it coming. He approached Mitchell in spring training that season and told him to set the goal of 100 RBI.

"I laughed at him," Mitchell recalled.

As it turned out, Craig undershot. Mitchell led the league with 125 RBI, 47 home runs, a .635 slugging percentage, and a 1.023 OPS. He had an astonishing early season hot streak, with 31 home runs and 81 RBI at the All-Star break.

"I didn't hit like that in the Pony League," marveled Giants catcher Terry Kennedy. "I don't even hit like that in my fantasies...I'm sure that when Willie Mays and [Mickey] Mantle were hitting 50 home runs, this is what they looked like."

There were lots of theories about Mitchell's breathrough. One came from Tony Kubek, who played with the Yankees when Roger Maris hit 61 home runs in 1961. Later an NBC broadcaster, Kubek noted the peculiar challenge of facing the 5'10", 186-pound powerhouse.

"I think one of the reasons you don't see pitchers knocking him off the plate is because they're thinking, 'If he comes after me, what's going to happen?'" Kubek told the *San Jose Mercury News*. "Everybody knows Kevin's background, that he's a tough guy, and I think with some pitchers there is a fear factor."

Boogie Bear had help from The Thrill. Clark, hitting third with Mitchell at cleanup, batted .333 with 23 home runs and 111 RBI.

"We were like batteries for each other," Mitchell said. "Every day we'd go out and put a new battery in."

The Giants went 92–89 during the regular season, then steamrolled past the Cubs in the NLCS. Clark batted an absurd .650 with two homers and eight RBI in the series; Mitchell batted .353 with two homers and seven RBI.

The onslaught carried San Francisco to its first World Series since 1954, when the franchise was still in New York. There is more on the '89 World Series against the A's in Chapter 35, but it's worth noting here that Mitchell homered off Mike Moore in Game 4.

When Mitchell was announced as the MVP awardee that season, he wasn't exactly waiting by the phone. He was sure Clark would get the nod and told reporters he'd been keeping himself occupied by playing Wiffle ball.

But he was the Giants' first MVP since Willie McCovey in 1969, and that hit home.

"This means a lot. It means I can walk around with my head held up," he said. "I'm trying to represent my home town, and people will say, 'There's Kevin Mitchell, and he's MVP.'"

Mitchell had a strong follow-up, batting .290 with 35 homers and 93 RBI in 1990. But by the following season, he was testing the Giants' patience in a series of brushes with the law. Trouble never is far from him. The transgressions came in varying degrees, from missed workouts to a lawsuit in which he was accused of beating a woman friend to associations with gang members.

The Giants traded Mitchell (along with Mike Remlinger) to the Seattle Mariners in December 1991 in a deal that netted Michael Jackson, Bill Swift, and Dave Burba.

It was the closing bell for the Pacific Sock Exchange.

Mitchell bounced around after that, including a season with the Fukuoka Daiei Hawks in Japan.

He was still playing minor league ball as late as 2000, serving as a player/manager for the minor league Sonoma County Crushers. His lasting claim to fame there? Mitchell was suspended nine games for punching another team's owner in the face during a brawl.

25

MATT WILLIAMS

One of the most thrilling home run calls in broadcasting can be traced back to a guy who tried to make long balls boring.

Matt Williams treated homers as a business transaction, socking them over the seats before embarking on a brisk, almost apologetic trip around the bases. He kept his head down and his feet moving.

But up in the broadcast booth, Kuiper was giving the baseballs a proper sendoff: *"He hits it high.... He hits it deep.... He hits it outta here!"*

Two decades later, that's still Kuiper's signature line for home runs. But it began as a practical matter.

And it began with Matt Williams.

"He hit very high, arcing home runs," Kuiper explained late in 2015. "There were no line-drive home runs with him where you didn't have enough time to give a call.... They were all *high* and *deep* and *outta here.*"

Kuiper's call became so popular that listeners told him, "You know what? I think you should use that all the time."

And so he did. And with Williams, he had plenty of chances to practice. Williams hit 247 home runs in a San Francisco uniform. The only players with more are Barry Bonds, Willie McCovey, and Willie Mays.

The third baseman, who played for the Giants from 1987 to 1996, was also a five-time All-Star and four-time Gold Glove winner. He led the league in RBI in 1990 (122).

Williams hit a career-high 43 home runs in 1994. But a player's strike cut that season short, denying him the chance to hit many more high...and deep...and outta here. If not for the work stoppage, Williams had a shot at two long-standing records, the NL mark of 56 home runs (set by Hack Wilson in 1930) and the major league mark of 61 (set by Roger Maris in 1961).

Williams, though, kept his head down in that instance, too.

"I don't look back at it as a wasted opportunity," he shrugged. "I'd never hit that many home runs, so I don't know what I would have done if there wasn't a strike."

Before all those long balls, Williams had a few very short stays in the majors. The best third baseman in Giants history had gotten off to a lousy start.

Williams had a shot at two long-standing records, the NL mark of 56 home runs (set by Hack Wilson in 1930) and the major league mark of 61 (set by Roger Maris in 1961).

Taken with the third overall draft pick in 1986 and rushed to the big leagues by '87, the infielder batted just .188 and struck out 68 times in 245 at-bats. He spent the next two seasons getting bounced back to the minors so often, the transaction wire looked like his personal travel diary.

But here's the thing about Williams' rough beginning: his bosses never doubted there would be better days ahead. The talent was too obvious.

"He'll hit 30 or more home runs in the big leagues," general manager Al Rosen vowed. "He has that kind of power."

"As good as Will Clark or Robby Thompson played last year, this kid is just as good," manager Roger Craig said in the spring of '87.

Indeed, that kid proved worth the wait.

Williams topped the 30-homer mark four times with the Giants and finished in the top five for MVP voting twice. Together with Clark and Kevin Mitchell, he gave the Giants one of the most feared lineups of the era.

"He was the most sure-handed, accurate-throwing third baseman I ever had."

Williams also played absurdly good defense. He led the National League in double plays turned by a third baseman three times—in 1990, '92, and '93.

"He was the most sure-handed, accurate-throwing third baseman I ever had," longtime manager Dusty Baker said.

Williams won Gold Gloves in 1991, '93, and '94 with the Giants, then added another with Cleveland in '97.

That's Gold Glove, not old glove.

"He would use about five gloves a year," pitcher Mike Krukow recalled. "He'd get a glove completely out of the box, play catch with it twice and it would be in a game. He liked a stiff glove.

"I'd never seen that before. Then he'd go out there and have the sweetest, softest hands. The glove was as stiff as a board! We'd say, 'Okay, how is this guy going to go down low for a backhander?' And it was—whoosh!—not a problem."

Williams' defense is what kept him in the big leagues while his bat was still growing up.

He struggled to hit because he was a sucker for breaking balls in the dirt. Williams also had a critic always nagging at him, hammering for the slightest imperfection. If he struck out, the guy was all over him. If he had a bad game, the negativity was relentless.

That ferocious critic was Williams himself.

"It's a pride thing with me," he said late in 1989, when he was still trying to find his way. "To know that I can play as well as anybody in this clubhouse, to know I can play defense as good as anybody, to know I can hit home runs with anybody, to drive in runs with anybody for an average as good as anybody—to know I can do that?

"And to not be able to do it is pretty trying on your conscience, on your abilities as a player, and on your confidence level."

But the Giants needed him to hurry. Starting shortstop Jose Uribe sustained a hamstring injury just before Opening Day in 1987, so Williams was summoned to the majors.

An All-American shortstop at UNLV, Williams wasn't ready for big-league pitching, but he was outstanding defensively. During one stretch in April, the Giants set major league records for double plays in three games (13) and in four (15).

When the team won the NL West that season, Craig saluted the rookie's contribution: "We never would have won without him."

Things clicked at the plate for Williams midway through the '89 season, when the Giants were on their way to the World Series. Recalled from the minors one last time on July 23, he promptly torched the league for 11 home runs in August, finishing with 18.

In the playoffs against the Chicago Cubs, the third baseman batted .300 and set an NLCS record with nine RBI in a five-game series.

"My attitude was not different. My approach wasn't different. I was just getting the opportunity to show some of the things I can do," Williams said. "I worked hard to improve myself as a player, and I think that some of that hard work finally paid off."

There was more to come in 1990, his first full season as a major leaguer, when he batted .277 with 33 home runs and 122 RBI.

Williams also emerged as a leader. But that, too, had been a long time in the making. Veteran players in the clubhouse recognized early in his career that Williams was a key cog in the Giants' future wheel. So they pulled him aside.

"We told him, 'One day, this is going to be your clubhouse. You're going to be in charge here,'" Krukow recalled.

Williams initially balked at the idea, but Krukow pressed on until he drove the point home.

"And I think he felt a responsibility," the pitcher said. "He knew he could never be in somebody's grill about the way they played if he didn't play it right. And he took that seriously. He never believed in showing up an opponent, so he just didn't. Ever."

Krukow told that story as a way of explaining Williams' home run trot. And even that word—*trot*—has it all wrong. With Williams, it was more of a home run gallop.

"It was the most humble trot that I've ever seen—in an era where 'humble' wasn't really a word used a lot," Kuiper said. "We were just getting into that era when there were a lot more flamboyant players—the way they dressed, the way they walked, walk-up music, the way they watched home runs.

"But Williams was pretty humble in everything he did."

He even showed humility in explaining that home run trot.

"I was looking at my feet, trying to make sure I didn't trip," he insisted.

After his blockbuster, strike-shortened '94 season, when he finished second to Houston's Jeff Bagwell in MVP voting, Williams had two more productive seasons in San Francisco.

He remained as popular as ever right up until November 13, 1996. That's the day the man famed for avoiding controversy unwittingly found his name setting sports-talk radio ablaze.

Williams found out about the trade from his mother. Before the Giants could tell him that he was heading to the Cleveland Indians, Mom called.

"Matt," she said, "do you have something to tell me?"

"I don't think so,"

"I was looking at my feet, trying to make sure I didn't trip."

he replied. "Did I do something wrong?"

He had been traded to the Indians for second baseman Jeff Kent, reliever Julian Tavarez, and shorststop Jose Vizcaino, a move that Giants fans greeted with the kind of disdain usually reserved for a Tommy Lasorda sighting.

Ten minutes after hanging up with his mom, Williams got the call from general manager Brian Sabean.

"I was shocked," Williams said, "for a couple of days. Then I was ticked off for a couple of days. There were a number of emotions. And then I started to worry, because of all the newness I was going to [in Cleveland]."

Williams thrived in Cleveland and elsewhere, but he remains cemented in Giants history. He ranks on San Francisco's all-time lists for games, at-bats, runs, hits, homers, RBI, and total bases.

Not bad for a guy who started his career still searching for his swing. He may have run the bases with his eyes looking down, but Williams left town with his head held high.

26

HUNTER PENCE

Every reliable source lists Hunter Pence's birthplace as Fort Worth, Texas.

Alas, there is no listing for his home planet.

But wherever the distant universe is that spawned the wild-eyed, shaggy-haired, scooter-riding, kale-munching, wall-crashing right fielder, you can bet the Giants are looking for the territorial rights.

Pence arrived in San Francisco in 2012 as part of a trade-deadline deal with the Phillies. He hasn't stopped moving since, whether it's running, throwing, or hitting balls into a galaxy far, far away.

"He gets guys fired up," second baseman Joe Panik said. "And with his play, he's all-out and gives everything he's got. It's spectacular to watch."

Pence's contributions to the Giants include batting .283 with 27 homers and 99 RBI in 2013 and following it up by hitting .277 with 20 homers, 74 RBI, and 106 runs scored in 2014.

But measuring his value by statistics is like

evaluating rock 'n' roll with sheet music. Hunter Pence is something to be *experienced*.

Pence's body mechanics look goofy and sped up, as if he's a ballplayer in those 1920s newsreels. The awkwardness is part of what makes him endearing. But there's also a precision to his game, and he always seems to be in the right place—even if that place is jumping in the chain-link portion of the right-field fence at AT&T Park.

That grab in Game 4 of the 2014 playoff series against the Washington Nationals ranks at the top of his long list of incredible catches.

Jayson Werth of the Nationals made the mistake of hitting it Pence's direction that night, October 7, launching an arcing shot toward deep right field. Pence tracked back to his left, jumped into the chain-link fence, and elongated his elastic body just enough to make the catch.

For extra style, Pence snagged the ball with his tongue out, *ala* Michael Jordan.

The catch became so famous that the Giants turned it into a bobblehead doll.

"The games in San Francisco, it's really a magical atmosphere," he said of his instant connection to the Bay Area. "I think that the type of people that run this organization and the type of players that are here, it's just a group where I felt like I fit in. There are a lot of accepting people of different personalities. And, really, I'm extremely grateful to have had the opportunity to come over here and play in front of the fans and the energy that they bring.... So it just feels like a good fit to me."

The catch was Pence's most memorable contribution to the 2014 championship team, but chances are he'll be better remembered for what he did two years earlier. On October 9, 2012, the Giants arrived in Cincinnati already on the brink of elimination. They'd lost two home games against the Reds, and a loss in any of the next three would wipe them out in the best-of-five division series.

So before Game 3, manager Bruce Bochy gave his troops a few words of encouragement.

That's when Pence cleared his throat. And a legend was born.

"I just remember him saying, 'I have something to say,'" reliever Jeremy Affeldt recalled. "I didn't really think much of it."

For extra style, Pence snagged the ball with his tongue out, ala Michael Jordan.

And then?

"He just got loud. He got crazy. I thought he was going to start head-butting guys and all kind of stuff," Affeldt said. "I'm glad that he didn't."

Third-base coach Tim Flannery later posted the speech, in full, on his Facebook page. Among the highlights:

> "Look into each other's eyes. I want one more day with you. It's the most fun, the best team I have ever been on, and no matter what happens, we must not give in. We owe it to each other. Play for each other!"

As Pence worked himself into a frenzy, others in the room sat in stunned silence. Reliever Javier Lopez remembered, "You don't know if you're supposed to sit back there with popcorn or start screaming and yelling."

Marco Scutaro went the yelling route.

WHAT'S THE DEAL WITH THE SIGNS?

To look for the signs, most batters look toward a coach. Hunter Pence can look into the stands. That's where the Giants outfielder will see placards that are as hilariously cryptic as any gyrations from a third-base coach.

The Hunter Pence sign phenomenon was born in early August 2014, during a Giants road trip to New York. Pence and his girlfriend, Alexis Cozombolidis, visited a New York diner and posed for a picture with a coffee cup featuring a line from *Seinfeld*. It said: "These pretzels are making me thirsty."

When he got to Shea Stadium that night, two fans held up signs with two more *Seinfeld*-esque lines:

HUNTER PENCE PUTS KETCHUP ON HIS HOT DOG
HUNTER PENCE EATS PIZZA WITH A FORK

And so it began. And it just kept rolling, each sign more delightfully baffling than the next.

"It's the wildest thing," Pence told *ESPN The Magazine* after the season. "The other day someone tailgating at the Notre Dame football game held a sign that said 'Hunter Pence Gave Us Five Stars.' Someone sent me one from a concert—I don't even know where, but the lyrics were 'Are you human or are we dancer?' [from The Killers' song 'Human']—and the sign at the concert said 'Hunter Pence is Dancer.'"

Here are some other gems from the 2014 season. Consider them signs of the times:

HUNTER PENCE HATES BACON
HUNTER PENCE PREFERS BATHS
HUNTER PENCE IS SPONGE WORTHY
HUNTER PENCE WEARS SOCKS WITH SANDALS
HUNTER PENCE IS A GATHERER
HUNTER PENCE THINKS GAME OF THRONES IS JUST OK
HUNTER PENCE BRINGS 13 ITEMS TO THE EXPRESS LANE
HUNTER PENCE EATS SUB SANDWICHES SIDEWAYS
HUNTER PENCE CAN'T PARALLEL PARK
HUNTER PENCE GOES TO A BUFFET AND ORDERS A SALAD
HUNTER PENCE READS THE TERMS AND CONDITIONS

Other players followed Scutaro's lead, and soon everyone was screaming. And the Giants didn't pipe down until they were World Series champs.

They won three straight to snuff out the Reds, overcame a three-games-to-one deficit to topple the St. Louis Cardinals in the NLCS, then swept the Detroit Tigers in the World Series.

Pence didn't exactly shut up after that Game 3 sermon, either. Each subsequent win was fueled by another oratorical adrenaline shot. As part of the pregame ritual, he would lead a huddle in the middle of the dugout. All the players would press into each other—Belt and Scutaro and Crawford and Romo all forming one giddy, adrenaline-fueled pile.

Audrey Huff had his famous "Rally Thong" in 2010.

This was the Rally Throng of 2012.

"The best way to describe it: there seems to be some excitement 30 minutes before it's time to go out on the field," catcher Buster Posey said. "Everybody knows we're going to go out there, and we're doing it together, and I think that's been helpful in winning these six games, because it's been a collective effort."

"When Hunter gave that unbelievable speech before that game, it really inspired everybody," reliever George Kontos said. "We realized what we were here to accomplish. Nobody wanted to go home."

The message never varied, but the intensity did. On some nights, it was fairly restrained. Other nights, the Giants looked as if they were ready to take on the Green Bay Packers.

"What are they like?" infielder Ryan Theriot said before the World Series. "Have you ever seen *Friday Night Lights*? It's kind of like that."

Silly as it sounds, the football-style pep talks represented something larger about the team that won't lose. There was a bond that has helped the Giants walk the tightrope of elimination. "A band of brothers–type thing," reliever Affeldt called it.

As the playoffs went along, Giants players got more creative. One night, just for the heck of it, Sergio Romo began firing sunflower seeds into the happy union, like rice at a wedding.

As it turns out, sunflower seeds were the least of it.

"I got hit in the head with some coffee creamer. It's wild, yeah. Those things are out of control."

"I got hit in the head with some coffee creamer," Theriot said. "It's wild, yeah. Those things are out of control.

"You kind of have to watch yourself. I try to stay on the outskirts. I don't want to get smoked with one of those Gatorade bars. Those things are hard."

The Giants admitted their routine was a bit of a shock to the baseball culture. Pence's speeches were being compared to those of Ravens linebacker Ray Lewis, Saints quarterback Drew Brees, and even Notre Dame coach Knute Rockne. Scott Ostler of the *San Francisco Chronicle* compared him to a preacher, dubbing him, 'The Reverend Hunter Pence.'"

But no one ever compared him to a ballplayer.

"That's what makes it unique," Pence said. "There's not a lot of rah-rah in baseball. But it seems to make us feel good, so I don't know. I can't really explain it."

Pence, of all things, struggled for words when it came time to explain why it did. Surrounded by reporters at AT&T Park, he was clipped in some answers. There was neither fire nor brimstone. Summing up his speeches, he said, "It's like, 'Win or go home.' It's just adrenaline."

Some of the *Friday Night Lights* vibe probably owes its roots to Pence's upbringing. He grew up in Arlington, Texas, playing ball at Texarkana College and the University of Texas at Arlington.

The Lone Star native signed with the Houston Astros after they made him a second-round pick in 2004. Pence was a two-time All-Star for the Astros and a terrific player in Philadelphia, but nowhere was he a better fit than in San Francisco.

The Giants recognized that almost immediately, signing Pence to a five-year, $90-million contract extension late in the 2013 season.

How trippy is this guy? In Game 1 of the World Series, Pence set the tone by blasting a two-run homer in the first inning. A once-raucous crowd in Kauffman Stadium suddenly went quiet.

Well, mostly quiet.

"It was really loud in my head," Pence said.

27

ONE FLAP DOWN

J effrey Leonard kept his trophy, which makes for an awkward souvenir. The distinction of being one of only three players to win a League Championship MVP award while playing for a losing team leaves him cold.

So whenever his individual prize catches his eye around his home in Rocklin, California, the player known as "Hac Man" gets a little hacked off.

"Every time I look at that thing it's like, 'ARGGGH!'" Leonard said.

The funny thing is, St. Louis Cardinals fans have that exact reaction when they see Jeffrey Leonard.

In October of 1987, the Giants and Cardinals engaged in a nine-day duel that was part National League Championship Series, part epic melodrama. Leonard played the enthralling villain in the black-and-orange hat.

He talked trash, and the Cardinal fans threw it. By Game 6, after a week of escalating tensions, fans in left field tried pelting him with frozen hot dogs, cowbells, money, and beer.

"It was light [beer]," Leonard sniffed, unimpressed.

At issue was Leonard's home run trot, that gloriously defiant stroll in which he essentially turned his left arm into a middle finger. Leonard would blast a ball into the seats and round the bases while his left arm dangled lifelessly at his side.

He called the move One Flap Down.

And just to make sure everyone noticed it, Leonard took his not-so-sweet time, sometimes shifting into a lower gear at each subsequent base. "There it is, the flap is down!" NBC color analyst Joe Garagiola bellowed during Game 3. "And when he gets to third, it's going to take him two or three minutes to come around!"

The Cardinals hated it, but they had a hard time stopping it. Leonard batted .417 with a .917 slugging percentage over seven games and opened the series by homering in each of the first four games—an LCS record.

The Cardinals won the series in Game 7, but the flap will go down as one of the signature moments in Giants playoff history.

In all, Hac Man spent 14 years in the major leagues, including eight with the Giants (1981–88). He batted .266 with 144 career home runs and 723 career RBI, making the All-Star teams of 1987 and '89. But he was never a bigger star than he was during those absurdly hot playoffs.

The crazy part is he wasn't even supposed to play. When manager Roger Craig penciled out the Game 1 lineup in St. Louis, he slated mild-mannered Mike Aldrete as his starting left fielder.

Craig wanted the left-handed hitter at the plate against right-hander Danny Cox, the Cardinals' scheduled starter, which is part of what put Leonard in a bad mood a day before first pitch.

"I'm mad. Leave it at that," he told reporters who approached for comment.

Fans, coaches, and players look to the stands after Jeffrey Leonard is doused with beer during Game 6 of the 1987 NLCS in St. Louis, a game which would be stopped multiple times because of things thrown at Leonard. (Eric Gay)

But on October 6, Cox awoke with a pain in his neck. Soon, all of St. Louis would share that condition.

Greg Mathews filled in for the Cardinals with a Game 1 start, pitching admirably in a 5–3 victory. But Leonard went 2 for 4 with a home run and further antagonized St. Louis with his postgame analysis.

Davis knew that Leonard wasn't nicknamed "Penitentiary Face" for his genial demeanor.

Asked what kind of pitch he'd blasted 414 feet to center field, Leonard poked fun.

"I thought it was his fastball," he said. "It was 70 mph, 80 mph—I don't know. But it looked like a fastball, if you can call it that. But if he says tomorrow it was his changeup, I won't argue with him."

Leonard dismissed the Cardinals' entire offense, too: "They got all the things, the bounces they needed to win. But you can't win day in and day out with those kinds of things."

Leonard went deep in Game 2, as well, this time off left-hander John Tudor. Will Clark also homered in support of Dave Dravecky, who pitched a shutout 5–0 victory.

But the subplot also thickened. Fans in the Busch Stadium outfield seats, annoyed by Leonard's Game 1 trot, let him have it from the start. And when the left fielder poked them a little more, catching a routine fly ball with a needless flourish of his glove, they stood up behind him and jeered.

"Mostly, they just insulted me," Leonard said later. "Yelled my name, asked me if '00' [his uniform number] was my IQ or something."

Over in center field, Chili Davis heard the ruckus and shook his head. He knew the Cardinal fans were making a tactical error. Davis knew that Leonard wasn't nicknamed "Penitentiary Face" for his genial demeanor.

"What the fans out there have to understand is that all they're going to do with that taunting stuff is make [Leonard] mad," Davis said. "He's just going to stick it up their [backsides]. He's going to say, 'Shut up, and just go retrieve the damn ball I'm going to hit up there.'"

That is exactly what Leonard did in the fourth inning. For the second consecutive game he hit a home run into the center-field bleachers, where only a few balls had been hit all season.

Davis knew what was coming because, like other Giants, they'd already seen Leonard angry. He sometimes feuded with the press and with his own teammates. In August that year, Leonard fought with Will Clark when some standard baseball needling got out of hand.

But in the clubhouse after Game 2, Davis joined Leonard in making fast enemies. Mark Purdy, a columnist from the *San Jose Mercury News*, wrote that Davis asked an assembled group of reporters whether any of them were from St. Louis.

Nobody raised a hand, so Davis said: "The fans are [bleeping] cow-towners, man. I go back to the hotel, and my bedspread is bright red, with a picture of two cardinals above it."

(Remember that cow-towners line. By the end of this series, it's going to ring a bell.)

As the series returned to San Francisco, Craig abandoned any notion of starting Aldrete, regardless of who was on the mound. The manager also had no intentions of curbing Hac Man's style.

"When he's hot, he can do what he wants to," Craig said.

St. Louis won 6–5 in Game 3, a showdown that delivered the requisite Leonard homer—a solo shot in the third, followed by a slow home run trot—and more bad blood. Reliever Bob Forsch drilled Leonard with a fastball in the fifth.

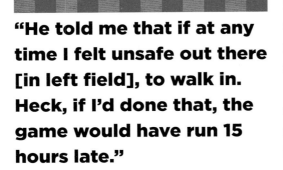

"He told me that if at any time I felt unsafe out there [in left field], to walk in. Heck, if I'd done that, the game would have run 15 hours late."

It sure looked as if Forsch hit Leonard on purpose, to send a message about those slow home run trots.

"That was an accident," Cardinals manager Whitey Herzog said.

Um, sure.

"I was just pitching Leonard inside," Forsch said. "I'm sure he could have gotten out of the way if he didn't dive into the ball."

Leonard provided his retort in Game 4. The Giants won that one 4–2 to even the series, as Leonard belted a two-run go-ahead homer in the fifth off Cox.

After the game, a reporter asked Leonard whether the Cardinals had been paid back for hitting him with a pitch. "In my personal opinion, they haven't," Leonard said.

Either way, it was the first time a player ever hit a home run in four consecutive LCS games. The only players to do it over three straight games were Hank Aaron (1969) and Gary Matthews (1983).

That was Leonard's last homer of the series, but the drama was hardly over.

The Giants won 6–3 in Game 5, meaning they headed back to St. Louis needing to win one of the final two games to reach their first World Series since 1962.

"There's no pressure," Leonard said. "This is fun to me."

But the Giants never scored again. Tudor led a 1–0 victory in Game 6 and Cox pitched a 6–0 shutout in Game 7.

Along the way, the fans treated Leonard to a hostile serenade. Some brought signs that said, "Scum Baby 00"—mocking the Humm-Baby ethos of the Giants. They booed Leonard, flipped him off, and rattled cowbells. (Never mind that it was Davis who cracked about the cowtown, not Leonard.)

A local reporter approached a kind-looking woman to ask her opinion of the Giants left fielder. "I hate him. He's the ugliest player in baseball."

Another fan, when asked what he wanted to see Leonard do on the field, said, "Step in a cowpile, I hope."

After Leonard's third at-bat in Game 6, plate umpire Bob Engel let him know that they were watching out for him.

"He told me that if at any time I felt unsafe out there [in left field], to walk in," Leonard said. "Heck, if I'd done that, the game would have run 15 hours late."

Leonard went 3 for 7 over those final two games, all singles. It wasn't enough, but it was astounding nonetheless. For the series, he was 10 for 24 with five runs, four homers, five RBI, and a 1.417 OPS. The only other players to win an LCS MVP award for a losing team are Mike Scott of the Houston Astros (1986) and Fred Lynn of the California Angels (1982).

GIANTS POSTSEASON MVPS

League Championship Series
1987: Jeffrey Leonard
1989: Will Clark
2002: Benito Santiago
2010: Cody Ross
2012: Marco Scutaro
2014: Madison Bumgarner

World Series
2010: Edgar Renteria
2012: Pablo Sandoval
2014: Madison Bumgarner

"He got the MVP and he can have it, because we got what we wanted," Cardinals shortstop Ozzie Smith said.

With that sentiment, Leonard agreed. When he came out to visit AT&T Park in 2012—for a Giants-Cardinals NLCS, no less—I asked him if he ever looks back to his amazing MVP series.

Leonard waved a dismissive hand.

"That was an individual accolade," he said. "I was a team player. It's about winning. That [losing] feeling will never go away."

In retirement, Leonard has redefined what winning means. He and his wife, Karen, created a charity that supports single parents with cancer. Based on the challenges faced by Karen's daughter, Christine, the organization provides resources ranging from laundry services to treatment-appointment transportation.

It's called the One Flap Down Foundation (oneflapdown.org).

"I started this foundation to bring awareness that cancer can happen to anyone at any age, and is especially tragic when a young, single parent has been told, 'You have cancer,'" Leonard said. "I've been extremely fortunate with a blessed life. It is my time to give back and help others."

28

2002 WORLD SERIES HEARTBREAK

The parade was to start at the Transamerica building, glide across Market Street, and wrap at City Hall. Local television coverage would hit the airwaves at 3:00 PM, with the ceremony at 4:30.

"I was already practicing my wave," Willie McCovey later confessed.

That's how inevitable the championship looked for the Giants late in the evening on October 26, 2002.

Instead of a parade through the streets of San Francisco, however, the Giants made a wrong turn and wound up in a seven-game pileup of a World Series.

Leading 5–0 with one out in the seventh inning of Game 6, manager Dusty Baker came to the mound to pull starter Russ Ortiz after he surrendered consecutive singles. As the right-hander began his walk toward the dugout, Baker stopped him and thrust a ball into his glove. It was a souvenir for a job well done.

For the record, Ortiz really did save the ball, just as Baker intended. The pitcher keeps it on display in his memorabilia room at his home in Mesa, Arizona.

"It's a good conversation piece," Ortiz said a decade later.

People are still talking about it, alright.

That Baker-to-Ortiz exchange came to symbolize the instant when everything went horribly wrong, the tug on the thread that made the entire championship banner unravel.

The Angels roared back for an improbable 6–5 victory in Game 6 before cruising 4–1 past the knocked-cold Giants in Game 7. After the final out, streamers fell from the Anaheim sky and Angels players mobbed each other in celebration. The Giants simply grabbed their bats, picked up their gloves, and fled the dugout.

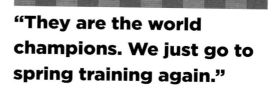

"They are the world champions. We just go to spring training again."

"They are the world champions," left fielder Barry Bonds said that night. "We just go to spring training again."

Bonds understood better than anyone the magnitude of the wasted chance. No one in baseball history had ever hit more home runs (613) or played in more games (2,439 over 17 seasons) before getting to his first World Series. He was 38 years old.

"It's something I've worked for my whole life," Bonds said.

Over his five previous trips to the playoffs, Bonds had been one of baseball's most infamous postseason flops, batting .196 with one homer in 97 at-bats. He was Mr. *Not* October. And it was beginning to feel like a curse. In 2000, he told ESPN how the drought gnawed at him even as he slept.

"Every time I dream about the World Series, I'm not there," Bonds said. "I'm trying to get there, but I'm stuck in traffic. I'm on a plane. Or I'm in jail. It's my turn at-bat, but I'm stuck in jail."

Bonds' reality was finally different in 2002. Upon reaching the Fall Classic, he did his best to make up for lost time. Bonds homered in his first-ever World Series at-bat, a solo shot in the second inning of Game 1.

"The dream came true," Bonds said after that one. "Finally."

That homer gave the Giants their first run of a 4–3 road victory that had all the makings of a tone-setter.

"For Barry to start off like that, in a series like this, that's a very good sign," Baker said that night. "He was really, really focused and kind of quiet today."

But Anaheim punched back hard in Game 2, winning 11–10 behind their own old man, Tim Salmon. The longtime face of the franchise hit a two-out, two-run shot off Giants reliever Felix Rodriguez to break an eighth-inning tie. Rodriguez tried to beat Salmon with a 96-mph fastball on the outside corner.

Where was the pitch supposed to be?

"In my glove," catcher Benito Santiago said.

The Series headed north for Game 3, the first World Series game in San Francisco since 1989. There was no earthquake this time, but the Angels' bats registered big on the Richter scale: Anaheim won 10–4, becoming just the fourth team in World Series history to score 10 or more runs in consecutive games.

A night later, the crazy pinball-machine series slowed down long enough for a baseball game to break out. Pitching and defense returned in the Giants' 4–3 victory. David Bell delivered the key, a single to drive home J.T. Snow for the go-ahead run in the eighth.

The series was tied 2–2.

"We knew we had to save face after yesterday's game," second baseman Jeff Kent said. "We needed to show that we can do this thing."

The Giants rolled 16–4 in Game 5, best remembered for Snow rescuing little bat boy Darren Baker, the manager's son, at home plate. It was part of a night that felt like a party at Pacific Bell Park, as Kent went 3 for 5 with two homers, and Bonds, Rich Aurilia, and Benito Santiago combined to go 7 for 13 with 7 RBI.

The Giants headed to Anaheim needing to win one of two games for the franchise's first title since 1954, when the team was still in New York.

"We all understand how much the city wants it," left-handed reliever Chad Zerbe said after the Game 5 victory. "But we don't

In one of the most iconic moments from the 2002 World Series, J.T. Snow drags Darren Baker out of the path of oncoming baserunner David Bell in the seventh inning of Game 5. (Kevork Djansezian)

care if it's been five years or 10 years or 100 years. We just want to win it as bad as anyone."

Ortiz was lined up as the Game 6 starter. A reporter asked him what to expect

"Obviously, the plan is to jump to an early lead and then hang on," Ortiz replied.

Nen was secretly pitching with a torn labrum, although the Giants spent October fibbing about his health.

How are those for famous last words?

The first part of the plan worked just fine. The Giants broke a scoreless tie in the fifth inning, when Shawon Dunston belted a two-run homer for another storybook twist. Like Bonds, Dunston had waited a lifetime for this chance. At 39, he was the Giants' oldest player, having broken into the big leagues in 1985 with the famously futile Cubs.

As the Giants built the lead to 5–0 on Kent's single in the seventh, Dunston just started repeating the same word in his mind: *outs, outs, outs.* But they didn't come quickly enough. When Ortiz wobbled in the seventh, allowing consecutives singles to Troy Glaus and Brad Fullmer, Baker made his infamous stroll to the mound.

The oft-repeated narrative is that players in the Angels dugout drew inspiration from seeing the Giants manager making a big show of handing Ortiz the souvenir baseball.

Salmon, years later, called that tale pure poppycock. In 2010, he told Henry Schulman of the *San Francisco Chronicle* that he didn't even see Ortiz get the ball, and if anyone else in the Angels dugout did, he didn't say a word.

"It wasn't like a rallying cry. 'Let's go get them!'" Salmon said. "I don't recall that. I was so in the zone I never heard it."

In fact, Salmon said he eventually tracked down a game tape just to see the exchange—and still wasn't ticked off. "The kid pitched an awesome game," Salmon said. "Would it have been bad to do that?"

The Angels weren't mad; they just played like it. Scott Spiezio greeted reliever Felix Rodriguez with a three-run homer at the end of a long at-bat that featured nothing but fastballs.

Spiezio's homer cut the score to 5–3, and a crowd full of so-called rally monkeys suddenly went bananas. Darin Erstad helped the Angels close to within 5–4 with a homer off reliever Tim Worrell in the eighth. Later that inning, Troy Glaus blasted a two-run double off Robb Nen and the Angels took the lead for good.

Nen was secretly pitching with a torn labrum, although the Giants spent October fibbing about his health. "It's not bothering him. He just needs more time to get loose," Baker said during the playoffs.

The Game 6 collapse transpired so quickly that by the time the Giants players got back to their lockers, clubbies were still scrambling to remove the protective plastic tarps put up in anticipation. They'd been preparing for a Champagne celebration.

Players tried to shake it off.

"It's fine," Dunston reasoned. "We're happy to have a Game 7. [The loss] wasn't heartbreaking because we have a game tomorrow."

But the air had gone out of the room, and the decisive Game 7 felt like little more than a nationally televised sleepwalk. The Giants' hopes hinged on Livan Hernandez, who had led the National League in losses during the regular season and had been hit hard in Game 4.

The team was hoping that the 1997 World Series MVP could find one last gasp of October magic, but the Angels pounded Hernandez for four runs in two innings.

Kirk Rueter—the players' choice to get the start—eventually entered in relief and delivered four shutout innings. But by then the Giants bats were quiet, managing nothing after the second inning off rookie starter John Lackey or the Angels' stellar bullpen of Brendan Donnelly, Francisco Rodriguez, and Troy Percival.

When the 2002 team returned to San Francisco for a 10-year reunion, I asked Rueter how badly he had wanted the start that day.

"If you were any kind of competitor, you wanted to pitch, so yeah, I wanted to do it," he said. "I would have liked to have seen what would have happened [if I'd started].

"But we know Livo. He was a big-game pitcher. That's what they set him up to do, and you have to go with that."

Starting Hernandez was just one of Baker's decisions that will be forever second-guessed. The manager also made a few curious choices at designated hitter, choosing light-hitting defensive specialist Tsuyoshi Shinjo for Game 1 and Pedro Feliz (with a .278 on-base percentage during the regular season) for Game 7.

It was the last game Baker ever managed with the Giants. As a lousy souvenir, the Angels handed him one last blast of pain.

29

ROBBY THOMPSON

At spring training in 1986, the big battle for the Giants' second-base job was supposed to be between Brad Wellman and Mike Woodard.

But Wellman hurt his foot. And while he was recovering, outfielder Jeffrey Leonard got a glimpse of some sparkplug rookie named Robby Thompson taking ground balls and spraying line drives.

"Brad Wellman was a friend of mine, so I went into the training room and said, 'You'd better get up off that table! It's going to be too late!'" Leonard once told me. "Brad goes running out, saying, 'I'm not hurt anymore!'"

Leonard laughed as he recalled the story. It was, of course, too late for Wellman or Woodard or anybody else.

Thompson became the Giants' Opening Day starter for the next 11 seasons and entrenched himself as one of the most popular players in San Francisco history. The second baseman was selfless and steady, willing to move runners along or belt them home himself.

Thompson won a Gold Glove for fielding excellence in 1993 and might have had even more big things in store, had a series of injuries not essentially ended his career at age 31.

Giants fans appreciated him while his body lasted. Thompson spent his entire 11-year career in San Francisco. When he was introduced as part of the final-game ceremonies at Candlestick Park in 1999, the crowd responded with an almost shocking ovation for the lifetime .257 hitter. The roar for Thompson was louder than the ones for Juan Marichal and Orlando Cepeda, surpassed only by the ruckus showered upon Willie Mays.

Duane Kuiper, another former Giants second baseman, was standing near Thompson on the field that day. He was close enough to see the big tears rolling down Thompson's cheeks as fans chanted, "ROBBY, ROBBY, ROBBY!"

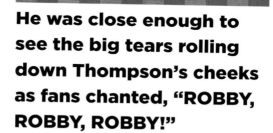

He was close enough to see the big tears rolling down Thompson's cheeks as fans chanted, "ROBBY, ROBBY, ROBBY!"

"It was really emotional for him," Kuiper said. "He never really had a send-off [when his Giants career ended in 1996]. I could tell he just wanted to get off by himself and take in that emotional ride.

"I honestly think Robby was a little surprised. And I think he appreciated it more than anybody. He wasn't the leading home-run hitter; he was just a steady guy who played extremely hard and played the game right."

Thompson later told me: "That was a very touching moment.... I was never the quote 'superstar' of the club. I was just a guy giving my all, day in and day out.

"I always figured that a game is three hours, and for three hours I was going to give it all I could. If sometimes I left the winning run at third or struck out, I still knew I was giving it all I could. I could look in the mirror and knew that I gave it all I had."

Giving it all he had was how Thompson made the Giants roster in the first place. Despite having not played a single game higher than Double-A ball, the University of Florida product wrested away Wellman's spot on the roster in '86. But the Giants were coming off a 100-loss season, and new manager Roger Craig was open to the young and the hustling.

At 23, Thompson was part of a wave of invigoratingly fresh faces. Will Clark was at first base, Thompson at second, and Chris Brown at third—none older than 25. A Giants ad campaign that year chirped, "You Gotta Like These Kids."

Thompson had surprising sock for someone his size.

No one argued.

Fans quickly embraced Thompson, whose lack of minor league seasoning never showed. The right-handed hitter batted .271 with seven home runs and 47 RBI that first season, leading the team with 149 hits, 73 runs, and 18 sacrifices. The *Sporting News* named him the National League Rookie of the Year.

Thompson had at least one hiccup, though: On June 27 that year, he became the first player in major league history to get caught stealing four times in one game. (The good news? It took him 12 innings to do it.)

But the hard-charging approach was part of the Giants' new style. They played fearlessly, with the fundamentals of gray-haired veterans. The team went 83–79 in 1986, signaling the beginning of a competitive new era.

"Everybody says 'scrappy,' and I think that pretty much says it all," Thompson said during the 1989 playoffs, when asked how he would describe himself as a player. "I've always been that way. I love to play the game. Deep down, I have a big heart."

Thompson had surprising sock for someone his size. Upon seeing him listed generously at 5'11", 170 pounds, columnist Mike Downey of the *Los Angeles Times* cracked in print that the only way that could be true is if Thompson were "measured in cowboy boots after eating two Fisherman's Wharf crabs dripping with butter.... Meet Robby Thompson, the little wick of Candlestick."

But Thompson grew up fast. He forever credited Bob Lillis, a longtime Giants coach, for showing him how to play the game right. Lillis had grown up in the Dodgers organization before becoming a respected scout, manager, and coach. Craig hired him to the Giants staff in '86. Lillis had been a little guy, too—at 5'11", 160 pounds, he was nicknamed "the Flea"—so he spoke Thompson's language.

"Flea, he was a guy I feel was as much responsible for me getting to the big leagues as anybody," Thompson told me in 2000, when he'd become a coach himself. "He had this incredible patience, and he was one of the first guys who went to [general manager] Al Rosen and Roger Craig and said, 'Hey, we might have found something in this guy.'

"Flea spoon-fed me knowledge all the time. He was even-tempered, a good communicator.... If I can be half the coach that Flea was, I'm going to be in good shape."

At the time of his retirement—i.e., before Jeff Kent came along—Thompson was the all-time leader among San Francisco second basemen in most categories, including hits (1,187), doubles (238), home runs (119), RBI (458), and stolen bases (103). In 1999, fans voted him as the second sacker for San Francisco's all-time team.

Thompson made the All-Star team in 1988 and '93, and captured the Silver Slugger Award as the best hitter at his position in '93.

Thompson helped anchor one of the most dynamic infields in team history. Bill James ranked Thompson and shortstop Royce Clayton as the best double-play combination of the 1990s.

His Gold Glove, though, was most certainly a metaphor. The actual glove Thompson used at second base was a gnarly beast. He used the same leather for almost his entire career, much to the horror of Rich Aurilia, an infielder who came along just as Thompson's career was winding down.

Bill James ranked Thompson and shortstop Royce Clayton as the best double-play combination of the 1990s.

Aurilia told writer Larry Stone in 2004: "I think by the time Robby was done, the glove mainly consisted of pine tar and chew spit. I don't even know how much leather was left in it. I know for a fact Robby still has that glove."

But the glove, like Thompson, always got the job done. And the undersized hitter had a knack for big hits. In the 1989 National League Championship Series against the Chicago Cubs, he homered twice, including a seventh-inning shot against Les Lancaster in Game 3. That two-run blast provided the winning margin in 5–4 victory, helping propel the Giants toward their first pennant since 1962.

Thompson never thrived under pressure more than he did in 1993, when the Giants were in an epic regular-season duel with the Atlanta Braves. Thompson batted .312 with 19 home runs and a .870 OPS for that team and teamed with Barry Bonds to keep San Francisco's playoff hopes alive down the stretch.

Thompson's magic was disrupted, though, on September 24 that season when Trevor Hoffman of the San Diego Padres delivered a high-and-tight fastball that smashed into Thompson's face. The batter collapsed in a horrifying thud, silencing a crowd of 24,351 fans at Candlestick Park.

A broken left cheekbone was supposed to wipe out the rest of Thompson's season.

Instead, he couldn't stand watching as the Giants faltered. He pleaded with manager Dusty Baker to let him play and talked the team's medical staff into creating a hard plastic mask he could wear to protect his face. (Stone wrote that it looked like "something straight out of *Phantom of the Opera*.")

Thompson went 0 for 4 against the Los Angeles Dodgers that day in a 12–1 defeat, but his toughness left his teammates in awe.

"It's going to hurt whether I play or not," Thompson reasoned. "So why not play?"

That '93 season was the last time Thompson was ever 100 percent. He stuck around for three more seasons, but injuries never allowed him to top more than 95 games or 336 at-bats. A torn right hip flexor. A strained side muscle. Whiplash syndrome. A shoulder injury. All of those things kept him from playing with the high-energy enthusiasm that once helped reignite the franchise.

After he played his final game with the Giants, someone mentioned to Baker that Robby Thompson was one of his favorites.

"Robby is one of everybody's favorites," Baker replied.

30

DRAVECKY'S COMEBACK

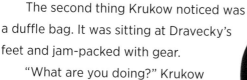

When Dave Dravecky sauntered into the Giants clubhouse at the start of spring training in 1989, fellow pitcher Mike Krukow figured he was merely stopping by to say hello.

Dravecky's career had been declared over months earlier when doctors had to remove 50 percent of his deltoid muscle to extract a tumor from his throwing shoulder. He was now a pitcher with half a shoulder, an artist with half a brush. When the left-hander plopped down at his Giants locker early in '89 and began to undress, the first thing Krukow noticed was the scar.

"He took his shirt off," he recalled, "and you could see the shark bite."

The second thing Krukow noticed was a duffle bag. It was sitting at Dravecky's feet and jam-packed with gear.

"What are you doing?" Krukow asked.

"I'm going to pitch again," Dravecky replied.

The statement was so absurd, so heartbreakingly naive, that Krukow couldn't even muster a response. He nodded politely for a time and walked away.

Krukow told this story from the outfield grass in the summer of 2014, as a way of introducing the AT&T Park crowd to the 25th anniversary of the greatest comeback story the San Francisco Giants have ever known. On the field were Will Clark, Kevin Mitchell, Willie McCovey, and other ex-players whose eyes still moistened at the memory of Dravecky's return against improbable odds.

"I knew he couldn't pitch again," Krukow said. "And he knew that he could."

In truth, Dravecky came back twice, once on the field and once in life.

Cancer merely nicked him that first time. By leaving him with half an arm but his whole heart, Dravecky still had all he needed. He worked his way back slowly, throwing a tennis ball for 15 feet...then a football for 30 feet...then a baseball for 60 feet...then his doctors for a loop.

On August 10, 1989, at Candlestick Park, Dravecky delivered eight strong innings against the Cincinnati Reds, each out more stirring than the last. "I've been in five World Series. I saw Don Larsen pitch his perfect game," manager Roger Craig said that day. "But I don't think any game had as much drama as this one."

Cancer pushed back hard, though, and this time the shark bite took everything. The miracle comeback story started to unravel five days later, when Dravecky's arm broke as he delivered a pitch against the Montreal Expos. Subsequent X-rays revealed a return of cancer. To prevent its spread, doctors removed his arm, his shoulder blade, and the left side of his collarbone in 1991.

The operation saved his life.

The operation took his reason for living.

"My ability to provide for my family was not based on how smart I was or how hard I worked. It was based solely on what my arm could do on game day," Dravecky wrote in his autobiography. "When people talked with me, it was the center of conversation. 'How's the arm today, Dave? Is your arm ready for tonight?'

"My arm was to me what hands are to a concert pianist, what feet are to a marathon runner. It's what made me valuable, what

Dave Dravecky warms up for his return against the Cincinnati Reds at Candlestick Park on August 10, 1989. (Eric Risberg)

gave me worth in the eyes of the world. Then suddenly my arm was gone."

Dravecky, of course, would make it back from this, too. The Youngstown, Ohio, native became a Christian motivational speaker as well as an official community ambassador for the Giants.

But after the amputation, there were no answers in the bottom of a duffle bag. Without a baseball career to fight for, he sank into a deep depression. As Dravecky recounted to me in a phone conversation years later, there was one wretched low point when he turned to his wife, Jan, and asked: "How can you love me? I'm not even a whole man anymore."

But Dravecky had always been able to win the tough ones. The 6'1", 195 pounder went 64–57 with a 3.13 ERA. He made an All-Star team in 1983, while with the San Diego Padres.

In those early days, Al Rosen, then the general manager of the Houston Astros, grew to admire Dravecky's fastball/slider combination as well as his bulldog competitiveness. So in 1987, when Rosen needed a bold move as the GM of the Giants, he pulled the trigger on a July 4 deal and hit the jackpot.

The Padres got infielder Chris Brown and pitchers Mark Davis, Mark Grant, and Keith Comstock.

The Giants got the NL West crown.

Bolstered by the additions of Dravecky, reliever Craig Lefferts, and utility man (and future MVP) Kevin Mitchell, the Giants went on to win their first division title since 1971.

They lost in the NLCS to the St. Louis Cardinals, but Dravecky did his part. In 15 innings over two starts, the left-hander gave up one run (0.60 ERA) and struck out 14.

"He was a very strong Christian man. But if you put a dollar bill at home plate, he would cut your ears off for it," Krukow recalled. "It was contagious. We loved that about him. The bigger the game, the better he was."

Krukow noticed something else about Dravecky: "Even his autograph was better than everybody else's. It was beautiful."

The gorgeous, readable signature could be traced back to Dravecky's son. Jonathan Dravecky noticed one day that his dad was hastily scrawling his autograph on a stack of baseball cards.

He said, "Dad, aren't you proud of your last name?"

The operation saved his life. The operation took his reason for living.

Dravecky said of course he was. "Then why don't you write it so people could read it?"

Dravecky signed plenty after the peak of his career in those playoffs, but by the end of 1988 he was dealing with his first cancer diagnosis. Doctors told him it would be a miracle if he could ever pitch again.

Dravecky needed 10 months.

When he climbed atop the Candlestick Park mound on August 10, 1989, he looked into the crowd with tears in his eyes. The 34,810 fans stood and cheered.

Through seven innings, he gave up just one hit. He gave up just three runs—all on an eighth-inning homer by Luis Quinones. In all, Dravecky gave up four hits, struck out five, and walked one over 92 pitches and eight innings.

The most impressive unofficial stat: 12 standing ovations.

In an emotional press conference after the game, Dravecky waved off a question to say: "Before we go on, I want to say, give all the praise to Jesus Christ. Without Him, there is no story." Then

Dravecky continued. "I hope everything I shared today gives hope to everyone who has had cancer. I hope it gives them reason to fight. After all I've been through, today was the easiest thing I've done in the last 10 months."

After the final out that day, Clark was among the first to meet Dravecky. He grabbed the pitcher and held on tight, because that was easier than finding the words. "I didn't know what to say, I couldn't give him enough. So I just grabbed him and told him, 'Welcome back, man.' I hope he knows how I feel."

The most impressive unofficial stat: 12 standing ovations.

Clark was also the first to rush to the pitcher in his next start, but this time under chilling consequences. Dravecky was pitching to Tim Raines of the Expos on August 16, when he felt a sharp, painful pop in his arm. The ball flew grotesquely toward home plate as Dravecky collapsed to the ground in agony.

Clark rushed to him from first base, struggling again for words. "I just said, 'Dave, breathe, breathe. In through your nose, out through your mouth. They're coming, buddy. They're coming.'"

Craig, the manager, remembered something just as stark. In an interview with MLB.com years later, Craig recalled that as doctors carried Dravecky off on a stretcher that day, the last thing the pitcher said was: "Hey, skip, we still have a chance to win this thing."

The Giants beat the Expos 3–2. Dravecky got the win.

But at 33, his career was over.

Shortly after his arm was amputated in 1991, Krukow bumped into his friend at Candlestick Park. As they talked, a young child approached Dravecky for an autograph.

Krukow, who had admired the way the pitcher once signed baseballs better than everyone else, watched as Dravecky held the ball steady between his knees and scribbled illegibly with his right hand.

"He scratched out something that didn't say 'Dave' and it didn't say 'Dravecky,'" Krukow recalled. "And I cried. It teared me up."

Dravecky had his share of tears, too. After his initial injury, rehab took 10 months. After his amputation, he was in counseling for 30 months. He struggled with anger issues and clinical depression.

Eventually, he came to understand that his left arm was a piece of him. But it wasn't him.

When he speaks to audiences now, Dravecky urges audiences to focus on the important things in life—family, friends, and relationships.

"Jobs are going to come and go. Stuff is going to come and go, especially in this economy," Dravecky said when we spoke. "People need to remember that it's not what you do, it's who you are."

Years later, Krukow looked on as the scene played out again: a child approached Dravecky for an autograph and the pitcher held the ball firm between his knees.

This time Dravecky's right hand began swooping across the baseball making his typically clear, florid strokes.

When he handed the ball back to the boy, the autograph looked perfect.

31

ROGER CRAIG

Beaten down by two dreadful seasons in the mid-1980s, the Giants went searching for a manager who could usher in an air of optimism.

It's safe to say they found their man.

Humm-Baby, did they ever.

"Being on a Roger Craig team," catcher Bob Brenly once said, "means that you hear him on the bench predicting that we're going to win a game with nine runs, and that's when we're down 8–1 in the eighth inning."

Arriving in 1986, Craig promptly turned the Giants' standings sunnyside up, engineering a 21-game improvement for the team that season, a National League West title in 1987, and a trip to the World Series in 1989.

He breathed life back into the Giants with some memorable catch-phrases—notably "Humm-Baby" and "Don't get your dauber down"—and by pressing more buttons than an elevator attendant. He stole signs, encouraged daring on the basepaths, and taught pitchers the newfangled split-fingered fastball.

In a strategy that symbolized both his aggresiveness and his outlook on life, Craig was known to give the sign for a hit-and-run *with no one on base.*

"It's a good way to make a hitter aggressive at the plate, to get him to start swinging," he explained in his North Carolina drawl.

In all, Craig managed the Giants from late in 1985 to 1992, compiling a 586–566 mark over eight seasons.

The more important record to know: 62–100. That was San Francisco's record the year before Craig arrived. This was a franchise whose dauber was very much down.

General manager Al Rosen hired Craig to replace Jim Davenport as manager in a move initially viewed as more ho-hum than Humm-Baby. Craig had had only one previous managing gig, a forgettable stretch for the San Diego Padres from 1978 to 1979, and was better known as Sparky Anderson's pitching coach with the Detroit Tigers.

"But his reputation had preceded him," Rosen said not long after the hiring. "And to tell you the honest truth, I'd been thinking about Roger Craig and his talents for some time. And when we talked, I came to realize very quickly that he's the type of fellow I like to be around. He's a straightforward man. He's an honest man, and he's a no-nonsense kind of man."

After the slow dirge of the '85 season, the '86 team arrived with the freshness of a boy band. Will Clark and Robby Thompson were among the 13 rookies to debut that season, and they played with an electrified air that brought Candlestick Park back to life. The team even unleashed a chirpy advertising campaign: "You gotta like these kids!"

But the true face of the change was a 56-year-old Lyndon Johnson lookalike who'd been around so long, he'd made his own major league debut at Ebbets Field with Pee Wee Reese at shortstop.

Craig grew up in Durham, North Carolina, where the kids playing infield filled the diamond with chatter: "Hum baby, hum baby, shoot fire rock."

The Dodgers spotted Craig pitching at a semi-pro game in 1950 and signed him to a contract. The right-handed starter broke in with Brooklyn in 1955, and you had to like this kid. As a rookie, Craig started Game 5 of the '55 World Series, a decision that puzzled reporters who wondered why manager Walter Alston would entrust a pitcher with just 91 innings of big-league experience.

"Because he's not afraid and because I know he'll give me 150 percent."

"Because he's not afraid and because I know he'll give me 150 percent," Alston replied.

Craig pitched six solid innings that day in a 5–3 win over the New York Yankees. Brooklyn won the Series in seven games.

Craig was often asked why he got along with his players so well. He pointed to his own major league career: "I've been through just about everything," he said, and the record bears him out. He would win two more World Series as a player (in '59 with the Dodgers and 1964 with St. Louis) and another as a coach (1984 with Detroit).

Those were the highs.

The lows were no less historic. Craig threw the first pitch for the worst team of modern times, as the Opening Day starter for the 1962 expansion New York Mets. Craig lost 24 games that year and 22 more the next. At one point in 1963 he lost 18 in a row.

In all, his 38–67 mark gave him a .355 winning percentage, the worst of the 1960s. The record wasn't all his fault, of course.

To be the winning pitcher for those disgraceful early Mets teams practically meant throwing a no-hitter.

But seeing the highs and the lows over his 12 seasons as a player taught Craig a thing or two.

"I've learned a lot of things from a lot of people," Craig said as Giants manager. "But the one thing I learned the most was that negative stuff doesn't help anyone. You stress the positive."

Craig liked at least one thing down, however. He was a guru of the split-fingered fastball, a pitch that looks just like a heater until it takes an abrupt dip. The pitch was invented by Fred Martin and first mastered by Bruce Sutter. But it was Craig who popularized it, first as the Tigers pitching coach and then as Giants manager.

CRAIG'S RING

When former Giants catcher Bob Brenly got his first managing gig, with the Arizona Diamondbacks, he turned to his old mentor for help. Brenly hired Roger Craig to serve as a consultant.

It was a small role, but an enormous help. So after the Diamondbacks won the 2001 World Series in Brenly's first year, he talked to Craig again.

"By the way, what's your ring size?" Brenly asked. "I've talked the owner into giving you a ring."

Brenly told the former Giants leader how much he meant to him as a player, coach, and manager.

Oh, and he lied. The owner had nothing to do with this.

One of Brenly's Diamondbacks coaches at the time—and another former Giant under Craig—Bob Melvin, later told Craig: "I'm not supposed to tell you this, but Bob paid for that ring himself."

"I called him and asked, 'What the hell did you do that for?'" Craig told writer Scott Miller of CBS SportsLine. "That was an awfully rewarding thing for an old guy like me."

The grip was similar to a forkball, with the index and middle fingers spread wide, but thrown harder. Rivals worried about the long-term effects on the arm, but Craig wrote in his book, *Inside Pitch*, that it was safe enough even for Little Leaguers: "This pitch doesn't put any strain on the arm and requires only an average-sized hand. The key to an effective split-finger is to think fastball."

The split-fingered fastball perked up the careers of pitchers ranging from Scott Garrelts to Roger Mason to Mike LaCoss. That '86 team finished third in the NL with a 3.33 ERA.

In terms of the Giants' offense, Craig's hallmark was aggressiveness on the basepaths—even if it meant 93 caught-stealings (the second worst mark in the league). Craig was so active in the dugout, so cagey about his intricate strategies, that even his players had a hard time keeping up with his sign.

"The guy has got some sort of computer brain or something," Brenly said. "I don't know how he remembers it all."

Catcher Bob Melvin, a Cal product, half-joked: "It's lucky I'm a scholar from Berkeley."

Craig once explained the madness to writer George Shirk, whose late-80s reporting for the *San Jose Mercury News* provides most of the quotes for this chapter. "I observe," Craig told Shirk. "I observe, and I watch everything. I watch the other manager. I watch their catchers. I watch their coaches. And then I keep my coaches busy.

"One of my coaches watches one thing, another watches for another thing. We concentrate.

"That's why we need about eight coaches."

Craig's complex sign-stealing techniques made the Giants an unpredictable team with an uncanny ability to crawl back into games.

"It's funny sometimes," pitcher Mike Krukow said. "Watching other teams not get their own signs because they've had to change them twice already in one game because Roger already was reading their signs better than they were at the start of the game."

In Craig's second full season as manager, the Giants went 90–72 to capture the team's first division championship since 1971. He was selected as the Manager of the Year by the Associated Press.

In 1989, the team went 92–70 and reached the World Series for the first time since 1962. But the magic faded after that. After three more years of declining finishes, the Giants replaced Craig with a younger blast of energy—promoting an exuberant batting coach named Dusty Baker.

Craig left his mark. At the time of his departure, before the eras of Baker and Bruce Bochy, he held San Francisco records for most games managed (1,252) and won (586). In seven full years as manager, Craig had five winning seasons.

His risk-taking paid off away from the diamond, too. Growing up near Durham, North Carolina, Craig once flipped a coin with a buddy to settle a debate.

At stake: which of them would get to ask out a girl named Carolyn Anderson.

Craig won. He took Carolyn on a hayride and unleashed the same type of daring base running he would later show as manager.

"He really tried to impress me, so he told me he was going to jump this creek," Carolyn Craig recalled. "He did, but he didn't quite make it to the other side."

No wonder he's an optimist. They've been married for more than 60 years.

In 1932, a smooth-talking kid named Russ Hodges got a job playing hillbilly music as a disc jockey at a Kentucky radio station. Hodges thought he was pretty good, so he asked station manager L.B. Wilson for a $5-a-week raise.

"Hodges," Wilson replied, "I can go down any alley, fire a shotgun, and hit 30 guys who are better than you."

The boss probably should have paid up. Hodges would grow up to become a Hall of Fame baseball broadcaster immortalized for his call of Bobby Thomson's 1951 pennant-winning home run. The homer was dubbed, "The Shot Heard 'Round the World."

That's right Mr. Wilson, *world*. Not the shot heard 'round the alley.

When the Giants moved west in 1958, Hodges was paired with a broadcasting upstart named Lon Simmons, and, for more than a decade, the duo became the Bay Area's summer soundtrack.

This was back in the 1960s, when live streaming meant hiding a transistor radio under your pillow after bedtime so you could hear Simmons and Hodges capturing the late-inning drama.

Hodges died of a sudden heart attack at age 60, in 1971; Simmons in 2015 after a long illness. But their voices echo still. Consider the reaction of Jon Miller on the day he won the Ford C. Frick Award, the top broadcasting honor from the Hall of Fame in Cooperstown.

"The first people I thought of were Lon Simmons and Russ Hodges—and Willie Mays," Miller said. "If it wasn't for Russ and Lon telling me about the great Willie Mays—and Willie McCovey, Felipe Alou, Juan Marichal, and the rest of those wonderful Giants—I wonder if I would be where I am now.

"It's all kind of astounding to me."

Ironically, the broadcasters who helped say hello to baseball in San Francisco are best known for saying farewell.

Ironically, the broadcasters who helped say hello to baseball in San Francisco are best known for saying farewell.

"Bye-bye, baby!" was Hodges' signature home run call.

"Tell it goodbye!" was Simmons'.

But these phrases were only a teeny fraction of what made them memorable. They were storytellers and educators, comedians and dramatists, partners on the air and off. Hodges was fond of telling Simmons: "If we win, we're gonna drink after the game because we're happy. If we lose, we're gonna drink after the game because we're sad. The only reason we won't drink is if we're tied."

As fate would have it, though, the Giants wound up with a deadlocked game in Philadelphia on June 28, 1961. The score was still tied in the 15th inning, and the game was called for being past curfew.

Simmons recalled: "Russ scribbled something, handed it over to me, and it said, 'We're just gonna break the rule.'"

Hodges was already an established name by the time he arrived in San Francisco, even if listeners knew him only as that madman shouting, "The Giants win the pennant!"

As always with Hodges and Simmons, there's a funny story behind that. On the eve of the most famous call in baseball history, Hodges' voice was a wreck. He had developed a cold not long after the Giants' regular-season finale and was struggling with a scratchy throat as the team prepared for a best-of-three

He was healthy enough by 3:58 PM on October 3, 1951.

showdown with the Brooklyn Dodgers to determine who would advance to the World Series.

So on the night before he'd be heard 'round the world, Hodges stayed up late gargling. "To test my voice, I kept talking into an imaginary microphone at home," Hodges wrote in his 1963 memoir, *My Giants*. "I had trouble breathing, my nose was running, and I was sure I had a fever."

But he was healthy enough by 3:58 PM on October 3, 1951. That's when Thomson struck his three-run blow against Ralph Branca with two out in the bottom of the ninth inning. The shot beat Brooklyn 5–4 and sent the Giants to the World Series.

This is how it sounded on radio station WMCA, and forevermore:

> "Branca throws. There's a long drive! It's going to be, I believe.... The Giants win the pennant! The Giants win the pennant! The Giants win the pennant! The Giants win the pennant! Bobby Thomson hits into the lower deck of the

left-field stands.... The Giants win the pennant and they're going crazy! They are going crazy!"

It's safe to say his voice was feeling okay.

Hodges called plenty of other home runs in his Giants career, and many of them were handled with his indelible, "Bye, bye baby!"

He knew that other broadcasters had expressions that caught on, such as Mel Allen's famous, "How about that?" So he liked it when Giants fans embraced his home run call. He'd been using it since '54 in New York, without much fanfare, but the San Francisco crowd dug it so much that "Bye, Bye Baby" became a song in 1962.

But early on there was just one problem. Hodges originally used his phrase for the other team, too. You can imagine how this went over when Hodges said, "Bye, bye baby!" after home runs by the Dodgers' Duke Snider and Dick Gray early in 1958.

"Before the game was over, we began getting phone calls from fans objecting to my using 'Bye, bye baby' in describing Dodgers' homers," Hodges wrote in *My Giants*. "When I stopped in at the studio later, I found out that people had been calling up all afternoon about it, and the next day we had an absolute flood of letters.

"If you're going to say 'Bye, bye baby' at all," a woman wrote from Marin County, "use it just for our side. We don't want to hear it when somebody else hits one."

"Her letter was typical of the hundreds that came in. So when I went to the ballpark that day, I saw my duty and I did it. Gino Cimoli of the Dodgers hit one out of the park in the second inning and I simply called it a home run. But when Bob Schmidt of the Giants banged one in the fourth, I gleefully howled, 'Bye, bye baby.' I guess everybody was happy, because the mail was predominantly favorable.

"And that's how 'Bye, bye baby' was officially born as the exclusive home run call of the San Francisco Giants on Thursday, April 17, during the third game of the 1958 season."

Simmons' signature line was no less distinctive, as he used his "Tell it goodbye!" for players ranging from Mays to Barry Bonds during a career that spanned 23 years over three stints (1958–1973, '76–'78, and 1996–2002).

"If you're going to say 'Bye, bye baby' at all, use it just for our side. We don't want to hear it when somebody else hits one."

But it was Simmons' down-to-earth accessibility that truly made him a fan favorite.

"Everybody felt they knew Lon," the late A's broadcaster Bill King once said. "You always felt: Here's another guy just like you. That's the way he always came across on the air."

Born July 19, 1923, Simmons grew up in Burbank, California, with dreams of becoming a big-league pitcher. The Philadelphia Phillies signed him shortly after he finished a stint in the U.S. Coast Guard, but the hard-throwing right-hander suffered a back injury in his first minor league game and was never the same.

Simmons launched his radio career in 1952, operating the switchboard, handling news updates, and spinning records for a station in Elko, Nevada. He would later work as a disc jockey for small stations in Marysville and Yuba City, California, where he volunteered to do play-by-play for high school sports teams for free.

Listeners always got the sense that he'd take the same rate for doing major league baseball. His regular-guy act was genuine. After he retired, when Giants officials and the likes of Joe Morgan and Vin

Scully pushed hard for his Hall of Fame candidacy, Simmons urged them to tone it down.

"I had felt, and still feel, I don't rate up there with people like Scully, [Ernie] Harwell, and Russ Hodges," Simmons said shortly after his inevitable election. "People can tell you things and make statements about how you do your job, and that's gratifying.

"But I'd finish broadcasts and be driving home and be really upset with myself because of something I didn't say or some mistake I made.... I never thought of myself as being a polished announcer."

Although he rejoined the Giants as a community ambassador in 2006, Simmons essentially retired from broadcasting after the '02 season. When he did, he used his trademark deadpan humor to defuse the ensuing tributes.

"To the people who have voiced the opinion that they enjoyed my work, I can only say, 'Thank you.' It's always pleasant to hear that they grew up enjoying listening to me," Simmons said. "To those that hated me—and believe me, there are a lot of them—I want to apologize for sticking around so long."

As it turned out, there was no need for Hodges or Simmons to ever say goodbye. The broadcast booth at AT&T Park is named in their honor.

33

BRIAN WILSON

We'll get to his preposterous beard. And Mohawk haircut. And his cleats with "too much awesome." And his spandex tuxedo. And the time he dressed as a sea captain. And the time he yelled at the owner.

But before we board the crazy train, let's get the most important thing out of the way: Brian Wilson could flat-out pitch.

The flame-throwing right-hander saved 163 games between 2008 and 2011, the most in the majors during that four-year span. Wilson made three All-Star teams, tied the Giants' single-season record with 48 saves, and pinned down some of the most important wins in franchise history.

In the 2010 postseason, he delivered 11.2 scoreless innings and earned a save in each clinching game through every round of the playoffs. Most notably, Wilson recorded the final out of the World Series, blowing a fastball past the Rangers' Nelson Cruz and promptly describing the moment in his best Wilsonese: "San Francisco is going nuts, we're going nuts, and it feels really good."

Before a torn elbow ligament hastened the end of his Giants career, he was eccentric even by closer standards—heck, even by *San Francisco* standards. But on the mound he was anything but a clown. Wilson and Robb Nen are the only Giants to post multiple 40-save seasons. Wilson is the only pitcher in team history to lead the league in saves (in 2010).

His ridiculously bushy black facial hair prompted a "Fear the Beard" slogan, but what batters really feared was a 97–100 mph fastball that cut to the corners. He worked hard at his craft after early bouts of wildness, both cutting his walk rate and boosting his strikeout total every season from 2008 to 2010.

Laugh at your own peril.

"When I'm on the field my one thought is to completely annihilate you and do everything in my power to make you fail," Wilson told Bob Nightengale of *USA Today* in 2010. "I don't have a single thought about what my hair looks like, what my shoes look like, why my shirt's unbuttoned. I don't care who you are or what you've done in this game. Right now it's a one-on-one battle and nothing's going to stop me from doing what I need to do to get the game over.

"I got three chances to get you out, three strikes. I got four chances to walk you. I like my odds. If I can't get that guy, I'll get the next guy."

Got it? Good.

Okay, now, about that beard...Wilson began growing it during the Giants' playoff run in 2010. It came out charging fast and wild, like a creature in a horror movie. He liked the lumberjack look so much he decided to leave his razor in storage just as long as the Giants kept winning.

The beard delighted San Francisco fans and appalled fashionistas. Jason Gay and David Biderman of the *Wall Street*

Brian Wilson celebrates after striking out Ryan Howard to end Game 6 of the 2010 NLCS, putting the Giants in the World Series. (Eric Gay)

Journal described Wilson's visage thusly near the end of the 2010 World Series:

> Years from now, he may rub his cheeks and wonder: "What in the name of Zeus was I thinking?... It begins innocently, with neatly manicured, natural brown sideburns. But then it gives way to a thicket of jet-black, apparently dyed madness that encircles Mr. Wilson's lower jaw like a box of Brillo pads.
>
> "It looks like a car crash involving Wayne Newton and country folk," said the celebrity hair stylist Rodney Cutler. "I'm confident it is a great distraction to the batters he is facing."
>
> Mr. Wilson's beard isn't the work of a celebrity stylist. It looks like the work of a nine-year-old bank robber.

But the hirsute look suited Wilson's personality. He was different. That was as plain as the beard on his face. He grew up in Londonderry, New Hampshire, where one of his summer jobs included straightening gravestones at a cemetery. The kid was a star in all of his pursuits, excelling in baseball and golf and reaching the 12-year-old regional finals of the NFL Punt, Pass, & Kick contest, where he got to show his stuff at halftime during a Patriots game.

Oh, and he was in the chess club.

It should surprise no one that Wilson was voted class clown of his high school graduating class. But behind the scenes there was sadness. Wilson was 12 when his dad, Mike, a career Air Force man, told him that he had kidney cancer. From that point on, the father taught his son as many life lessons as he could before the clock ran out.

His father died at 52. Wilson was 17.

The pitcher recounted his upbringing for *USA Today* in 2010 as a way of explaining his life philosophy, on the mound and off.

"I'm able to accept things better," Wilson said. "It's not easy to lose anybody, but I was brought up to realize that this is what happens in life. As soon as you're born, you're dying. So enjoy yourself. Don't be so selfish that you hold a hard grudge through life. You don't want to face death, but the last thing you want to do is fear it, because it's inevitable."

"San Francisco is going nuts, we're going nuts, and it feels really good."

The approach helped navigate the obstacle course awaiting Wilson in the Giants organization. They took him out of Louisiana State University in the 24th round of the 2003 draft, envisioning him as a starter.

But Wilson missed the entire season after undergoing a ligament replacement operation, better known as Tommy John surgery. He made a handful of starts in the minors, but blossomed as a reliever. Given his first extended chance to close in the majors, late in the 2007 season, Wilson promptly converted six of seven chances and batters hit only .188 against him.

Within a year, he was an All-Star. In 2008 Wilson became just the eighth Giants reliever to be selected for the Mid-Summer Classic, joining Stu Miller, Gary Lavelle, Greg Minton, Scot Garrelts, Jeff Brantley, Rod Beck, and Robb Nen.

Wilson followed in those footsteps by debuting a pair of absurdly shiny orange cleats at the All-Star Game. Wilson continued to wear them in the regular season, too, prompting Florida Marlins manager Edwin Rodriguez to call them "a little too bright, too flashy."

The league agreed with Rodriguez and fined Wilson $1,000.

Rodriguez eventually apologized for starting the flap, but Wilson was already ticked. "The fact that he thinks these shoes throw 97–100 with cut might be a little far-fetched," the pitcher said. "I guess we should probably have these checked for performance-enhancing cleats."

Ann Killion, writing for *Sports Illustrated*, later quoted Wilson as saying he was punished "for having too much awesome on my feet."

Wilson took his job seriously, especially when it came to fitness. The Giants 2012 media guide lists his regimen as including kickboxing, yoga, stretching, and weights. But they left out one thing: Wilson once left me waiting nearly an hour for an interview as he worked out maniacally to the video game Dance Dance Revolution.

"Richard Simmons has nothing on him," teammate Jack Taschner said, emerging from the training room in awe.

This was during spring training in 2008, before Wilson's first full season as a closer, and he explained the science behind the sweat: His goal was to get his heart rate up to 140 beats a minute but not over 168 and keep it there for an hour. Why? Because he'd recently read a study that showed 140 to 168 was the heart rate of a major league closer in the ninth inning.

His training, Wilson said, was designed to make "pitching easy. You've pushed yourself so hard, you're accustomed to toughing it out mentally."

Wilson sometimes sent manager Bruce Bochy's heart rate soaring in his early days, when he gave up a lot of base runners. But he was always at his best when the pressure was at its worst. Only 15.1 percent of his inherited runners scored over a four-year stretch (2008–11), the best mark in the majors during that span.

In the 2010 postseason, Wilson saved six games, one short of Robb Nen's 2002 team record for a postseason. He allowed only one hit over three scoreless outings in the World Series.

By the final out of that championship, Wilson's beard made him about as recognizable as Abe Lincoln. When comedian George Lopez asked for a Giant with "a little personality" for his TBS talk show, Wilson arrived with his beard dyed gray and dressed in a nautical outfit, complete with a pipe.

Wilson also appeared on *The Tonight Show* with Jay Leno, where he discussed a character known as "The Machine" (a silent, leather-clad dude who would pop up in the background of Wilson's other media interviews, just to keep things weird).

But the pitcher famous for successfully finishing off games had trouble with his ending in San Francisco. Wilson had a solid 2011 season but blew out his elbow against the Colorado Rockies on April 12, 2012. He never pitched for the Giants again, resurfacing as a free agent and signing with the Los Angeles Dodgers midway through the 2013 season.

Upon returning to AT&T Park in late September, he went a little berserk—and this time it was no act. After the Giants' 3–2 victory, he approached Giants CEO Larry Baer for a strange and heated discussion. With Baer in the front row of the stands, the pitcher screamed and gestured wildly toward the CEO from just in front of the Giants dugout.

The next day, Baer went on KNBR radio to explain the rage: Wilson was apparently ticked about not receiving his 2012 World Series ring. Baer said he'd tried several times—including in the days leading up to Wilson's return to San Francisco—to arrange a meeting, but Wilson never responded.

"Well, it was very unusual," the radio host said. "You just don't see that, usually. These things aren't handled in front of everyone."

"Unusual and Brian," Baer said with a laugh, "is that a surprise to you?"

34

CAIN'S PERFECT GAME

About the closest thing to an error in Matt Cain's perfect game on June 13, 2012, was a laughable violation of the baseball code. After finishing off a white-knuckle ride of a seventh inning, the pitcher returned to the dugout only to discover that Brandon Belt had stolen his spot.

It was a curious seating choice by the first baseman: Cain's spot was already far away from teammates and coaches for the specific purpose of avoiding human contact.

There are unwritten rules for this kind of thing. The rules dictate that you don't risk jinxing a pitcher in the midst of making history. Yet there was Belt, blissfully unaware and perfectly comfortable.

"You goofball," Cain remembered thinking. "Some of the things that guy does...that's Belt. It was priceless."

Cain didn't say a word. But fellow pitcher Ryan Vogelsong gave Belt a look that could have melted the helmet off Darth Vader.

Belt moved.

"I think Vogey was ready to kill me," he said.

And with that, Cain was on his way to a

Matt Cain waves to the crowd after his 14-strikeout perfect game beat the Astros 10–0. (Jeff Chiu)

permanent seat in baseball history. The Giants right-hander silenced the Houston Astros for the first perfect game in the history of the franchise.

Christy Mathewson never did it. Juan Marichal never did it. But Cain finished off 27 consecutive batters and raised a triumphant fist after a 10–0 victory at AT&T Park.

It was the 22nd perfect game in major league history and a doozy, even by perfect game standards. Cain struck out 14, tying Sandy Koufax's record for a perfecto set in 1965.

The man who grabbed the final out? Belt, of course. He snagged a long throw from third baseman Joaquin Arias and, now into the spirit of the day, tucked the ball into his pocket for safekeeping.

So Belt explained the next day to beat writer Alex Pavlovic that he was ready when Cain came looking for the souvenir baseball in the clubhouse.

"I thought maybe I could get something out of it. I asked him for a Corvette," Belt cracked.

He settled for a photo of himself with the pitcher and the ball. But Cain was much more eager to strike a bargain with Gregor Blanco, the right fielder, who made a sensational catch in deep right-center field in the seventh.

"He asked me what I want—a watch, car, house," Blanco said. "I just told him I'm always there for you. What happens between those lines happens for a reason."

Cain had pitched in big games before—he'd thrown 20.4 scoreless innings in the 2010 postseason—but this night at AT&T Park felt like a career coronation. Since breaking in with San Francisco in 2005 at age 20, the right-hander had dealt mostly with rotten luck.

Lousy run support made for losing records—7-16 one year, 8-14 the next—but Cain always blamed himself for each defeat.

But for 2 hours and 36 minutes on this chilly Wednesday night, Cain got everything he needed.

"Couldn't happen to a better guy," general manager Brian Sabean said a day later. "I've always considered him our John Wayne, kind of a big, reliable hero. Lincecum is our Johnny Depp, but Cain is our rock."

> **"He asked me what I want—a watch, car, house. I just told him I'm always there for you. What happens between those lines happens for a reason."**

This was the 14th no-hitter in Giants history, as well as the first to begin with a pitcher launching a magnificent tee shot. Dustin Johnson, the PGA star, was on hand at AT&T Park that day to throw out the first pitch.

Johnson was goofing around during batting practice by hitting golf balls from home plate. Cain thought it looked like fun and decided to give it a go. He put a ball on a tee, grabbed a driver, and whacked the ball 310 yards into McCovey Cove.

After that he was ready for the back nine.

Cain opened the game by throwing nine of his first 11 pitches for strikes, establishing a 93-mph fastball that would carry him throughout the night. He registered consecutive strikeouts of Jordan Schafer and Jose Altuve before getting Jed Lowrie on a foul out.

The Astros hit just one ball beyond the infield over the first five innings, when J.D. Martinez flied out to center leading off the second.

It was early, but it was special.

"The first time through the lineup, I felt like something could happen," Cain said.

Cain, whose career had been defined by a lack of support, suddenly had help coming from all corners. With one out in the sixth inning, Astros catcher Chris Snyder socked a ball to left field that looked destined to end both the perfect game and the shutout.

"I thought it was gone," manager Bruce Bochy said. "It almost seemed like it went over the wall and came back."

"Oh, yeah," Cain said, nodding in agreement. "I thought it was a homer. I have no idea why it stayed in the park."

Instead, left fielder Melky Cabrera zoomed back toward the wall and made a leaping catch. Cain raised both arms in celebration, then slapped his glove in delight.

Turns out that was merely the warm-up act.

Schafer, leading off the seventh, blasted a deep fly ball to right-center field, an area known as Triples Alley. But on this night, it was Blanco Boulevard—a dead-end street.

TOP 10

As a perk of throwing a perfect game, Matt Cain was invited to deliver the Top 10 list on *The Late Show with David Letterman*. Tonight's topic? The Top 10 Things I Want to Achieve Now That I've Pitched a Perfect Game:

10. Throw a perfect game with my other arm.
9. Convert the mound into an organic vegetable garden.
8. Discover a cure for groin pulls.
7. Open my dream salon.
6. Catch a line drive with my mouth.
5. Fix the economy, just kidding, that's impossible.
4. Pitch an inning without my pants.
3. Appear on Jay Leno's "Ten at Ten."
2. Throw a hole in one.
1. Win the contest to replace Regis Philbin.

The Giants right fielder, unlike a certain first baseman, was in tune with the history in the making. Blanco had already made a private vow as he took his position.

"I was aware of what was going on," he said. "I said to myself, 'If it's hit out here, you'd better catch it.'"

Schafer's ball kept going. Blanco kept running. Bochy's heart kept sinking.

"I just put my head down," the manager said. "And then I looked up and saw Blanco, and he was relentless."

Blanco, a center fielder by trade, launched into a headlong dive and came up with the catch. Just to make sure he was to be believed, he held the ball aloft for all to see. Blanco recalled that second-base umpire Angel Campos had to pause a few extra beats before signaling the out.

Schafer's ball kept going. Blanco kept running. Bochy's heart kept sinking.

"He was just staring at me," Blanco said, impersonating Campos' surprised expression.

The catch was so spectacular that Cain himself risked a jinx. He hugged Blanco in the dugout and asked him why he had positioned himself so far toward the alley.

"What are you doing playing there? How'd you make that catch?"

"I'm there for you, man. I did it for you."

That was the last spectacular defensive play, but hardly the end of the suspense. For one thing, Cain was on his way to 125 pitches—the most ever thrown in a perfect game. As the pitch count mounted, Bochy was ready to pull the pitcher if someone broke up the perfect game.

But he could hardly let Cain know that. So he secretly dispatched long reliever Shane Loux to warm up—in a cage behind the dugout, not in the bullpen where he might be seen.

In the end that was a needless precaution. Cain pitched an efficient eighth, leaving him just three outs from baseball immortality.

Cain knew what was at stake. He'd previously taken five no-hitters into the seventh inning without finishing the deal.

"I was having to recheck myself to see the signs that Buster [Posey] was putting down," Cain said. "I was thinking about it. It felt like it was the World Series, but it almost felt a little louder."

Posey said of heading into the ninth: "I was as nervous as I've ever been on the baseball field."

Brian Bogusevic fouled out to left. Snyder flied out to left. Then Jason Castro hit a bounding ball toward third, where Joaquin Arias made a looooooong throw across the diamond.

Twenty-seven up. Twenty-seven down.

Forty-two thousand fans on their feet.

"It's such a hard thing to do—to be part of it is special, a night we well all remember," Bochy said. "He's had some hard luck in the past, and he's been close. For him to be the guy that gets it makes it all the more special."

35

EARTHQUAKE WORLD SERIES

The Loma Prieta earthquake struck at 5:04 PM on October 17, 1989. And suddenly Game 3 of the Bay Bridge World Series took a backseat to scenes of devastation.

"We found out where the priorities of life are," Giants catcher Terry Kennedy said in the aftermath. "The World Series doesn't mean anything compared to what happened in this city. It makes me feel sick."

The quake registered 6.9 on the Richter scale, causing 63 deaths and 3,757 injuries. So brutal was its toll on the Bay Area that Major League Baseball considered canceling the remainder of the World Series. That would have been fine with the Giants.

"Personally, I don't care," outfielder Brett Butler said as the deliberations were underway. "As far as baseball goes, I can take it or leave it right now. We're talking about a disaster here, a national tragedy.

"Your heart just melts for the city and for the people who have died and their families. If the commissioner wants us to play Tuesday, I'll play and give my best effort. But if Tuesday comes

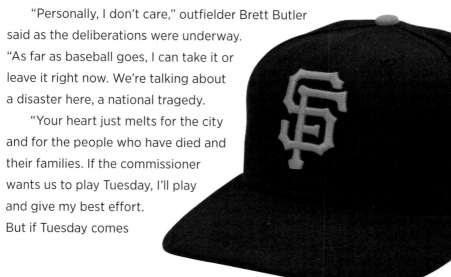

and they don't feel it's right to play the game of baseball, I'm all for that."

After a 10-day delay, the Series did resume. For the record: The Oakland A's manhandled the Giants over a 4–0 sweep. They outscored the Giants 32–14 over the Series, led by MVP Dave Stewart, who went 2–0 with a 1.69 ERA.

The A's celebrated. But barely. No Champagne in the locker room. No victory parade.

"It was an earthquake Series, and there were some unfortunate things," Stewart said years later. "But I do believe through it all that it brought the two sides of the Bay together. And that was a good thing."

Stewart was the star of the Series. But he was not the hero.

That role belonged to a young police commander whose quick thinking and calm under fire made sure that a blend of 60,000 fans, a damaged stadium, and darkening skies did not descend into chaos at Candlestick Park.

Isiah Nelson III orchestrated the evacuation after the Game 3 quake—a smooth, if surreal, exodus that former commissioner Fay Vincent recalled as "the American public at its best."

Vincent was in his field-level commissioner's box with his wife just 27 minutes before Game 3, when the ground shook for about 20 seconds. A lifelong East Coaster, Vincent was so bewildered he looked up to the sky.

"I thought that's where the noise was coming from," Vincent recalled when I phoned him on the quake's 25th anniversary. "It sounded to me like someone had scheduled a flyover of jet bombers. That's how loud the roar was.

"My wife, who is much smarter than I was, said, 'Fay, I think this is an earthquake.' And sure enough I was lurching from side to side."

The flag is flown at half mast in honor of victims of the Loma Prieta earthquake as Game 3 of the 1989 World Series resumes at Oakland Coliseum on October 27, 1989. (John Swart)

In the immediate aftermath, with the stadium awash in confusion, Vincent was among the first to learn the extent of the quake's reach. He was sitting near a flock of television cameramen and had access to their live feeds from around San Francisco. Peering into the tiny playback screens, Vincent saw scenes of devastation.

This was a major moment for the novice commissioner. He had been MLB's deputy commissioner until September 1, when his friend A. Bartlett Giamatti died of a heart attack. Now he had to navigate the postponement of a World Series game amid an epic natural disaster.

That's when Commander Nelson stepped out of his car.

"He drove up in that scout car, right after the earthquake, I would say within five or 10 minutes. And it was chaos in the ballpark. People were milling around in the field," Vincent said.

"He said, 'I'm Isiah Nelson and I'm in charge of the police detail here. Commissioner, we have a major problem. We have all these people here. Our lighting system is down and it's getting dark. I'm strongly recommending that you cancel this game.'"

Vincent assured Nelson the game was already canceled. With that, Nelson set the course of action: He would drive around in his scout car and use the loudspeaker to alert fans of the cancelation. And he would ask them to exit as calmly as possible.

Still, Nelson knew that the commissioner's demeanor would set the tone, so he told Vincent:

"If they panic, it's going to be tough. Here's what I want you to do. I want you to stay right here. Don't go indoors. Don't go under the stands. Don't go anywhere. Stay right here. As long as you're visible and calm and talking to people, we have a good chance."

The sense of panic was understandable, even for those who were watching on TV. Up in the ABC broadcast booth, announcers

Al Michaels and partner Tim McCarver were busy discussing the Giants' chances of bouncing back after losing the first two games.

"And then all hell broke loose," Michaels told me years later.

The duration of the quake was short, but "it felt five times as long," the broadcaster said. "Right after the quake, if you'd asked me how long it was, I would have said well over a minute."

The broadcast crew had its backs toward the open window, and Michaels remembered the "petrifying split-second when we thought that we were going to get pitched out of the booth and on to the mezzanine."

"We have a major problem. We have all these people here. Our lighting system is down and it's getting dark. I'm strongly recommending that you cancel this game."

It was during this time that the picture went out, startling viewers across the country. This was the first earthquake broadcast live on national television.

Once ABC finally restored audio via telephone, Michaels sounded calm. "Well, folks," he said, "that's the greatest open in the history of television, bar none!"

But he was more shaken than he let on.

"The question is," Michaels recalled thinking, "is that the big jolt that is now subsiding? Or is it the beginning of a bigger rumble?"

Michaels, a California native (and former Giants broadcaster) had been through earthquakes before. But for many of the out-of-towners and family members on hand for the Fall Classic, the shaking was too much to bear. The iconic *Sports Illustrated* cover from the Series featured Giants right-hander Kelly Downs cradling his young nephew as he walked off the field. The headline: "The Day the World Series Stopped."

The World Series started again, but it was obvious that the enthusiasm was gone. Before the quake, the Giants talked about the thrill and excitement of hosting their first World Series since 1962. After, they talked about it as nothing more than a job they had started and were obligated to finish.

"From what I hear about the stadium, it's perfectly safe, and I'm not afraid of it—really. But I'm managing from second base."

"We worked hard to get here, and in a lot of ways it would be a disappointment to see it end unfinished," reserve outfielder Pat Sheridan said. "But by the same token, even if we came back to win, how could we really even celebrate?"

There was also the question of how venerable Candlestick Park was holding up.

"From what I hear about the stadium, it's perfectly safe, and I'm not afraid of it—really," manager Roger Craig said. Then he wryly added, "But I'm managing from second base."

Enthusiasm flagged across the country, too. Game 4—which the A's closed out 9–6—was the lowest-rated primetime World Series game ever. On the East Coast, it was outdrawn by *The Golden Girls*, *Empty Nest*, and *Hunter*.

While the baseball was forgettable, the actions of that young police commander were not. Vincent thinks of Isiah Nelson III often.

"I do because it's such a poignant story," Vincent said. "He died so young and he had such a terrific future. It's just one of those awful aspects of life. It's a tragedy."

As a distant aftershock of the Loma Prieta quake, the hero of Candlestick Park died a few months later on a closed-off stretch of freeway just after midnight. He was en route from the stadium on April 14, 1990, when he crossed a portion of I-280 that had been shut down for earthquake repairs. He struck a cement barricade he hadn't seen. He was 40.

Art Agnos, the mayor at the time, ordered city flags to half-staff and called him "a brilliant police officer whose professional future had no limits."

Since 1990 the Giants have given out the annual Commander Nelson Award to the employee who best exemplifies Nelson's "spirit, dedication, and professionalism." The team also presented the family the bases from the World Series Game 3 that was never played.

His wife, Dorian, said she looks at them every day.

36

JACK CLARK

Yes, his most famous home run came while wearing a St. Louis Cardinals uniform. But the ferocity behind Jack Clark's memorable swing in Game 6 of the 1985 NLCS can be traced back to the cold and swirling winds of Candlestick Park.

His three-run, ninth-inning blast off Tom Niedenfuer propelled the Cardinals into the World Series. And because it had the added perk of coming against the Los Angeles Dodgers, Clark knew instantly how much the moment would resonate back in San Francisco.

"I wasn't a Giant at the time, but I think I was pretty sure that I told everybody—including the great Cardinal fans—that it was for a lot of frustrating years against these guys," Clark told KNBR radio host Marty Lurie in 2015.

"I was glad to break [the Dodgers'] hearts on national TV in front of millions of people. Tommy Lasorda always talked about bleeding Dodger Blue. And he spilled all kinds of blood out there. There was Dodger blood everywhere."

This is why Clark was known as "Jack the Ripper."

For his bat.

And for his mouth.

Either way, Clark kept things lively during a Giants career that lasted from 1975 to 1984. Whether letting 'em rip or giving 'em lip, the outspoken right fielder was regularly the best player on a bad team.

Clark hit 163 of his 340 career home runs as a Giant and made two All-Star Games in San Francisco. His best year was in 1978, when he batted .306 with 46 doubles, 25 home runs, and 98 RBI.

He had 11 seasons with at least 20 home runs, matching the total shared by the likes of Joe DiMaggio, Jim Rice, and Johnny Bench.

In 1982, he kept the Giants afloat in the N.L. division race by batting .274 with 30 doubles, 27 home runs, and 103 RBI.

"Jack was a clutch man," said former Giants manager Dusty Baker, who watched most of Clark's heyday as an opponent from the Dodgers dugout. "For a guy his size [6'2", 175], Jack probably had one of the shortest, quickest strokes around. You couldn't shoot a bazooka and get it past Jack Clark."

While his bat speed was revered, his penchant for bluntness didn't always sit well with managers. *Sports Illustrated* once dubbed him "baseball's all-time leader in boats rocked." Clark complained. He clashed with Frank Robinson. He called the Giants organization "a loser." Once, Clark was asked to name something that would improve Candlestick Park.

"Dynamite," he replied.

But for all the controversy, Clark was also, for the better part of a decade, the man the Giants wanted at the plate with the game on the line. One of the most feared right-handed hitters of his time, Clark delivered when it mattered.

Consider the all-time leaders in most career extra-inning home runs:

1. Willie Mays (22)
2. Jack Clark (18)
3. Frank Robinson (16)
4. Jimmie Foxx (14)
5. Mickey Mantle (14)
6. Hank Aaron (14)
7. Ted Williams (13)

That's some quality company. It's also about as far as you can get from Clark's actual supporting cast while with San Francisco. The Ripper never played in a postseason game during 10 seasons with the Giants. Instead, he was part of only three Giants teams that finished above .500—in 1978 (when Clark finished fifth in MVP voting), 1981, and '82 (seventh in MVP voting).

It was far more likely in any given year for Clark to be the best paddler on the Titanic. He played on four teams that finished at least 20 games out of first place.

Still, the Ripper was often the bright spot among some dim fog. His 26-game hitting streak in 1978 remains the Giants team record, standing the test of time against the likes of Barry Bonds and Buster Posey.

In all, Clark finished his career as a four-time All-Star who led the league in walks three times. More solid company: He had 11 seasons with at least 20 home runs, matching the total shared by the likes of Joe DiMaggio, Jim Rice, and Johnny Bench.

His nickname—"the Ripper"—came from Vida Blue, and from some early career tinkering with his batting stance. Clark made his debut with the Giants on September 12, 1975, and over time came to realize that Candlestick Park was no place for towering fly balls.

Moon shots that he thought were home runs off the bat weren't coming close to clearing the fence. The wind and fog and cold stood in the way.

"And I got frustrated with it," Clark told Lurie on October 3, 2015. "So I started top-handing everything and trying to hit hard, low groundballs. The sound off my bat started making a different sound. I had more bat speed. I was 'cleaning' the baseball better—hitting it more consistently on the sweet part of the bat.

"As a result, I didn't hit a lot of home runs but I started really slugging because I started driving it through the wind and hitting it into the gaps."

Clark was surrounded by expectations from the start. The Giants elected him in the 13th round of the 1973 draft after he batted .517 for Gladstone High School in Azusa, California.

At first, the Giants wanted to get a look at his arm, too: Clark opened his professional career as a 17-year-old hurler for Great Falls of the Pioneer League. He went 0–2 with a 6.00 ERA over five games. He fared better at the plate for that team, batting .321 with 9 homers and 54 RBI.

He never pitched again.

Clark was hardly an imposing sight but he had bat speed galore. He also had an aggressive approach, honed by Giants batting instructor Hank Sauer, who told players, "Don't be nice to the ball."

Clark was less conscientious in the field, sometimes throwing to the wrong base or forgetting the number of outs. When Clark devoted himself to Christianity, a Giants teammate quipped: "Why is it that Jack Clark can find God but not the cutoff man?"

That lack of polish was at the root of a prolonged, ugly feud between Clark and hard-nosed manager Frank Robinson. The Hall of Famer annoyed his star player by questioning his all-around game.

"A Pete Rose scares you. He can do so many things to hurt you," Robinson told reporters in 1982. "But Jack Clark, if he's not at the top of his game, can't help you. I'm not putting him down, but his whole game is his hitting."

BOO

In a nod to the inevitable, Johnnie LeMaster once changed the name on the back of his uniform to "Boo."

It's what Candlestick Park fans were going to call him anyway.

The Giants shortstop of the late 1970s and early '80s was a lifetime .222 hitter with no power who twice ranked among the National League leaders for errors.

"I started getting booed a lot around 1980," LeMaster told writer Ed Attanasio for the website This Great Game. "So I was laying in bed one night and my wife sat up and said, 'You should just change your name to Boo!'"

It took a while to work up the jersey—and the nerve—but LeMaster pulled off an all-time prank by sneaking into the clubhouse right before a game and swapping uniforms. He actually wore "Boo" onto the field for three outs before general manager Spec Richardson saw it and blew a gasket.

The Giants fined LeMaster $500. In retrospect, it was a small price to pay.

"I started getting booed a lot less after that," he told Attanasio in 2015. "I've been asked several times by the Giants to return for the events over the years and I always do. When I go on the field now, it's more of a gentle boo because all the fans remember. I still have that 'Boo' jersey and collectors from New York call me all the time wanting to buy it, but I can't part with it."

Ouch.

Clark, never one to back down, promptly fired back when he appeared a guest on a radio show, saying: "The Giants have to look at themselves in the mirror and say whether they are even trying. I'm not a loser...but the organization is a loser."

By 1985, he was gone. The Giants traded Clark to the St. Louis Cardinals for first baseman David Green, pitcher Dave LaPoint, outfielder Gary Rajsich, and shortstop Jose Uribe. The Cardinals got a crucial piece to their '85 and '87 pennant winners.

Because his grumbling got headlines, it's easy to forget the Clark of happier times. He was the first ever winner of the Willie Mac Award, given annually to the player who best exemplifies the spirit and leadership consistently shown by Willie McCovey throughout his long career.

Clark earned the first one in 1980.

He says now that the trophy is a mess—the wood is chipped, the cup sometimes falls off the plaque—but it's about the only personal award from his career that he keeps on display at his home in St. Louis. He likes it because it bears the name of his friend, and because it was voted upon by his Giants teammates.

Clark told Lurie that people sometimes look at the beat-up keepsake and offer to do a repair job.

"I say, 'No! Just leave it!' I like it like that."

37

JOE MORGAN'S HOME RUN

Before they had trophies to polish and parades to plan, the Giants set the bar a little lower.

Sometimes, a great season simply meant making Tommy Lasorda sad.

That's how Joe Morgan became a folk hero in San Francisco. He belted a three-run homer to beat the Los Angeles Dodgers on the last day of the season, October 3, 1982, a shot that Morgan said ranked among the greatest homers of his Hall of Fame career.

Nope, the Giants didn't advance to the playoffs with the victory. But the Dodgers didn't either. Morgan's homer ensured that Los Angeles would finish behind the division champion Atlanta Braves.

"I've been in the big leagues 19 years, and I've learned a lot of humility," Morgan said that day. "It's tough to be over there with your head down because you needed to win that last game and you couldn't do it. I have a lot of respect and admiration for the Dodgers.

"But I wanted this one for the Giants and the fans."

Morgan's bash came on the anniversary of Bobby Thomson's 1951 home run to beat the Dodgers for the National League crown. The play-by-play call this time might as well have been, "The Dodgers don't win the pennant! The Dodgers don't win the pennant!"

Why such an exuberant celebration? In an otherwise dark era of Giants baseball, seeing the Dodgers suffer tasted nearly as sweet as

Champagne. The highlight clip, played often in San Francisco to this day, always comes in two parts: Act 1: Morgan blasts a pitch from reliever Terry Forster over the right-field fence as Candlestick Park fans go crazy; Act 2: Lasorda, the Dodgers manager, rubs his weary eyes in despair.

"I still remember Joe between first and second base," Duane Kuiper told the *San Francisco Chronicle* years later. "He raised his right arm to say, 'If we're not going to win this, you're not either.'"

A crowd of 47,457 showed up at Candlestick Park

> **"I still remember Joe between first and second base. He raised his right arm to say, 'If we're not going to win this, you're not either.'"**

that day. And if the final celebration looked over the top for a third-place team, it can be explained by all that came before. By the time Morgan stepped to the plate in the seventh inning, Candlestick Park was a fizzy mix of frustration, elation, gratitude, and *schadenfreude*. It was already shaken up. Morgan just twisted off the cap.

The fans had come to cheer *something*. The Sunday game was supposed to be the end of a miracle ride. The Giants were 13½ games behind the Atlanta Braves on July 30 before putting together a hot streak for the ages, going 20–7 and putting some heat on the Dodgers and Braves.

Jack Clark kept the team afloat with one of his finest seasons, batting .274 with 27 home runs and 103 RBI. Veteran Reggie Smith, in the final season of his All-Star career, put together a torrid second half, including batting .354 with seven home runs and a .615 slugging percentage in August.

And, as with all successful teams, there were some unlikely heroes. On September 30, the last game before the crucial Dodgers series, the Giants trailed the Houston Astros 7–6 heading into the bottom of the ninth.

With two out, bases loaded, and Astros closer Dave Smith on the mound, manager Frank Robinson dispatched Ron Pruitt to pinch-hit for Jonnie LeMaster. Never mind that the 30-year-old backup catcher hadn't had an at-bat in two weeks.

By Sunday, only the Dodgers were alive.

Ronald Ralph Pruitt dumped a little droplet of a fly ball behind second base and it fell as softly as summer rain, prompting one of broadcaster Hank Greenwald's greatest calls:

"Three-one pitch…. Swung on…. A little looping fly ball back of second base…. It's gonna drop! Base hit! Evans scores! Leonard scores! The Giants have won the ballgame! They're back in the race!"

Indeed, the Giants were tied with Los Angeles, one game back of Atlanta, with three to play.

"I don't want to think about the Dodgers," Robinson said that night. "I want to savor this. That's almost unreal."

Those were the only two RBI of Pruitt's season, and the last of his career. Twenty years later, reporter Steve Kroner of the *San Francisco Chronicle* tracked down Pruitt to ask him about his signature moment.

"You mean that drive I hit off Dave Smith that one-hopped the center-field wall?" Pruitt cracked.

Whatever it looked like, the hit gave the Giants a pulse heading into that final weekend. That was a rarity for a zombie of a franchise that went from 1972 through 1986 without winning a thing. There were no division titles during that span. No finish higher than third place. Instead, there were 10 teams with losing records.

But here they were entering a Friday night series with a chance to go head-to-head against the Dodgers—and with home-field advantage no less. Pruitt's hit had put a faint whiff of destiny in the air, and the fans came ready to rock.

It did not go well. Rick Monday hit a late grand slam on Friday night, backing Jerry Reuss' shutout in a 4–0 victory. Then the Dodgers eliminated the Giants on Saturday with a 15–2 victory that all the Pruitt bloop singles in the world wouldn't have been able to save.

By Sunday, only the Dodgers were alive.

But the Giants hardly played that way. Kuiper got a sense of the stakes when he arrived at the ballpark to see Robinson's lineup card.

"I knew it was a big game when I saw I wasn't in the lineup," Kuiper, a backup second baseman, told the *Chronicle*. "We were eliminated, but all the big guys were in there. I felt going to the ballpark I actually had a chance to play, but Joe Morgan was the starting second baseman."

With two on, two out in the seventh and the score tied 2–2, the future Cooperstown resident came to the plate against Forster. Morgan, who was 39 that season, had plenty of bigger moments in his career. Countless bigger moments. He was the sparkplug for the Big Red Machine, winning back-to-back MVP awards in 1975–76, the years the Cincinnati Reds won back-to-back World Series.

Listed at just 5'7", 160 pounds, he had improbable power, once hitting 27 homers in a season. During his Hall of Fame induction speech, he said: "I take my vote as a salute to the little guy."

Forster was not a little guy, listed at 6'3" and (cough, cough) 200 pounds. No less an authority than David Letterman guessed it was closer to 300 and repeatedly referred to the lefty as "a fat tub of goo."

As in, tell it goo-bye.

Forster hung a slider and Morgan jumped all over it. He sent a line drive over the right-field fence, where Dodgers outfielder Monday all but deflated as he ran out of room.

"Whatever Joe Morgan wants, it's my treat."

An airplane-engine-size roar erupted. The Giants led 5–2 by the time Morgan touched home plate and stepped into a bear hug from Clark. With a stellar bullpen led by Greg Minton, the Giants held on for a 5–3 victory. And the Dodgers were done.

Morgan recognized the significance of what he'd done. He understood the Giants-Dodgers rivalry. Though his best days had been in Cincinnati, he'd grown up in Oakland and appreciated baseball history.

"I got a chance to see the great players. Willie McCovey. Yes, I was there the day he went 4-for-4 against Robin Roberts, and the great Willie Mays," Morgan said during his Hall of Fame induction speech. "I got to see these guys play each and every day…. And I think that watching them play, and the way they enjoyed the game, I was fortunate enough that I was infected with their enthusiasm for the game, and wanted to play the game the way that they did."

As if to rub it in, the Braves lost to the Padres that day. Meaning Los Angeles really had blown a chance to force a playoff.

"Whatever Joe Morgan wants, it's my treat," said Braves player Bob Horner when the news reached San Diego.

The homer would be Morgan's last act as a Giant. In the off-season, the team traded him to the Philadelphia Phillies in a deal that netted pitchers Mike Krukow and Mark Davis.

But it was a pretty good ending to his two years in San Francisco.

"I guess I'll remember that home run for the rest of my career," Morgan said. "It may not be one of the biggest I ever hit, but it will be one of the most memorable."

After the final out, Candlestick fans stood and applauded so long and loud that Morgan had to come back from the locker room for a curtain call.

He then walked along the grandstand railing, signing autographs and shaking hands. When he finally left the stadium that day, Morgan bumped into a Dodgers outfielder named Dusty Baker.

"You broke my heart," Baker told Morgan of the homer.

Which is why Giants fans will treasure it forever.

38

ROBB NEN

He was not as colorful as Rod Beck nor as wacky as Brian Wilson nor as outright goofy as Greg "Moon Man" Minton. But no Giant ever secured more white-knuckle victories than the coolly efficient Robb Nen.

The hard-throwing right-hander with a knee-buckling slider racked up 206 saves for San Francisco, seven more than Beck's previous team record.

Nen would have had more had he not given his right arm for the team. He knowingly (but quietly) put his career in jeopardy by pitching with a torn rotator cuff and a torn labrum during the second half of the 2002 season. Nen refused to surrender to surgery because the Giants were in a pennant race. That team indeed reached the World Series—thanks in part to his seven postseason saves—but Nen never pitched again.

He had inflicted so much additional damage to his shoulder that he was finished, at age 35. Nen tried for several years to rescue his fastball from his body's wreckage but to no avail.

"I don't have any regrets about anything I

did at any time," Nen told the *San Francisco Chronicle* on the day he announced his retirement. "I may regret some pitches, how I pitched to somebody, but as for pitching, I'd have done things the same way now.

"For me, I played this game to win and go to the World Series."

At his retirement, Nen ranked 13th on the all-time saves list. He made three All-Star teams fresh off the peak of his powers. At the All-Star break in 2002—before his undisclosed injury—he had 24 saves and a 1.58 ERA, with 40 strikeouts and only six walks in 40 innings. Opposing hitters had managed just a .182 batting average against him.

Nen was already an imposing figure—6'4", 200 pounds with a stare straight out of *The Terminator.* And the Giants amped up his aura by playing "Smoke on the Water" whenever Nen strolled in from the bullpen.

There was smoke all right. At his best, Nen reached the upper 90s with his fastball. But what hitters really feared was his slider.

"For me, Nen's slider is the toughest pitch in baseball," Colorado Rockies first baseman Todd Helton told me during the pitcher's prime. "It looks exactly like a fastball. I can't tell the difference. I've never had a hit off the guy. I'm 0 for 6, but it feels like I'm 0 for 30. He's definitely got my number."

How tough was that slider?

"I hit a ground ball to shortstop against him last year," Helton said, "and I was happy. At least I made contact."

Crazy as it sounds, Nen's slider was born out of failure. While with the Florida Marlins, the hard-thrower was in need of a secondary pitch to keep opposing hitters off balance. Marlins pitching coach Marcel Lachemann told teammate Richie Lewis, a curveball expert, to take Nen under his wing.

Lewis showed Nen his grip, but there was still one big problem.

"Robb was so super-human and he threw so damn hard, he threw right through the break," Lewis recalled.

Lewis had the same problem early in his career, before four arm operations sapped his fastball. Lewis turned to a solution his father taught him years earlier, telling Nen to lock the wrist to get a better downward pull on the release.

After weeks of practice in the outfield, the light went on.

"I'll never forget the day when he finally got it," Lewis said. "His face lit up. And his career took off."

In his ninth pro season, Nen's slider was born. It was a terrific, hard, late-breaking pitch. He went 5–1 with a 1.35 ERA and 35 saves in 1996, his first full year of throwing it.

The Giants acquired him for a song in 1998, sending minor leaguers Mick Pageler, Mike Villano, and Joe Fontenot to the Marlins in one of the best deals in team history.

Pageler and Villano never reached the majors. Fontenot went 0–7 with a 6.33 ERA for the Marlins in 1998 and never played in the big leagues again.

Nen, meanwhile, began racking up saves at a remarkable rate. He saved at least 40 games in four of his five Giants seasons. The only year he didn't was in 1999, when he had 37 saves.

When he recorded his 300th career save at age 32, he was the youngest to reach that milestone, surpassing John Wetteland, who had been 33. And by doing it in his 617th relief appearance, the right-hander became the fifth-fastest to accomplish the feat. (Former A's closer Dennis Eckersley was the quickest, at 499.)

"It's a comfortable feeling having Robb out there," Barry Bonds said that night.

When Nen started, however, he was far from comfortable. He spent his minor league career as a flame-throwing starter in the Texas Rangers' organization. He threw his fastball in the 90s, but his body was not built to do so for nine innings. He suffered injury after injury.

The Rangers traded Nen to the Marlins midway through the 1993 season. The Marlins stuck him in the bullpen, reasoning that his live arm might stay healthy if he faced only a handful of batters a few times a week.

That's when he learned the modified curveball from Lewis and became nearly unhittable. To throw it, Nen would hold his index and middle fingers across the part of the ball where the two seams are closest together. Then he'd shift them slightly to the right side of the ball.

Hall of Famer Willie Stargell once compared hitting a slider to "trying to drink coffee with a fork."

Though some pitchers make a twisting motion as they release the pitch, Nen simply added pressure—or "cut it"—by ripping down with his fingers as he released the ball. That sent it spinning like a gyroscope, with a tight spin and a mostly horizontal break as it reached home plate. (Curveballs break mostly vertically.)

Hall of Famer Willie Stargell once compared hitting a slider to "trying to drink coffee with a fork." In his masterful book, *The Art of Pitching*, Tom Seaver put it this way: "At its best, the slider utterly confounds the hitter who can never 'sit' and wait on this pitch. The slider breaks too much to be a fastball but is thrown too hard to be a curve. Since it breaks late in the hitting zone, the batter rarely has time to react to its sudden movement."

And therein lay the challenge of trying to hit off Nen. He threw his slider at the ridiculous velocity of 91 to 92 mph. The average major league fastball during that era was 88 mph.

"Hitters react at it thinking it's a fastball," Giants pitching coach Dave Righetti said, "and it's gone."

Righetti argued that Nen's pitch belonged in the pantheon of great sliders, joining those of legends such as Steve Carlton, Ron Guidry, and J.R. Richard. And even the best hitters of the 2000s didn't argue.

"His slider is filthy," said Luis Gonzalez, who struggled in his career against Nen. "Being a left-handed hitter, you usually feel more comfortable against a right-hander. But he has an unorthodox style and it's tough to get your timing."

The timing, though, turned out rotten for Nen, too. A few weeks before the 2002 All-Star Game, he pitched 1⅓ innings against the Toronto Blue Jays. He fell asleep on the team plane heading home. When he woke up, the top of his shoulder was aching.

That was the beginning of the end, although no one in the Giants' inner circle knew it. To help hide his injury, the mph reading on the stadium radar gun often not-so-mysteriously vanished when he came into the game.

But he clearly wasn't the same in the World Series. In the fateful Game 6 loss, Nen surrendered a ringing two-run double to Troy Glaus that gave the Angels a 6–5 lead in the eighth inning. The Giants never led again.

It was also the last time Nen ever took the mound.

"He was one of the best players, people, and teammates I've ever seen," Giants assistant general manage Ned Colletti told the *San Francisco Chronicle*. "He really died on the sword for the club and his teammates."

39

THE BRIAN JOHNSON GAME

fter Brian Johnson hit one of the greatest home runs in San Francisco history, people danced and shouted and frolicked in the aisles.

Barry Bonds came out of the dugout and shadow-boxed an invisible opponent. Portly reliever Rod Beck deemed the situation worthy of a sprint, blasting full-on into the celebration.

"That was some of the most partying I've ever seen at this park," manager Dusty Baker said that day from the relative calm of his office. "That was awesome. Just awesome."

But here's the thing.

Johnson's brain declined to join the fun that day, apparently skipping the party for a quiet night in. The hero swears he heard nothing as he rounded the bases, sound returning to his ears only after he reached the giddy mob awaiting him at home plate.

There were 52,188 lunatics screaming at Candlestick Park, yet Johnson's head was an abandoned library.

"It was so bizarre," the catcher told me, years later. "It was so loud that it was like my body was trying to protect me from the sound. As soon as I hit the bag, everything was muffled."

This was the Shot *Not* Heard 'Round the World. Still, it had a similar effect as the home run Bobby Thomson blasted in 1951. Johnson's, leading off the 12th inning on September 18, 1997, staggered the rival Dodgers and propelled the Giants toward an unlikely playoff spot.

"I've never recalled a game with so much emotion," first baseman J.T. Snow said.

Johnson, like Thomson, was hardly the guy you'd pick from the lineup to play hero. He'd spent three seasons as a backup catcher with the San Diego Padres and half a season with the Detroit Tigers before the Giants acquired him in a quiet trade-deadline deal on July 16, 1997.

"That was some of the most partying I've ever seen at this park."

Johnson lasted only a season and a half in San Francisco. On the other hand, he lasts forever.

Mention "The Brian Johnson Game" to a San Francisco fan and then duck. There's an emotional tidal wave coming. Johnson's homer on Mark Guthrie's first pitch of the inning culminated a four-hour saga that came to symbolize the shocking '97 NL West champions.

No, it didn't clinch anything. But the Giants moved into a first-place tie with the Dodgers that day and never saw second place again. Johnson's home run proved to a team that had finished in last place in '96 that they were ready for whatever the '97 pennant race had to offer.

"This is crazy. Everyone's jumping on the bandwagon," second baseman Jeff Kent said that day. "I hope the train is big enough."

Part of what made Johnson's final chapter so great was the prologue. Just a week earlier, it looked as if the sputtering Giants were about to run out of gas. They lost four straight, including a gut-punch loss in Atlanta, where Beck coughed up four runs in the bottom of the ninth.

More on Beck later.

By the time the Dodgers arrived at Candlestick Park on September 17, they led the division by two games. The Giants, knowing they needed to sweep the two-game series, won the opener on Wednesday.

That set the stage for the Brian Johnson Game.

"I told him to use his whole bag of tricks that he'd learned during his career."

On Thursday, the Giants took a 5–1 lead in the fifth after a three-run homer by Bonds, who did a little dance as his drive cleared the right-field fence. His gesture did not go unnoticed by the Dodgers.

"He's got his pirouette down," catcher Mike Piazza said. "I could care less. If he feels the need to entertain, that's his problem."

Giants fans, though, cheered wildly for Bonds, remaining on their feet in hopes of getting him to take a curtain call. Instead, teammate Stan Javier came out and took a bow as a goof.

The Dodgers promptly turned the comedy into a drama. They cut the score to 5–3 in the sixth, when Eric Karros and Todd Zeile delivered run-scoring hits.

Los Angeles tied it in the seventh when Piazza drilled a two-run single to left to make it 5–5.

Getting to Johnson's magic, however, required a little hocus-pocus from the bullpen. Beck, fresh off his collapse against the Braves, entered the game in the 10th inning. It did not go well. Piazza singled. Karros singled. Raul Mondesi singled. And the bases were loaded with nobody out.

For Beck it looked like Atlanta all over again. But this time, he supplied the grit.

"I told him to dig as deep as he could," Baker said, recalling his trip to the mound. "I told him to use his whole bag of tricks that he'd learned during his career."

The full account of what happened next is in Beck's chapter, but the quick version is no less astounding: He struck out Zeile on a 94-mph sinking fastball. Then he coaxed future Hall of Famer Eddie Murray to ground into an inning-ending double play.

Beck got an assist from Kent. The second baseman had spent two seasons as Murray's teammate with the New York Mets. Kent and Murray often discussed hitting scenarios, including the one here — bases loaded, infield drawn in.

"Eddie would say, 'Just see the ball, and if it's close try to take any pitch they throw and just push it up the middle, poke it through there,'" Kent said. "So I had a notion that Eddie would hit the ball to my right, trying to do that. But how often does it really happen that way?"

At least once, which is all the Giants needed. Kent scooped up the ball and gunned the ball to Johnson standing atop home plate for the first out. Johnson then pivoted and threw to Snow at first base. Double play. The 41-year-old Murray was late to the bag by a full step.

As the game snaked into the 12th, Johnson found a simpler way to stage a rally. It helped that he was in his lucky ballpark. As a prep star at Oakland's Skyline High, he'd once pitched a no-hitter at Candlestick against San Francisco's McAteer High.

Johnson went on to play at Stanford, where he was the winning quarterback in the 1987 Big Game against Cal. He also won two College World Series titles while at Stanford.

That was part of his baseball education.

"What I have taken from that experience is the reinforcement that a champion is not always the team that should win," he once said. "A champion is not the most talented always, nor the luckiest, but the most resilient. We were not the best team in the nation or even in our conference for that second championship, but when the money was on the table, we were very tough to beat."

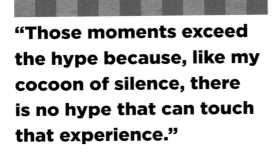

"Those moments exceed the hype because, like my cocoon of silence, there is no hype that can touch that experience."

And that takes us back to Johnson batting against Guthrie in the bottom of the 12th inning in the heat of a pennant race. He blasted one deep to left field. Johnson knew he hit it well, but worried a bit as he watched outfielder Todd Hollandsworth tracking the ball in flight; Johnson thought the wind might knock it down.

Instead, it sailed into Giants history, just over Hollandsworth's outstretched glove. Someone asked Johnson afterward to articulate what it felt like.

"My vocabulary is not that broad," Johnson said, despite his Stanford degree in political science.

Johnson took another swing years later, this time in an online Q&A with his friend and former *Sports Illustrated* baseball writer Jeff Pearlman. This time, Johnson's vocabulary seemed plenty broad.

"Those moments exceed the hype because, like my cocoon of silence, there is no hype that can touch that experience," Johnson told Pearlman. "It touched my soul and took me to another planet at the same time...and I was unable to do anything about it. The rawest and truest drug that only sports can produce."

The Giants went on to win the '97 division title, their first since advancing to the World Series in 1989. They fizzled next against the Florida Marlins, but new general manager Brian Sabean's first-ever playoff team had the electric feel that would set the stage for even more sparks down the line.

Johnson played one more season for the Giants, batting .237 with 13 home runs and 34 RBI. That off-season he signed as a free agent with the Cincinnati Reds and eventually finished his career—gasp!—in Los Angeles, where he played three games for the Dodgers in 2001.

In all, Johnson spent eight seasons in the big leagues and batted .248 with 49 home runs and 196 RBI. He also had one unforgettable trip around the bases.

"I had other moments in my career," Johnson said. "But I'm happy to be remembered for that one."

40

JOHN MONTEFUSCO

Technically, he was listed on the roster as a right-handed pitcher.

"I was more of an entertainer," John Montefusco clarified for me years later. "We didn't get very many fans out at our games at Candlestick. I didn't want them to be bored sitting in the stands.

"I wanted to put on a show while I was out there. If it took me striking out people for them to be happy, I tried to do it."

The Count put on a show all right. In his brief, spectacular, downright weird career, the right-handed entertainer dazzled with his fastball and mesmerized with his off-field quips. Instead of "Play ball!" the umpire should have yelled "Action!"

Even Montefusco's major league debut came with dramatic flair. He sauntered out of the bullpen on September 3, 1974, fresh from the minors, to inherit a bases-loaded, nobody-out situation against the rival Dodgers at Dodger Stadium.

Montefusco got Tom Paciorek on an RBI groundout, then struck out Steve Yeager and

Doug Rau to end the threat. Montefusco kept on rolling that day, pitching eight more solid innings to earn the win in a 9–5 victory.

Oh, and in his first at-bat, he belted a two-run homer.

As they say in show biz, a star was born.

"I got drunk the night before when I learned I was going up, because they told me I wouldn't pitch for at least a week," Montefusco said.

"When they called my name with the bases loaded, I was ready to turn around and walk out of there. I was shaking, but I got a grounder and two strikeouts and got out of the inning.

"I think I'm a pretty good pitcher. I could be rated with Tom Seaver or Don Sutton, I think. One of these days, I want to throw a no-hitter, too."

"I couldn't ask for anything better for breaking into the big leagues."

After that taste in September, Montefusco was back for an all-you-can-eat buffet in 1975. Relying mostly on a fastball and a slider/slurve, he went 15–9 with a 2.88 ERA and struck out 215 batters in 243.2 innings.

Montefusco won National League Rookie of the Year honors that season, edging out Gary Carter, the Montreal Expos' future Hall of Fame catcher. No Giants player would snag Rookie of the Year again until 2010, when a young catcher named Buster Posey took top honors.

In a Giants career that lasted from 1974 to 1980, Montefusco went 59–62 with a 3.47 ERA. He ran hot and burned out fast. But it was fun while it lasted.

The Long Branch, New Jersey, native was as brash as they come, once wondering: "Who am I hurting by popping off? What's the sense of keeping it in?"

He even had a cool nickname. Well, cool eventually. His original cumbersome moniker—"the Count of Monty Amarillo"—was a headline after he sizzled in a minor league game in El Paso. After his debut with the Giants, play-by-play man Al Michaels anointed him "the Count of Montefusco."

That one stuck.

How bold was he? Let us Count the ways.

Montefusco was still green when he tangled with the Big Red Machine. In his fifth career start, Montefusco silenced the Cincinnati Reds 6–0 at Candlestick Park on September 22, 1974. Along the way he struck out future Hall of Famer Johnny Bench three times.

"I should have struck him out a fourth time, but I hung a slider and he got a hit 0-and-2," Montefusco recalled during a visit to AT&T Park years later.

Before the Giants headed to Cincinnati in '75, a reporter asked Montefusco how he thought he'd fare in the rematch.

"I said, 'Well, I shut them out once before. I can probably shut them out again. And since I struck out Bench three times—I should have had him the fourth time—I can probably strike him out four times,'" he recalled.

Montefusco's shutout prediction vanished in the first inning, when Ken Griffey scored on a throwing error by first baseman Willie Montanez.

As for that bit about striking out Bench four times...

"In the second inning, I hung a slider 3-and-2 to Bench again and he hit the longest home run ever hit off of me in my life. And if it wasn't for the cement facade up in the third deck of Riverfront Stadium the ball would still be going," Montefusco said.

Bench's three-run shot was part of a miserable day for Montefusco, who didn't make it out of the second inning of an 11–6 loss.

When he got back to San Francisco, the Count came across a letter addressed to him on Cincinnati Reds letterhead.

"I opened it up and it was a bill for $946.74," Montefusco recalled. "It said, 'For damage done to the cement facade by Johnny Bench's home run.'"

Montefusco fumed. Who the hell did the Reds think they were?

Then it slowly dawned on the pitcher that one of his teammates had pulled off a big-league prank. "Chris Speier sent me that letter," he said, still laughing.

That Bench dinger aside, Montefusco fared just fine in '75. He threw 10 complete games, four shutouts, and finished fourth in the league in Cy Young Award voting. His 215 strikeouts were the most by a rookie since the Cleveland Indians' Herb Score in 1955.

"I think I'm a pretty good pitcher," he declared back then. "I could be rated with Tom Seaver or Don Sutton, I think. One of these days, I want to throw a no-hitter, too."

He was terrific again in 1976, going 16–14 with a 2.84 ERA and 172 more strikeouts. That was the year he made his lone All-Star appearance, at Philadelphia's Veterans Stadium.

As in his big-league debut, Montefusco had a daunting All-Star assignment. The 26-year-old came in as a reliever for future Hall of Famer Tom Seaver and promptly faced four more future Cooperstown enshrinees.

The right-hander got Carl Yastrzemski on a pop-up, walked Rod Carew (who stole second), retired George Brett on a fly ball to center, and coaxed Carlton Fisk to foul out to the catcher.

He pitched a scoreless seventh inning, too, including strikeouts of Fred Lynn and Phil Garner.

"My favorite part? Getting out there, doing my job, and getting it over with," Montefusco said.

Amazingly, there was even better to come that season. On September 29, 1976, he fired a no-hitter against the Atlanta Braves. He struck out four, walked one, and finished things off by getting Jerry Royster on a fly ball to right field. Then again, the batter could have been anybody.

GIANTS ROOKIE OF THE YEAR WINNERS

1951: Willie Mays
1958: Orlando Cepeda
1959: Willie McCovey
1973: Gary Matthews
1975: John Montefusco
2010: Buster Posey

"[The] adrenaline that was rushing through my body would have allowed me to get Willie Mays, Joe DiMaggio, Babe Ruth, Lou Gehrig, and anybody else in the ninth," Montefusco told author Bill Ballew. "I felt no pain and felt like I was 10 feet off the ground."

Montefusco also told Ballew: "At the end of that game, it was the greatest feeling in the world. It is the greatest high that I have ever experienced in my life."

It was also the high point of a career that would begin to falter. An ankle injury in 1977 prompted a change in repertoire. Montefusco now relied more on a sinker, changeup, and forkball. He would never win more than 11 games for the Giants again, never get his ERA back under 3.00 or strike out 200.

Upset that Dave Bristol removed him from a game against the Mets at Candlestick Park on June 18, the Count scuffled with his manager and wound up with a black eye. By December 12 that year, he was gone. The Giants traded him to the Braves in a deal for pitcher Doyle Alexander.

Still, his presence was hard to shake. For more than 20 years, Montefusco was the last Giants pitcher to throw a no-hitter. So every time a San Francisco hurler carried one late into the game, Montefusco's phone would start ringing off the hook.

It was no different on July 10, 2009, when Jonathan Sanchez ended the drought by throwing a no-hitter against the San Diego Padres. Yes, Montefusco was watching. But this time he didn't want to talk about it.

Eight months after Sanchez registered the final out, Andrew Baggarly of the *San Jose Mercury News* finally got the Count to open up. Montefusco said he had gotten the first call for comment while the game was still going on.

"It was the Giants' cable broadcast," Montefusco said. "They wanted me to go on the air. What am I going to say? It's the kid's game, not mine. For a couple days after that, my phone was ringing off the wall. I just didn't want to pick it up. First off, if I did one [interview], I'd have to do all of 'em. And it's the kid's day. Let him have it."

Plus, Montefusco wasn't sure how he'd sound in interviews. He'd have to admit the truth: that he'd miss his place as the last Giant to throw a no-hitter.

"You know, yes, I will."

Then Baggarly asked Montefusco if he worried about slipping a little further from memory now that Sanchez had replaced him as the trivia question.

"Nah, I did a lot of crazy stuff," Montefusco said. "So I know they'll never forget me."

THE
1962
WORLD SERIES

Because Willie McCovey hit the ball so hard it blurred, the ears told a better story than the eyes. Billy Pierce, the late Giants pitcher, remembered the end in two distinct jolts.

"You heard the smack off the bat," Pierce recalled, "and it wasn't a second later and you heard the smack again into the glove."

In San Francisco, that was the sound of breaking hearts.

McCovey's crackling liner to New York Yankees second baseman Bobby Richardson was the last out of the 1962 World Series. He hit it with two on, two out in the bottom of the ninth inning, allowing the Giants to think for a fraction of a second that they were going to win the World Series.

Instead, Richardson made a shoulder-high catch to preserve the 1-0 victory in the decisive Game 7 at Candlestick Park. So haunting was the final out that for years McCovey continued to have dreams about lining the ball toward Richardson.

"Unfortunately," McCovey lamented, "he kept catching it."

McCovey was not alone in his angst. That play marked the nearest a generation of Giants fans got to a World Series victory. Being that close somehow made it worse. So close to drinking Champagne, they got a bucket of ice water to the face.

Had McCovey's ball gone anywhere else than right at Richardson —anywhere in the 94124 zip code—Matty Alou would have scored from third and Willie Mays from second for a thrilling walk-off victory.

Alas, San Francisco would have to wait a little while longer for a World Series win. Just about a half-century.

McCovey went on to hit 521 career home runs, 18 grand slams, and earn a spot in the Hall of Fame. "But that out is what many people remember about me," he said. "I would rather be remembered as the guy who hit the ball six inches over Bobby Richardson's head."

Sometimes forgotten is that McCovey's at-bat was

McCovey was not alone in his angst. That play marked the nearest a generation of Giants fans got to a World Series victory.

merely the final step of an improbably cruel parade for the Giants—a botched bunt, a controversial base-running decision, and a Mays liner earlier in the seventh that also died in a Yankee glove.

The agonizing finish would come to symbolize the frustrations of the entire decade: The Giants of the '60s had Mays, McCovey, Orlando Cepeda, Juan Marichal, Gaylord Perry—five Hall of Famers. No rings.

"We were always the best second-place team in baseball," pitcher Mike McCormick said in 2012. "And many of those second-place years, we should have won the pennant. And, finally, it happened in '62."

That team remains one of the finest in San Francisco history, going 103–62 under manager Alvin Dark.

Mays enjoyed one of the top seasons of his career, batting .304 with 49 home runs and 141 RBI.

Cepeda added 35 home runs and 114 RBI. Right fielder Felipe Alou batted .316 with 25 homers and 98 RBI. Catchers Tom Haller and Ed Bailey combined to make one Buster Posey–like season, totaling 35 homers and 100 RBI.

"We had a damn good club," recalled Don Larsen.

Larsen, who is a tad better remembered for his perfect game for the Yankees in the 1956 World Series, was a middle reliever for that Giants team. There wasn't much room for him in a dazzling four-man rotation that featured

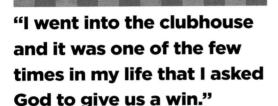

"I went into the clubhouse and it was one of the few times in my life that I asked God to give us a win."

Jack Sanford (24–7), Billy O'Dell (19–14), Billy Pierce (16–6), and Marichal (18–11).

Sanford had been a solid but unspectacular right-hander over his first few seasons, but in '62 he found a formula that worked— namely, a new slider and lots of luck. At one point in late summer, he won 16 consecutive decisions.

Sanford was hardly overpowering, striking out only 147 batters in 265⅓ innings and finishing with a 3.43 ERA. For the SABR Baseball Biography Project, writer Warren Corbett recalled that Dark told Sanford to throw as hard as he could for as long as he could and let relievers do the rest. As a result, one writer dubbed the pitcher "the composer of the Unfinished Symphony."

The Giants' mission looked unfinished, too, heading into the final weeks of September. With seven to play, they trailed Los Angeles by four games. But the Dodgers skidded toward the finish by losing four in a row, and the rivals were tied at 101–61 after 162 games.

That forced a three-game playoff, and, again, it looked as if the Giants would be the best second-place team in baseball. Los Angeles led 4–2 heading to the ninth inning of the decisive third game at Dodger Stadium.

"I went into the clubhouse and it was one of the few times in my life that I asked God to give us a win," Felipe Alou told writer Steve Bitker in *The Original San Francisco Giants.* "I went in and out in one minute. I said I couldn't believe we'd come that far to get beat, and then I went back out."

The Giants promptly scored four times in the ninth to capture their first pennant since 1954. The winning rally was aided by a bases-loaded walk, a wild pitch, and an error.

"You don't want your worst enemy to suffer through that," Alou told Bitker. "Of course, it happened to us in the World Series."

The showdown against New York made for the first coast-to-cost Fall Classic in history. Apparently intent on building the drama, Mother Nature rained out games in both cities. The World Series famous for its blink-of-an-eye finish took a then-record 13 days to play.

Over the course of the evenly matched series, the Yankees won the odd games (Games 1, 3, and 5) while the Giants took evens. That set the stage for a classic Game 7 at Candlestick Park.

Sanford did his part, allowing one run over seven gutty innings. The Yankees' only run scored in the fifth, when Tony Kubek hit into a bases-loaded double play as Bill "Moose" Skowron scampered home from third.

Terry, squaring off against Sanford for the third time in the series, allowed only two hits over the first eight innings. He got help from left fielder Tom Tresh, who made a terrific running catch in the left-field corner to rob Mays of extra bases in the seventh.

It remained 1–0 heading to the bottom of the ninth inning.

This is where more squeamish readers may choose to avert their eyes.

Matty Alou led off with an exquisite drag bunt toward second base for a single. So began a Sequence of Regrettable Events. Dark called upon Felipe Alou—who had a .513 slugging percentage during the season—to bunt the runner over.

Alou, looking lost, struck out.

"It wasn't the manager's fault," he told Bitker. "I should have bunted fair because I had a good runner, my brother, on first. But I hadn't been practicing my bunting. What I [did later, as a manager] is have my players practice a lot of bunting. *All* of them."

Hiller struck out, too, bringing the Giants down to their last out. Still, there was hope. Due up: Mays, McCovey, and Cepeda.

The next regrettable event in the Sequence came during Mays' double, which he whacked just inside the right-field foul line. As

CHARLIE BROWN

As the 50th anniversary of the '62 classic approached, *San Francisco Chronicle* reporter Sam Whiting visited Willie McCovey's home in Woodside, California.

Whiting knew the first baseman was preparing to be asked about the Bobby Richardson liner all over again so he showed up in person to pose the question of how he was coping with the memories.

By way of answering, McCovey reached into a plastic packet that contained reprints of *Peanuts* cartoon strips.

In the first, which originally ran on December 22, 1962, Charlie Brown sulks for three panels until he finally lifts his head and bellows to the sky, with all the Charlie Brown angst he can muster, "Why couldn't McCovey have hit the ball just three feet higher?"

In the second, from January 28, 1963, the caption is: "Or why couldn't McCovey have hit the ball even *two* feet higher?"

right fielder Roger Maris raced over to retrieve the ball, Matty Alou raced around the bases and had thoughts of scoring all the way from first.

That's when third-base coach Whitey Lockman put up the stop sign.

The decision to hold Alou at third would be debated for years. But Pierce, who had an unusual vantage point, told me that Alou had no chance. Pierce had been dispatched to

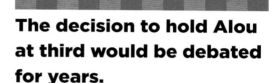

The decision to hold Alou at third would be debated for years.

warm-up in the bullpen along the left-field line in case the game went into extra innings. He had both Maris and Alou in his line of sight.

"I saw Alou coming around third. He couldn't have scored, no question about it," Pierce said in 2012. "Maris made a very good, quick recovery. He played it really well and got it into Richardson for the relay really quick."

The Yankees countered Lockman's stop sign with their own questionable decision. With first base open, New York manager Ralph Houk decided to let the right-handed Terry faced the left-handed-hitting McCovey even though right-hander Cepeda was on-deck.

Houk was apparently unfazed that McCovey had homered off Terry in Game 2 and tripled off him earlier in Game 7. "I was ready," Cepeda said in 2015. "I was ready to face Ralph Terry. So when they pitched to McCovey, wow. It blew my mind."

Houk's strategy almost backfired, twice.

On the first pitch from Terry, McCovey launched a long, slicing foul ball down the right-field line. The mighty blast was enough to catch the attention of the Yankees second baseman, who made one last crucial move in the Sequence of Regrettable Events.

Richardson, upon seeing McCovey pull the pitch with such power, concluded that Terry would try to throw a curveball, and that McCovey would pull it again.

"I moved over just a little bit, and he hit the ball right to me," Richardson told Tyler Kepner of the *New York Times* in 2001. "It was one of those balls like [Mickey] Mantle used to hit, with a lot of overspin. It looked like a base hit going to the outfield, but it came down in a hurry. He really hit it hard."

That's how the Giants' hopes ended. Not with a whimper, but with a bang.

42

J.T. SNOW

J.T. Snow won six Gold Gloves for his fielding excellence and along the way racked up 12,855 putouts and 1,016 assists. But there's no argument over his greatest grab.

In the seventh inning of Game 5 of the 2002 World Series, little Darren Baker, the manager's son, put himself in harm's way. The three-year-old batboy was so intent on retrieving Kenny Lofton's bat that he toddled as fast as he could toward home plate. But he forgot that grown-ups were still chugging around the bases. And they were chugging hard.

Snow was the first to score, and as he crossed the plate his alert eyes noticed Darren stepping into the middle of baseball's train tracks. The sure-handed fielder reached back, snatched the boy by the back of his warm-up jacket and hoisted him safely into his arms. A split-second later, David Bell plowed home on Lofton's two-run triple.

"I've got a four-and-a-half-year-old son of my own at home, so I know how to get ahold of them when they're running away," Snow said that night. "I didn't want him to get hurt. When I grabbed him, his eyes were huge. I don't think he knew what was going on."

In the manager's office after the game, Dusty Baker's phone rang. It was his mother, and she wasn't calling to congratulate him for a 16–4 victory over the Anaheim Angels. Christine Baker had already told Dusty—to no avail—that she worried about her grandson getting hurt on the field. She was calling to say "I told you so."

"Just listen to me this time," Christine said. "And thank J.T. for me."

Indeed, Jack Thomas Snow's heroics earned him a permanent place in Giants lore (not to mention boosting his stock with the coveted Worried Grandma demographic).

But the first baseman was far more than the best babysitter in Giants history.

From 1997 to 2005, the switch-hitter was among the most reliably valuable players on the roster. He had several solid years at the plate, including a 28-homer,

"I've got a four-and-a-half-year-old son of my own at home, so I know how to get ahold of them when they're running away,"

104-RBI season in '97. On defense, he turned playing first base into an Olympic gymnastics routine. Snow and Hall of Famer Willie McCovey are the only San Francisco first basemen to make nine straight starts on Opening Day.

He meant enough to the franchise that the Giants arranged for a special farewell. Snow had played his last game in 2006, for the Boston Red Sox. But the Giants signed him to a ceremonial one-day contract in 2008, allowing him to take his position in a game against the Los Angeles Dodgers. Snow was removed before the first pitch, then jogged off the field to one last roar from the San Francisco crowd.

"It's a good statement of what we think of him," general manager Brian Sabean said then. "He is one of the most popular players and one of the truest professionals we've had in uniform."

His Superman act with Darren Baker tends to overshadow all else, but in that very same World Series, Snow batted .407 with a .448 on-base percentage and a .556 slugging percentage. He had a 1.004 OPS for the Series, with at least one hit in all seven games.

So how did the comedian (and Giants fan) Robin Williams greet him upon seeing Snow before Game 6?

He called him, "the child savior."

Snow got used it.

"My friends kept saying, 'You had a great World Series, you hit .400 and made a great catch and all they remember is you saving Dusty Baker's kid,'" Snow joked when he reported for spring training in 2003.

For example: His 14 sacrifice flies in 2008 remain a San Francisco record. Sexy!

Snow had plenty of other big moments during his San Francisco career. Acquired in a heist of a trade (the Angels got forgettable pitchers Allen Watson and Fausto Macey), he drove in 90 runs at least three times and did a lot of little things that went unnoticed or overshadowed.

For example: His 14 sacrifice flies in 2008 remain a San Francisco record. Sexy!

For example: The biggest home run of his career went for naught. Snow blasted a game-tying three-run shot off Armando Benitez in the bottom of the ninth in Game 2 of the 2000 National League Division Series. One inning later, it meant nothing to him because the New York Mets went on to win 5–4 in 10 innings.

"You know, it doesn't really matter," he said, declining to talk about it. "We win as a team, we lose as a team. I don't remember much."

But over the long haul, his quiet moments made some noise on the Giants' all-time chart. Heading into the 2016 season, Snow ranked eighth on the list in doubles (228), eighth in RBI (615), and first in batboy rescues (one).

His offensive resume might surprise fans who remember him mostly for his glove.

"That's what happens when you're so very good in one department," Baker said in 2001. "Hank Aaron's defense got overlooked because he was a home-run hitter. There was a time when what Rickey Henderson did was overlooked because he was a stolen-base champion. Whatever your super strength is overshadows everything else."

In fairness, it's easy to understand why Snow's defense gets top billing. This was astounding, mind-blowing, acrobatic, wear-out-the-rewind-button stuff on a daily basis. The only first basemen to win more than Snow's six Gold Gloves are Keith Hernandez (11), Don Mattingly (nine), George Scott (eight), Vic Power (seven), and Bill White (seven).

"I just tell J.T. 'Good play' before every game because it saves me time," Baker said in 2004. "I asked him if he ever gets sick of hearing that, but he doesn't."

Snow even had a memorable catch in that 2002 World Series, a jaw-dropper in Game 1. Drifting over toward the Giants dugout in pursuit of a foul pop-up, he slipped on a slick surface, fell on his back, and coolly righted himself to make the catch.

Snow got his first glove as a fifth birthday present in 1973. A red-white-and-blue autographed Roberto Clemente model, the glove was so beloved he still has it.

Even in his prime, though, when he'd graduated to a Wilson 2002 model, Snow never stopped working relentlessly on his defense. He sometimes took up to 300 ground balls in a single workout, knowing that no hop could be taken for granted. Snow told me he learned that lesson in 1996, on the night the Angels presented him with his second Gold Glove in a pregame ceremony.

"Really early in that game, a guy hit a slow roller right between my legs, right under my glove," Snow said. "I just wanted to crawl under the base and hide."

But he caught just about everything else in his career, just like his father did—albeit on a different field. Jack Snow was a Pro Bowl receiver for the Rams, playing from 1965 to 1975. He led the NFL with 26.3 yards per catch in 1967, just ahead of Homer Jones (24.7) and Paul Warfield (21.9).

Growing up in Southern California, J.T. followed in his father's footsteps for a while. He was a star quarterback for the Los Alamitos High School football team. But he was even better on the baseball diamond, where his teammates included a skinny third baseman named Robb Nen.

And whenever Los Alamitos needed a reliever for a couple of key outs late in the game, coach would call on...Snow.

"He didn't have any pitches except strikes," Mike Gibson recalled years later. "He didn't have much of a curve or anything. But he never rattled out there."

Nen, of course, would go on to become one of the best Giants relievers of all time. He and Snow helped the team nearly win it all in 2002.

Instead, the lasting Giants legacy of that World Series wound up being a rule change: Starting in 2003, batboys had to be at least 14 years old. It's called the "Darren Baker Rule."

But if it's goodwill for kids' baseball wishes, there ought to be another rule, one with a deeper meaning: The J.T. Snow Rule would remind people that Darren wasn't the only kid he helped.

Inspired by the death of his mother, Merry Carole, who died of cancer in 1998, the first baseman created a lasting tribute. He arranged to buy 25 tickets for underprivileged children to come to every home game. It came to be known as the "Snow Pack" and was filled with young guests from the American Cancer Society, the Make-A-Wish Foundation, and the Lucile Packard Children's Hospital at Stanford.

He'd also invite kids and their parents into the dugout every Sunday for photographs, autographs, and major league memories.

"Really early in that game, a guy hit a slow roller right between my legs, right under my glove. I just wanted to crawl under the base and hide."

"I think anytime someone plays in a town and has a long-term commitment to a team, they should give something back," Snow explained. "I get some incredible letters and pictures from kids and their parents. It's amazing. Our society today is so busy and everything is rush-rush, but if a kid goes to a ballgame just one time it can make a lasting impression."

The Snow Foundation remains in full swing, long after the player's retirement from baseball.

"Sometimes players don't realize what we mean to kids. I just try to remind myself what it was like being in their shoes as a kid and how I looked up to players," Snow said. "Sometimes you think that you don't have that much of an impact, but you do."

Some of the kids who came to the park as Snow's guests couldn't have cared less about his Gold Gloves.

They just knew his heart was made of the same stuff.

43

SAVED BY OWNERSHIP

Like so many of the innovations spawned from the Bay Area in the early 1990s, this one started when someone started scribbling furiously during a bleary-eyed, late-night brainstorming session.

That's how the Giants wound up with their version of the Next Big Thing. That's how they broke out of baseball's dark ages and engineered a path that would lead to three World Series titles in a five-year span.

In true Silicon Valley style, it started with someone essentially grabbing a cocktail napkin and a pen. The setting was Peter Magowan's living room in 1992 on a night that should have been pure euphoria.

Magowan's group had just received word that their bid to buy the Giants was approved. In fact, their last-minute offer had rescued the team from moving to St. Petersburg, Florida.

And yet the room was oddly somber. As one investor put it: "I've got good news and bad news. The good news is that we just bought the team. The bad news is: What the hell do we do now?"

"We should have been celebrating," said Larry Baer, a fourth-generation San Franciscan who would become the team's president and CEO. "But what were we celebrating? We just spent $100 million on a team that was losing more than $10 million a year and that everybody told us had no future."

That night, Magowan and Baer sat down and created The List. It was audacious, bold, dreamy, and a little naïve. To those who knew the bleak parts

"I've got good news and bad news. The good news is that we just bought the team. The bad news is: What the hell do we do now?"

of Giants history—no World Series victories since 1954, an embattled home ballpark, lackluster home attendance—their to-do list might have looked like the silliest top 10 this side of David Letterman.

But one by one, the neophyte owners went on to cross off every item on their wish list.

Some were easy. Some were not. The last one to go was No. 4—"Win the World Series"—but they checked it off in 2010, then underlined it in 2012 and highlighted it in 2014.

Moreover, the Baer-Magowan group did it without resorting to a quick fix. They never stocked the roster with overpriced free agents or mortgaged their future by trading away too much of their farm system.

Instead they patiently laid the groundwork for a culture of success. Results? A gorgeous waterfront ballpark, epic attendance numbers, stability in the front office, a strong farm system, bankable stars, and a reputation for sustaining a winning chemistry.

"A leading venture capitalist told me once, when he invests, he would much rather put his money behind an A person values-wise with B talent than A talent and B values," Baer told the *Wall Street Journal* in 2015, not long after the Giants won their third World Series. "We are in a highly people-intensive business."

The ownership structure has changed several times over the years. Magowan stepped down as managing partner in 2008; Baer emerged as the control person for the franchise when Bill Neukom retired in 2012.

But the vision remained constant. Before the Giants could plan their victory parades, however, there were more pressing items on The List. For example, saving the franchise. In fact, the No. 1 item they scribbled on that pad was: "Keep the Giants from leaving San Francisco."

It was almost too late. On August 7, 1992, a *San Jose Mercury News* headline blared: "Bye-Bye, Giants: Lurie accepts offer, team is headed to St. Petersburg." Then-owner Bob Lurie had a $110 million deal in place from a Tampa Bay investors group. In November, however, National League owners overwhelmingly rejected the move, giving Magowan's group time to swoop in.

"There were a lot of people who thought we were just a temporary thing," Baer said. "They thought we were a Band-Aid until the team could be moved elsewhere.

"But the number one thing on our list was very real to us. Our whole goal at that time was to stabilize the franchise. We realized that we had to move away from the Candlestick economics. It was affecting everything from the payroll to the attendance."

No. 2 was about brain power—"Hire the best baseball management team." Magowan, a 1964 Stanford graduate with a master's degree from Oxford, was the chairman and CEO of Safeway Inc. Baer, a 1980 Cal graduate who went to Harvard Business School, was coming off a job at CBS.

These baseball neophytes were immediately left in the lurch. When they bought the team, their brain trust—general manager Al Rosen and manager Roger Craig—resigned. Even more daunting, they left behind a team that finished last in the National League West.

"We didn't profess to be baseball experts," Baer said.

In search of a new leader while at the winter meetings that December, Magowan and Baer kept hearing the same name pop up: Dusty Baker, their batting coach. They promoted Baker to his first managerial job and he responded by winning the Manager of the Year Award in his very first season and later won two more.

Baker was long gone by the Giants' World Series triumphs, but he proved to be the right man for an ownership group looking to reignite the franchise. The charismatic, high-energy Baker took over a team that had gone 72–90 in '92 and led it to a 103–59 finish in '93.

That sizzling turnaround also had a lot to do with No. 3: "Add to that team the best player in the game."

"We needed to at least give people hope," Baer said. "We needed to show some fans a commitment that we were going to make things better."

So the Giants called Dennis Gilbert, then representing Barry Bonds, a free agent coming off an MVP season for the Pittsburgh Pirates.

"Gilbert was incredulous," Baer said. "He said, 'You guys haven't even been approved as owners yet. It's nice of you to call, but I only have time to deal with more serious interests.'"

Eventually Gilbert agreed to let Baer call Bonds' number and try for himself. The Giants figured that the San Francisco connection alone would be worth taking a shot at reeling in one of baseball's most dynamic young stars. Bonds' father, Bobby Bonds, had been signed by the Giants as an amateur free agent in 1964 and later spent seven years at the big-league level in San Francisco.

Little Barry grew up about 25 minutes south of Candlestick Park in San Carlos, and idolized his father, as well as his godfather, Willie Mays.

That sizzling turnaround also had a lot to do with No. 3: "Add to that team the best player in the game."

"When we called Barry directly, he was almost choked up," Baer recalled. "He said, 'I can't tell you how much I'd love to come home.' It hit him emotionally."

Gilbert remembers the negotiations going a little less sentimentally: "Larry Baer was on me like a bad rash. He would call me three or four times a week, and sometimes he had nothing to say. He just wanted me to know how much they wanted Barry. It was a very passionate sales job."

Bonds signed for six years and $43 million, which turned out to be a bargain. The left fielder, like Baker, was gone by the time of the World Series runs. But over a 15-year run with his hometown team, Bonds won five MVP awards, set single-season and career home run marks, and electrified the fan base.

No. 4? That's the aforementioned World Series. Every baseball owner has the same goal, of course, but No. 4 held special resonance for the Giants. They hadn't won it all since 1954, when the team was still in New York, having reached the Fall Classic only twice since their 1958 move across the country.

By the time San Francisco won its first title in 2010, the only franchises with longer title droughts were the Chicago Cubs (1908) and Cleveland Indians (1948).

No. 5 was sweet, if calculated: "Become the most community-minded organization in baseball." Part of the reason voters had rejected four previous proposals for a new ballpark was because the Giants were all take and no give. The team complained about cold and dilapidated Candlestick and wanted taxpayers to bail them out.

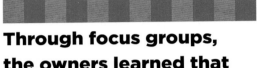

Through focus groups, the owners learned that people did not consider the Giants a public necessity along the lines of, say, the symphony.

Magowan and Baer decided that they could win more support from the community by reaching out. They began holding annual benefits at the ballpark for issues outside the game. "Until There's a Cure Day," first held in 1994, raises awareness about AIDS. "Stop Violence Day" does the same for victims of domestic abuse.

Every player on the Giants roster now regularly participates in a local charity. Baer was named the "Person of the Year" by the San Francisco Boys and Girls Club in 2012.

No. 6 and No. 7 were kind of a package deal. One was "Convince the voters to approve a new ballpark," and the other, "Pay for our facility with no public money."

This is where previous-owner Lurie had run into so many road blocks he surrendered. When a ballot initiative to build a new stadium in San Jose failed on June 2, 1992, it was the last straw.

Magowan and Baer recognized that most citizens voted as taxpayers and not baseball fans. Through focus groups, the owners learned that people did not consider the Giants a public necessity along the lines of, say, the symphony. Taxpayers weren't sympathetic to wealthy owners pleading for more money.

Still, no new major league ballpark had been privately financed since Dodger Stadium 38 years earlier.

Here, the Giants caught a break. From 1996 to '99, when Magowan's group was trying to get its ballpark off the ground, the Bay Area economy raged. "We had wind at our back," Baer remembered. "Wealth was being created, and companies were eager to sign up to help sponsor the ballpark."

They built their new home—originally known as Pacific Bell Park—for $357 million. The financing plan included $172 million from naming rights, other sponsorships, pouring rights for beer sales, concession rights, and the selling of charter seats. The ownership secured another $170 million through a bank loan, and $15 million in tax increment financing from San Francisco's Redevelopment Agency.

The Giants secured their park on a 13-acre site in the neighborhood known as China Basin. The spot was less windy than Candlestick Point—then again, so is the center of a tornado—and with an area primed for new restaurants and bars.

The only thing left to do was to make sure the new house was pretty.

No. 8 was "Design the best ballpark in the country." The goal at the time was to combine the old and the new—the soul of a place like Wrigley Field with the modern amenities of, say, Baltimore's Camden Yards.

"The best $50,000 we ever spent was on a model of what the park would look like," Baer said. "We took it out to the BART stations and to the lobbies of office buildings.... Until then, people had this vision of cranes picking up Candlestick and moving it to the corner of Third and King."

The park was an instant hit, with the glittering views of McCovey Cove and quirky features, such as the oversized glove and Coca-Cola bottle in left field. The *Sports Business Journal* in 2008 named it the "Sports Facility of the Year."

Still, the best part of the yard proved to be the people inside. That was No. 9: "Draw 3 million fans."

Before Pacific Bell Park, the Giants' television ratings were about twice the A's, according to Baer, but the A's won at the box office. More fans went to games at Oakland. In 1992, for example, when the new ownership group took over, the A's drew 2.49 million fans to the Coliseum, while only 1.56 million came to Candlestick Park.

"People thought we were smoking something when we said we could draw 3 million," Baer said.

But the Giants' new ballpark and improved team drew 3 million that very first season, and fans haven't stopped marching in yet. At least that many attended every year from 2000 to '07, becoming one of only four teams to exceed 3 million attendees in eight consecutive seasons.

That's why Magowan and Baer wound up surpassing their final item beyond their wildest dreams. No. 10: "Increase the value of the franchise."

At the time of the purchase, the group paid $100 million.

How'd their investment pay off? In March 2015, *Forbes* magazine valued the Giants franchise at $2 billion.

44

THE ALOUS

When Major League Baseball began widening its doors to Latin players in the 1950s, legendary Giants scout Alex Pompez struck quickly. Well connected from his days as an influential owner in the Negro Leagues, Pompez hired his former shortstop Horacio Martinez to serve as his eyes and ears in the Dominican Republic.

Together, Pompez and Martinez helped the Giants tap into a gold mine that would forever change the face of baseball.

This was no small thing in the days before Latin flair was a daily part of life at AT&T Park. This was before the statues of Orlando Cepeda and Juan Marichal, before reliever Sergio Romo took the mound to the mariachi sounds of "El Mechon," before you could order a Cha-Cha bowl at the concessions stands, before broadcaster Jon Miller bellowed *"Adiós, pelota!"* as a nod to the Spanish-speaking men who hit them.

This was before Felipe Alou.

"Felipe was really the first, the guy who cleared the way," Manny Mota told *Sports Illustrated* in 1985. "He was an inspiration to everybody."

The athletic and powerful outfielder helped pave the way for his countrymen—and his own household. Alou's brothers, Matteo and Jesús, would soon join him in San Francisco, occasionally cramming into the same outfield the way some siblings pile into the back of a minivan.

Felipe Alou became the first Dominican-born player in San Francisco history upon his debut in the summer of 1958. He was just the second Dominican in the major leagues, period—player Ozzie Virgil (another Pompez signee) had broken through with the New York Giants in 1956.

Virgil, though, had gone to high school in New York and was a utility player in the big leagues. Alou's journey to full-fledged star meant more to the players who followed.

Alou would make a name for himself, as a player and as a manager. But—as a sign of the times—the name he made was all wrong. It should have been Felipe Rojas, but he was too self-conscious to correct anyone upon arriving in the U.S.

Alou was born on May 12, 1935, in Bajos de Haina, San Cristobal, near the capital city of Santo Domingo.

His father was Jose Rojas; his mother, Virginia Alou. By Latin custom, each parent contributes half of a double surname—as in *Felipe Rojas Alou*. The paternal half is used in everyday life in the Dominican, which is why people knew the baseball-playing trio of Felipe, Matty, and Jesús as the Rojas brothers.

Mark Armor, whose writing on Alou's name for the SABR Baseball Biography Project informs this chapter, noted that even the last name that stuck around got lost in translation. "Alou" is supposed to rhyme with "allow" not "aloo," but young Felipe let it slide. Instead, he focused on playing ball.

Alou had been an astonishing all-around athlete in the Dominican. He ran sprints and threw the javelin as a track star. He was also the cleanup hitter for the powerhouse University of Santo Domingo baseball team, which is where the Giants connection kicked in.

The baseball coach was Martinez, who had played for Pompez with the New York Cubans. He tipped off Pompez to a lithe outfielder with a powerful line-drive stroke, and the Giants signed him in 1955 for $200.

Fortunately for Alou—and for baseball history—Pompez's role extended beyond his ink on the contract. He knew that his players would need guidance in this new frontier.

When Alou arrived late for his first spring training due to visa problems, Giants coaches told him to come back the next year.

"And Alex Pompez told the Giants that if I was sent back, he would quit," Felipe once told me.

Instead, Alou was dispatched to the Giants' Class C affiliate in Lake Charles, Louisiana, in 1956. But he lasted only nine at-bats before being shipped out again to Class D Cocoa of the Florida State League. It wasn't because of his play; it was because a Louisiana law prevented him from playing on the same field as whites.

Off the field it was no easier, especially in Florida in the mid-1950s. During a long conversation at his AT&T Park office, where he was the Giants' manager from 2003 to 2006, Alou told me that Pompez would shuttle dark-skinned players from the spring training barracks to the ice cream parlor rather than let them walk a mile and a half through a segregated town.

"We didn't know anything," Felipe remembered. "It was Pompez who kept telling us, 'You don't do this, you don't say that, you don't go there at that time.'"

Pompez's careful cultivation of his talent helped the Giants tap into the gold mine of Latin American players before the rest of the big leagues caught on. The Giants landed Cepeda, Juan Marichal, Jose Pagan, Tito Fuentes, and the Alou brothers, all of whom helped fuel a decade of success in the 1960s.

From left: Jesús, Matty, and Felipe Alou pose in a three-way handshake before a game against the Mets at the Polo Grounds.

By 1961, San Francisco had 47 Latinos at spring camp. Among them were 15 Dominicans, 10 Cubans, seven Venezuelans, and six Panamanians.

How far ahead of the curve was San Francisco? The next team to field a Dominican player was Milwaukee, with Rico Carty in 1963.

"The big door of the Dominican was opened by Pompez," Felipe said. "It's not only the talent that he brought in, it was a relationship. Anywhere and everywhere they played baseball—Panama, Colombia, Venezuela, Puerto Rico, Cuba—Pompez was a legend."

The wave made for a heck of a family reunion.

On September 15, 1963, all three Alou boys trotted out to the vast expanses of the Forbes Field outfield. Matty was in left, Jesús was in right, and Felipe was in center.

They are the only trio of brothers ever to occupy the same outfield.

It was remarkable to everyone but them.

They are the only trio of brothers ever to occupy the same outfield.

"At the time, it was the most normal thing for us because we played together in the winter league for years," Felipe told writer Steve Bitker in 2001. "All three of us dominated, with our club winning the pennant three or four years in a row.

"But with the more time that passes, playing together in the same major league outfield becomes to us a bigger accomplishment."

Contrary to popular belief, the three Alous never started in the same Giants outfield. Their togetherness was fleeting, a few innings here and there over three games.

Often forgotten, but no less cool, was that the Alou boys batted back-to-back-to-back on September 10, 1963. Manager Alvin Dark dispatched Jesús and Matty as pinch-hitters before Felipe stepped up. (They went 0 for 3 against New York Mets pitcher Carlton Willey.)

The Giants broke up the Alous after that season, trading Felipe to the Milwaukee Braves. But they kept swinging some mighty lumber from that family tree.

The Alous played in 5,129 games and collected more hits (5,094) than any other trio of brothers in big-league history. (Dom, Joe, and Vince DiMaggio are the closest, at 4,853).

Including Felipe's son, Moises, all four members of the family played in at least one World Series. Felipe and Matty were in the 1962 World Series with the Giants; Jesus played for the '73 and '74 A's, and Moises was with the '97 Florida Marlins.

When Matty won the NL batting title in 1966 with a .342 average for the Pirates, Felipe was the runner-up at .327. It's the only time brothers have finished one-two in a big-league batting race.

Bill James, the writer and baseball historian, determined in 1999 that the Alous were the greatest ball-playing family of all time, concluding that they ranked safely ahead of the DiMaggios, Waners, Boones, Delahantys, and any of baseball's other royal families.

"What makes the Alous number one is that they have had four guys who could actually play, at least some," James wrote. "Several families have had four members reach the majors, but none of the others had four guys who actually stuck around and contributed the way the Alous have."

Felipe was a three-time All-Star who finished his career with 2,101 hits and 206 home runs. He had a monstrous year in 1962, helping San Francisco to its first World Series by batting .316 with 25 home runs and 98 RBI.

"After you get past Willie Mays, he's as good as anyone," manager Alvin Dark said that year.

Felipe also reached the 20-homer mark four times and, while with the Braves, twice led the National League in hits.

Matty, the middle brother, was the second Alou to reach the big leagues. He never found regular playing time with the Giants from 1960 to '65 because he couldn't crack that loaded outfield. "I signed one year after Felipe, but he never told me about Willie Mays—and I was a big center fielder," he told writer Nick Peters.

Matty's finest moment in San Francisco was his rally-starting pinch-hit bunt single in the final game of a three-game tie-breaking playoff series against the Dodgers in 1962.

He had better days elsewhere. A speedy 5'9", 160-pound center fielder, Matty was a lifetime .307 hitter, who had 1,777 hits over 15 seasons with six different teams.

His swing did not, however, win any beauty contests. Matty choked up on a big bat and relied on his wrists to flick the ball. "The worst .300 hitter I've ever seen," Steve Carlton once called him.

Jesús, who broke in during the 1963 season, had a rough start in the majors. For one thing, he had a name issue, too. Some reporters called him "Jay Alou," apparently uncomfortable with the religious connotations of his first name.

"What is wrong with my real name—Jesús?" he asked. "It is a common name in Latin America. My parents named me Jesús, and I am proud of my name. This Jay, I do not like. It is not my name."

During his rookie year, Jesús stepped in against Dodgers ace Don Drysdale and started twitching his neck and shoulders. This was a nervous tick, but no one told the pitcher. Drysdale promptly leveled Jesús with a brush-back pitch. He thought he was being taunted.

But there were better days ahead. Jesús went 6 for 6—five singles and a home run—against the Chicago Cubs on July 10, 1964. He went on to hit .280 over 15 seasons and, with 1,216 hits, gave the Alous a triumvirate of brothers with at least 1,000 hits apiece.

"It's a family legacy," Felipe said. "The Alou legacy is a legacy in itself."

THE 1993 SEASON

They had the four Gold Glove winners, the MVP, the manager of the year, and a pair of 20-game winners.

And in the end, they had nothing.

The 1993 Giants went 103–59, but winning the most games in franchise history wasn't enough. San Francisco finished one game behind the Atlanta Braves for the National League West division title.

This was back before baseball expanded the playoffs to include wild-card teams. This was back when finishing second did as much good as finishing last.

"I guess it just wasn't meant to be," pitcher Bill Swift said, packing his locker and struggling for words the day after the final out. "To have that kind of year and then not having anything to show for it...."

Swift paused.

"And to think," he said. "I was going to pitch tonight."

Instead of loosening up for a playoff game, Swift and the rest of the Giants were left to fathom their impossibly bad luck. Only three other teams in 20th century baseball history—the 1909 Chicago Cubs, the 1942 Brooklyn Dodgers, and the 1954 New York Yankees— won as many games without making the postseason.

"We didn't lose to Atlanta," left fielder Barry Bonds insisted after the Giants were eliminated. "The Braves just won more than we did, and we just happened to be in the same division."

Perhaps worst of all, the Giants' speedboat of a season ended with a Titanic of a loss. On October 3, 1993, the last day of the regular season, manager Dusty Baker entrusted slumping rookie pitcher Salomon Torres to start against the Dodgers. The result was a tire fire: Los Angeles torched Torres en route to a 12–1 victory.

So ended one of the greatest

Instead of loosening up for a playoff game, Swift and the rest of the Giants were left to fathom their impossibly bad luck.

scoreboard-watching summers in Bay Area history. It was like a double-feature every day, with one eye on the Giants and the other on the Braves, who were buoyed by the late-season acquisition of Fred McGriff.

Consider that the Giants went 14–3 down the stretch but still couldn't close the gap.

So addictive was the NL West race in September that even as the Braves boarded the team plane to fly to Philadelphia for the playoffs, third-base coach Jimy Williams turned to broadcaster Pete Van Wieren and asked, "How are the Giants doing today?"

"That was the question we'd been asking for two months, and it was a great relief not to have to think about it anymore," Van Wieren told writer Robert Weintraub for ESPN.com years later. "That was when it really sank in that we'd won."

As late as July 10, San Francisco led Atlanta by 10 games in the standings. Then they fell *behind* by as many as four as late as

September 17. But for the most part, the Giants and Braves were matching each other win for win for win for win for...well, until that last part.

"It was a hell of a year," catcher Kirt Manwaring said. "And we still came up short."

"Best team I ever played on," second baseman Robby Thompson said.

"It was a hell of a year. And we still came up short."

"We did everything but win the title," Baker said. Still, it was fun while they blasted. Bonds hit 46 home runs, drove in 123 runs, and batted .336 for the best season of his young career. The left fielder had already won two MVP awards with the Pittsburgh Pirates before signing with his childhood team, the Giants, where his father, Bobby, and his godfather, Willie Mays, once patrolled the Candlestick Park outfield.

Bonds celebrated his homecoming by becoming the first player to lead the league in slugging percentage (.677) *and* on-base percentage (.458) since Stan Musial of the St. Louis Cardinals in 1948.

"I've had the opportunity to watch the likes of Eddie Mathews, Henry Aaron, Stan Musial, and others, and Barry ranks right up there," Giants general manager Bob Quinn said shortly after Bonds won his third MVP award.

"You can't compare his season to any one season of theirs. [Barry] embodies a combination of their talents."

Bonds represented the first major roster investment by a new ownership group, led by Peter Magowan. The other big move was promoting hitting coach Baker to manager.

Baker instantly infused the franchise with an electric vibe that revived a team coming off of a 72–90 finish. Players loved Baker, whose enthusiasm and smarts endeared him to veterans and younger players alike.

"I think we were characterized by Dusty, who held up all year long," Will Clark said after the season.

Baker became the first rookie manager to win 100 games since Sparky Anderson did it in 1970.

As one of Baker's first acts, he approached pitcher John Burkett in spring training and asked: How many games are you going to win this year?

Baker had done this as the batting coach, too, and Burkett usually replied he'd win something in the 15 range. This time, Burkett said "20."

It was an audacious goal. Burkett had never won more than 14 games in a season and would never win more than 14 again. But in 1993, he underestimated himself: The right-hander wound up the NL leader in wins, tied with future Hall of Famer Tom Glavine, by going 22–7.

Burkett, who was also an elite bowler, kept setting 'em up and knocking 'em down. Relying on four pitches he could throw for strikes—fastball, slider, curve, and splitter—he allowed only 1.554 walks per nine innings and let the Giants stellar defense do the rest.

"One reason I like baseball better than bowling is that bowling is an individual sport," Burkett said on the day he won No. 20. "You can share something like this. Bowling a perfect game isn't close to winning 20."

Burkett was the first Giants pitcher since Mike Krukow in 1986 to win 20 games. And he soon had company. Three days later, Swift would win his 20th game as well.

Like Burkett, Swift was a right-hander who put it all together in '93. He had never won more than 10 games—and would never again win more than 11—but in that magical season, he allowed only 1.074 walks + hits per nine innings. The only NL pitcher better that season was the Braves' Greg Maddux, the future Hall of Famer, at 1.049.

Swift reached milestone win No. 20 on September 26, when he arrived at Candlestick Park early enough to listen to some Frank Sinatra in the clubhouse in honor of his father, a Sinatra fan, who died the previous winter.

Burkett was the first Giants pitcher since Mike Krukow in 1986 to win 20 games. And he soon had company. Three days later, Swift would win his 20th game as well.

"Any time I hear Frank, I think of my dad," Swift said after the 5–2 win. "I always wanted to pitch for my dad. Of 15 kids in the family, I was the one who made it to the big leagues. I learned everything from him."

While Burkett and Swift won big, no one else on the staff started more than 18 games or threw more than 120 innings that season. That the Giants stayed in the race was a testimony to Baker's managing skills, the performance of closer Rod Beck (48 saves), and a defense that covered the field like a tarp.

Bonds, Thompson, Manwaring, and third baseman Matt Williams were all honored for defensive excellence in '93, making the Giants just the 15th team to have four Gold Glove winners in the same season. No team had done it since the 1981 Philadelphia Phillies.

The Giants could have had five: Center fielder Darren Lewis set a major league record that season by extending his streak to

316 consecutive errorless games. In all, the Giants led the league in fielding percentage (.984) for the first time since moving to San Francisco.

There was, however, one thing the Giants couldn't catch that season: the Braves.

"This team is only going to get better next year," Bonds shrugged. "The Giants are going to be good for a long time, maybe a dynasty, if they keep this team together."

Instead, it was the end of the line for that nucleus. Clark, the face of the franchise since '86, signed a free-agent deal with the Texas Rangers in the off-season. Thompson, who broke in as a rookie with Clark, stuck around for three more years, but injuries essentially ended his career. Thompson never played more than 100 games in a season or batted better than .223 again.

The Giants' 103 victories matched the franchise record established in 1962, but the '62 team had the benefit of three games as the result of a tiebreaker with the Dodgers, winning two to decide the NL pennant.

Had the Giants beaten the Dodgers again this time, they would have forced an extra game against the Braves.

Instead, they finished 103-and-no.

"But that's what life is all about," Baker said. "How do you handle the hurt? How do you handle the disappointment?"

46

RICH AURILIA

Rich Aurilia learned baseball from a man who wore a uniform in the Army, not the big leagues. His high school coach at Xaverian High School in Brooklyn spent 30 distinguished years in the service, accomplishing something of a military Triple Crown—surviving World War II, Korea, and Vietnam.

All those tours of duty taught coach Ed Murach lessons about discipline, honor, loyalty, and perseverance. And in turn Murach taught those lessons to a kid who never forgot, not even after he established himself as the most prolific offensive shortstop in San Francisco history.

"He taught me that baseball was secondary," Aurilia told me in 2001. "He wanted to mold his players into being good men. It was almost done in a military sense. At the time, you think he's really harsh on you. But when you look back afterward, you realize what he was doing."

Aurilia grew up to become a fan favorite in San Francisco, largely because of his play but also because of his class. He always acted the right way, even when proving people wrong.

Rich Aurilia singles in a run during Game 4 of the 2002 World Series. (Kevork Djansezian)

The Texas Rangers had taken Aurilia in the 24th round of the 1992 draft. Not long after, a team official approached the young shortstop with some advice. He told Aurilia to focus on his glove work because his bat would be too weak to get him to the big leagues.

That scouting report would get an "E" on the scoreboard.

The Rangers traded Aurilia to the Giants when he was still a minor leaguer, and San Francisco remains eternally grateful. Aurilia became the first National League shortstop since Dave Concepcion to lead all NL shortstops in both home runs and RBI for three consecutive seasons. (Concepcion did it for the Cincinnati Reds from 1978 to 1981; Aurilia did it from 1999 to 2001.)

When Aurilia hit 37 home runs in 2001, he became just the third shortstop in NL history to top 30 homers in a season. The two previous players to do it are in the Hall of Fame: Ernie Banks (six times) and Barry Larkin (in 1996).

Aurilia is one of three San Francisco players to amass 200 hits in a single season, joining Willie Mays and Bobby Bonds.

Not bad for a mid-level draft pick with a supposedly weak bat.

"I was a guy who was told what I couldn't do rather than what I could do," Aurilia said. "I tried to use that stuff to motivate me.

"Now, when I look back on things, I know why I'm in this position. It's because I've worked hard for it. It's also a matter of being in the right place at the right time and finding a team that has confidence in me."

The right place? That was easy. San Francisco acquired Aurilia and infielder Desi Wilson by trading pitcher John Burkett to the Rangers on December 22, 1994.

The right time? Well, that part took a while.

Aurilia barely cracked the roster over his first three seasons with the Giants. He was a September call-up in 1995 and limited to a reserve role over the next two seasons because of a stress fracture in one of his vertebrae.

The allegedly light-hitting kid from St. John's University showed occasional pop—including, ahem, a home run off Burkett in 1996—but he mostly rode the bench.

But Aurilia made a point of keeping his brain in the game even when his body wasn't.

"I don't mean to go on, but what a breath of fresh air this Rich Aurilia guy is."

"When you're not playing every day, sometimes you can get down," he said, looking back. "But I tried to learn a little bit about the other team. I'd ask some of the other guys questions about the pitchers they were facing.

"If you can sit there and learn while the game is going on, even if you're not playing, you'll be better in the long run."

From 1998 to 2003, Aurilia became the first San Francisco shortstop to play in six consecutive Opening Days. He established himself as a force in 1999, when he batted .281 with 22 home runs, 80 RBI, and a .780 OPS. But he struggled defensively, leading NL shortstops with 28 errors.

"I'm still learning as I go," Aurilia shrugged. "Every year I want to do better at something, whether that's a point higher on my average or one less error or one more run scored. My goal is always to say, 'I did better than last season.'"

He'd been doing the same thing since he was a kid in Brooklyn, under the guidance of his military-minded coach. Murach died in 2004 and was buried with full military honors at Arlington National Cemetery.

But he lived long enough to see Aurilia become an All-Star in 2001.

The skill that impressed Murach most? Aurilia's politeness during interviews. The retired U.S. Army sergeant major was watching a Giants-Mets game one night when his former protégé fielded questions from Ralph Kiner, the Hall of Famer turned broadcaster.

Aurilia was so respectful—repeatedly calling his interviewer "Mr. Kiner"—that Kiner continued to touch on it throughout the broadcast.

"I don't mean to go on," Kiner told his audience, "but what a breath of fresh air this Rich Aurilia guy is."

Murach's reaction: "I'm so proud of him. He is really and truly a hero. He's a family man. He's a gentleman. You never see him throw tantrums like so many ballplayers these days."

Aurilia got plenty of practice with the media during his sensational year of 2001. He batted .324 with 37 home runs, 97 RBI, and a .572 slugging percentage. That home run total was the most by a NL shortstop since Banks hit 41 in 1960.

Aurilia also shattered the Giants' single-season record for shortstops, previously held by Alvin Dark (23 in 1953).

It wasn't just the long ball. Aurilia led the NL with 206 hits that season, joining Mays and Bonds as the only San Francisco players to top 200.

"I think all every player really wants is consistency, hopefully successful consistency," Aurilia told Henry Schulman of the *San Francisco Chronicle* on October 2, 2001, the day after the shortstop reached the milestone. "To get 200 hits and be mentioned with Bobby Bonds and Willie Mays is an incredible feeling."

Of course, that season Aurilia also had the unprecedented benefit of batting ahead of a player on his way to hitting 73 home runs. Aurilia hit second in the lineup, one spot ahead of Barry Bonds.

Pitchers were so intent on not putting anyone on base before Bonds came to the plate that they pounded the strike zone with Aurilia at the plate rather than risking a walk.

But teammates sometimes rankled at that convenient theory. They said Aurilia deserved more credit for his growth as a hitter. The guy could hit, whether he had Bonds as his bodyguard or not.

Aurilia's final numbers over 15 seasons include a .275 average, 186 home runs, and 756 RBI.

"I think his patience has paid off more than anything," said Jeff Kent, another player whose power emerged late. "He's being selective at the plate. He's going up there with a game plan and then following through."

General manager Brian Sabean said: "Good things happen to good people. [His] success didn't happen by accident."

Whatever the reason, Aurilia is the only Giants shortstop to have three different 20-homer seasons (only Alvin Dark had two). And he and Kent became the first pair of middle infielders to each hit 20 home runs in three consecutive seasons.

Aurilia's production dipped to 15 home runs and 61 RBI during the 2002 regular season. But he saved something for dessert: He had 17 RBI during the postseason alone, a binge that put him back among elite company. Those 17 RBI were the most by a shortstop in a single playoffs since 1974, shattering the previous mark (11) shared by Bucky Dent, Nomar Garciaparra, Orlando Cabrera, and Tony Fernandez.

That feat is barely remembered for two reasons. One, the Giants lost the 2002 World Series to the Anaheim Angels. Two, Aurilia always made his feats easy to forget by sailing under the radar.

"I'm not a high-profile guy," he said back then. "I don't like a lot of attention. When I'm out of this game, and guys I played against say I played the game the right way, that's all I really need."

Aurilia signed a free agent deal with the Seattle Mariners in 2004, going on to spend a few seasons with the San Diego Padres and Cincinnati Reds. But for his final two seasons in the big leagues (2008–09), he returned home, to San Francisco.

Of course he did.

"Bringing Richie back to San Francisco is a truly exciting day for the Giants," Sabean said in announcing the signing. "He clearly is a highly productive player...while his character and desire to win are unquestioned."

Aurilia's final numbers over 15 seasons include a .275 average, 186 home runs, and 756 RBI.

He now works occasionally as a broadcaster for Comcast Sports Net Bay Area and is active in the Make-A-Wish Foundation.

Aurilia and Dave Roberts, another former Giant, are also part of the team behind Red Stitch Wine in Napa Valley. There's a note on their website about how Red Stitch should be enjoyed. They want their fans to raise a glass to "memories of love and laughter with those who make up the fabric of your life." Murach would surely be one of those.

47

BOBBY BONDS

Bobby Bonds blended power at the plate, speed on the bases, and grace in the outfield.

About the only weakness in his game was timing. Bonds arrived in the majors in the late 1960s, when being a supernova Giants outfielder meant being anointed as "the next Willie Mays."

"When they told me that, it was an honor," Bonds told the *Los Angeles Times* in 1990. "You're talking about a guy who I considered the greatest player to ever wear shoes.

"I probably had more success than anyone they ever put that label on. You show me another guy who's going to do 30-30 five times.

"But all the writers kept talking about was potential. 'You haven't reached your potential yet,' they say. Well, unless you win a Pulitzer Prize, you're not living up to your potential either, are you?"

Bonds' career would also be eclipsed by his famous son, Barry. But those who resist the temptation to compare Bobby Bonds to anyone else can appreciate him on his own merits.

And in that light, teams would be lucky to find "the next Bobby Bonds."

"So much power, so much speed," Hall of Fame pitcher Juan Marichal told the *San Francisco Chronicle* in 2003, shortly after Bonds died at age 57. "Bobby had everything to become a great ballplayer, and he played hard to win."

In a career spanning 14 major league seasons—his first seven in San Francisco, from 1968 to 1974—Bobby Bonds hit 332 home runs and stole 461 bases. He was a three-time All-Star and won three Gold Glove Awards.

Bobby Bonds wasn't the first to join the 30-30 Club, but he remains among the most prominent members. The right-handed hitter delivered at least 30 home runs and stole at least 30 bases in the same season five times. The only other player to have done it five times is his son.

Bobby was just the third National League player to reach the 30-30 plateau, following Mays and Hank Aaron. Bobby did it for the first time in 1969 then again in '73, when he fell one homer short of establishing a 40-40 club. (Four players have since done it, including Barry Bonds in 1996.)

"Bobby had that world-class speed," former infielder Sonny Jackson told Bonds' hometown paper, the *Riverside Press-Enterprise*, in 2001. "With his quick acceleration, he was going full speed in a heartbeat. He was as fast as anyone I've ever seen. He had great power, and he was a terrific outfielder with better arm strength than Barry."

Bonds also racked up strikeout totals that would make Rob Deer blush. A leadoff hitter who swung hard and unapologetically, he whiffed a major league record of 187 times in 1969. The next year, he broke his own record by striking out 189 times. (He also struck out at least 120 times in eight other years.)

His single-season strikeout mark stood for more than 20 years—withstanding the wild cuts of Deer, Reggie Jackson, and Steve Balboni—before Adam Dunn claimed the dubious crown with 195 in 2004. (The record now belongs to Mark Reynolds, with 223 in 2009.)

Did it bother Bonds to strike out that much? Nope, he was A-okay with all those Ks.

"He was the first guy that I ever played with that did not sulk after he struck out...for the third time," said Giants broadcaster Duane Kuiper, who played with Bonds in 1979, when both were with the Cleveland Indians.

Bobby and Barry Bonds walk off the field at the Giants' spring training facility in 1993. (Gary Stewart)

Kuiper pointed to Bonds' well-known response for whenever managers urged him to make better contact. Bonds once said, "If you get 200 hits a season, you're going to hit .333 and you'll still have 400 outs. I don't see why you have to run down to first base every time you make an out."

He really did get those 200 hits, albeit just once. Bobby hit exactly that milestone in 1970; the only other two San Francisco players with 200 hits in a season are Mays (208 in 1958) and Rich Aurilia (206 in 2001).

Bonds also stole 48 bases in '70. The only Giants to surpass that total are Billy North (58) and Brett Butler (51).

Because of Bonds' speed, managers insisted on using him as a leadoff hitter. In one respect, it worked: The same season he broke the strikeout record, Bonds also scored 134 runs—a San Francisco record that still stands. The next best total in team history? The 131 Bonds scored in 1971.

He opened a game with a home run 35 times, which ranks seventh on the all-time list. Bonds' 11 leadoff homers in '73 stood as an NL record until Alfonso Soriano broke it in 2007. Bonds was MVP of the All-Star Game that summer in Kansas City, and the *Sporting News* named him major league player of the year.

"He was one of the first of the new breed of leadoff guys who could steal bases and hit home runs," Hall of Famer Willie McCovey told the *Chronicle* in 2003. "It was perfect for us when he came along."

Bonds made it clear right away that he had a knack for strong starts. In his major league debut on June 25, 1968, the 22-year-old kid started in right field against the Los Angeles Dodgers at Candlestick Park.

Bonds came to bat against John Purdin in the sixth inning with the bases loaded—McCovey at third base, Mays at second, and

Jimmy Ray Hart at first. He blasted one into the seats to become the first player with a grand slam in his debut game since Bill Duggleman in 1898.

Bonds, who had been leading the Pacific Coast League with a .367 average, said he was just happy to bring his hot streak to the majors.

"I had three grand slams in a month at Phoenix," he explained that day.

Even before the memorable intro, there was plenty of "next Willie Mays" hype around the fleet, powerful outfielder. Bonds grew up

The right-handed hitter delivered at least 30 home runs and stole at least 30 bases in the same season five times. The only other player to have done it five times is his son.

with expectation. He was such an astonishing star growing up in Riverside, California, that young athletes now play at the Bobby Bonds Park & Sport Complex Center.

His exploits as a four-sport star at Riverside Poly High School—baseball, football, basketball, and track—captured the imagination of another promising young ballplayer in the city.

"He was my childhood hero," Dusty Baker remembered, years later. "I wanted to be Bobby Bonds."

After Bonds' grand start with the Giants, they ultimately cleared the path for the flashy center fielder by trading Mays to the New York Mets in 1972. Bonds eventually teamed with Garry Maddox and Gary Matthews in what Bonds often said was "the fastest outfield in baseball history."

But after he had an off-year in 1974, the Giants traded Bonds to the New York Yankees for Bobby Murcer. The deal was widely viewed as a swap of "the next Mays" for the one who was to be "the next Mickey Mantle."

So began a vagabond career for Bonds, whose abrasive personality and personal problems battling alcoholism often led to short stays. He bounced from the Angels (1976–77) to the Chicago White Sox ('78) to the Texas Rangers (also '78) to the Indians ('79) to the Cardinals ('80) to the Cubs ('81).

Bonds did not sustain his superstar stats, but he still had his moments. Giants broadcaster Mike Krukow, who played with Bonds on the Cubs, recalled a late-season series against the Cardinals that year. Unbeknownst to the other Cubs, Cardinals president August Busch Jr. had said that Bonds was absolutely through as a player.

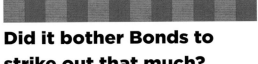

Did it bother Bonds to strike out that much? Nope, he was A-okay with the all those Ks.

Bonds responded by going 4 for 15 with four homers and eight RBI in the series, leading Chicago to a three-game sweep.

"Back then, it was a big deal to hit the ball off the Marty Marion Restaurant. And he hit like six balls off the face of it—three were fair; three were foul," Krukow recalled. "He just had the most amazing series. He just went off. He made his point to Augie Busch."

Bonds returned to the Giants as a batting coach under Baker from 1993 to '96. There was no question about his prize pupil. It was the same powerful left-hander he'd been teaching since the kid was in the third grade.

"My dad was always the eyes behind my head," Barry Bonds told MLB.com writer Barry Bloom in 2007. "He'd keep me motivated better than anybody. There was always something I had to prove to my father."

Bobby and Barry hold the all-time father-son homer record by a comfortable margin. They combined for 1,094, far ahead of Ken Griffey Sr. and Jr. (782). The Bondsmen also combined for 17 All-Star selections and 11 Gold Glove Awards.

But Bobby's connection to the Giants went beyond his bloodlines. When he died on August 23, 2003, it hit San Francisco hard.

"Losing someone like Bobby is like losing family," McCovey told the *Chronicle*. "You hear that from some teams, but for us it was true. We were family when we played, and we thought we'd always stay together.

"It's a tough loss, but I'm glad he and Barry were close at the end. That meant a lot to me, to see them close like that."

48

STU MILLER

Whenever people start talking about the howling winds at Candlestick Park, someone inevitably brings up the time Stu Miller got blown off the mound at the 1961 All-Star Game.

Don't be a sucker.

For one thing, the story is wildly exaggerated. The Giants reliever swayed noticeably, rocking three inches or so, but he did not get whisked away like some tumbleweed.

For another, the myth obscures the most important thing to know about the man, the reason he was on that All-Star mound to begin with: Stuart Leonard Miller threw arguably the greatest change-up of all time.

"He made the big hitters look like they were swatting at flies," Billy Pierce said.

"Oh, it was incredible," Mike McCormick said.

"The best I've ever seen," Felipe Alou said.

Miller spent 16 years in the major leagues and had some of his best years with the Giants, in both New York and San Francisco. He led the National League with a 2.47 ERA in 1958, the team's first year on the West Coast.

Saves were not an official stat until 1969, but applied retroactively Miller would have led the league twice. He went 14–6 with a 2.66 ERA and 17 "saves" in that All-Star year of 1961 and later put up outstanding numbers for the Baltimore Orioles.

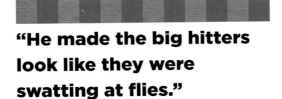

"He made the big hitters look like they were swatting at flies."

Miller did it all with a fastball so slow that his mom probably let him throw it in the house. His weapon wasn't the heat, it was the stupidity. He told me that he always counted on hitters to look for a fastball, especially in pressure situations.

"Even if they have a Ph.D. in physical education, most hitters are idiots once they get in the batter's box," he told me.

Hitters were smart enough to eventually give him his respect. A 1987 book called *The Players Choice* asked 645 former players to name the pitcher with the best change-up. The honor went to Miller, who'd been retired since 1968.

Later, writers Rob Neyer and Bill James compiled an exhaustive guide to pitchers' repertories. *The Neyer/James Guide to Pitchers* also ranks the hurlers who had the best version of every pitch. The writers determined that the best curveball in history belonged to Sandy Koufax, the best slider to Steve Carlton, the best screwball to Carl Hubbell—and the best change-up to Miller. (The best fastball was broken down by half decade, with names such as Walter Johnson, Bob Feller, and Nolan Ryan making the cut.)

But there's no need to read an entire book. Those who saw Miller pitch during his Giants days say they can define the pitcher by one batter.

"The best way to explain his change-up is this: Frank Howard," said Gaylord Perry, the Hall of Fame pitcher and Miller's teammate with the Giants.

Howard was a 6'7", 255-pound beast who looked like he ate a middle infielder for lunch. He was precisely the type of behemoth Miller drove crazy with a repertoire described as "slow, slower, and slowest" by former Orioles teammate Milt Pappas.

Miller told me his change-up probably traveled at about 75 mph, but former players swear it never touched 70 mph. Ed Bailey, one of his catchers, used to say that he could catch Miller with a pair of pliers.

Whatever the speed, Howard couldn't hit it.

"Honest to goodness, I remember a time Howard swung at Stu's change-up and the ball wasn't even halfway to home plate," said Juan Marichal, the Giants Hall of Famer.

Miller struck out Howard the first four times he faced him in '61. The reliever threw a total of 12 pitches in those at-bats—all strikes, according to Baseball-Reference.com—and Howard didn't come close to making contact, according to the Giants who saw it.

"We would just laugh until the game was over," Perry said.

"Even some of the Dodgers would start laughing," third baseman Jim Davenport said. "Frank would say, 'Throw a fastball!' But Stu didn't have a fastball."

Technically, Miller did have a fastball. By most estimates, it would have barely topped 80 mph had there been radar guns. And Marichal said Miller rarely dared to throw it in the strike zone: He would show it to hitters mostly as a way of establishing the change of speed.

In 2007, the Giants threw a party for all of their former All-Stars. More than two dozen players came back, including players like

Marichal, Willie Mays, and Will Clark. I approached Miller that day, notebook in hand, and assured him I had come in peace.

"I don't want to ask you about wind," I said.

"Good," he replied.

Instead, we shot the breeze about his dragon-slayer of a pitch.

Miller, who was 79 at the time, said he was at Class D in the St. Louis Cardinals farm system when manager Vedie Himsl summoned his pitchers for a meeting.

"He said, 'You have to come up with a change-up. And the key is to make it look like a fastball.' That's all he said. And I thought, 'That sounds good.'

"I went out and threw one and he said, 'Oh, my gosh.' It came that naturally."

The ball floated unpredictably. Alou, who played with Miller from 1958 to 1962, recalled playing catch with Miller in the outfield one day and asking Miller to throw his change-up. It nailed Alou in the chest.

"I couldn't catch it," Alou said. "You call it a change-up, but it was really more of a breaking ball."

Just as the pitch itself came easily to Miller, so did his grip on a new philosophy. He learned that big hitters in big situations geared up for the heat. So Miller threw cotton balls.

"The harder you throw, the better they like it," he said. "You hum one by them for strike three, and they think, that's fine."

But beat them with something slow?

"They wanted to eat that bat and me along with it," he said.

Roberto Clemente hit .125 (5 for 40) against Miller. Harmon Killebrew hit .167 (3 for 18) and Mickey Mantle .188 (3 for 16 with six strikeouts). Howard hit .250 (6 for 24 with a home run and six strikeouts).

As if hitters weren't flummoxed enough by the slow ball, Miller had another quirk. When he began his windup, his head popped around his shoulders like a jack-in-the-box.

"He had this little—I don't know how else to explain it—jerk action with his neck," said McCormick, the 1967 Cy Young Award winner. "Most batters were fooled by that, started to commit, and then here comes the change-up.

"He made some fool-looking hitters out of some pretty big names over his career."

But beat them with something slow? "They wanted to eat that bat and me along with it."

Miller said he developed that delivery the same way he came up with everything else—almost by accident.

"It was involuntary," he said. "I couldn't help it.... But if my head disturbed them a little bit, all the better."

Miller is most known, of course, for one particularly involuntary movement on the All-Star mound on July 11, 1961.

Oh, yes. That.

Indeed, he committed a costly balk during the ninth inning while trying to preserve the NL's 3–2 lead. (He relieved Koufax, the best curveball of all time being replaced by the best change-up.)

With Rocky Colavito at the plate, the story goes that a hurricane-force wind caused Miller to tumble from the rubber. But the actual gust—the genuine Miller draft—caused what the pitcher called "a little sway." A young Giants fan watching on TV said it was more than that.

"Oh, it was noticeable," said the college student, Peter Magowan, who is now grown up and owns the team. "He toppled enough to make it an obvious balk."

Umpire Stan Landes agreed, sending Al Kaline to third and Roger Maris to second; Kaline scored the tying run on an error by third baseman Ken Boyer.

The Miller incident has become legendary over time, with the myth steadily eroding reality. It is common for people to talk about the time Miller "was blown off the mound" as a casual statement of fact. And even when the accounts are accurate, the long-ago gust seems to blow away everything else he did.

When Miller died on January 6, 2015, the *New York Times* headline said: "Miller, All-Star Who Committed a Windblown Balk, Dies at 87." The first line of his Associated Press obituary began, "Stu Miller, who committed perhaps the most famous balk in All-Star Game history at windy Candlestick Park...."

Fortunately, some of Miller's famous friends are more protective of his memory. I once watched a radio reporter ask Willie Mays about the time Miller got blown of the mound.

"Stu didn't get blown off the mound," Mays shot back. "Get it right, man."

Mays has a point. When it comes to Stu Miller, here's hoping people remember his career as it should be remembered.

For a change.

JIM
DAVENPORT

They gave Willie McCovey the nickname "Stretch" because of the first baseman's ability to extend his arms for a late or wayward throw.

With Davenport at third base, there was no stretching necessary.

"He gave you a perfect throw all the time," McCovey said.

The slick-fielding Davenport was one of the Giants' early, if underappreciated, stars. Overshadowed in the era of McCovey, Willie Mays, and Orlando Cepeda, the soft-spoken Alabaman was a steady contributor to the powerhouse teams of the early 1960s.

By the time Davenport retired after the 1970 season, he'd played 1,501 career games—all for the Giants. The only men to play more games in a San Francisco uniform are McCovey (2,256), Mays (2,095), and Barry Bonds (1,976).

"Jimmy is as much a part of the Giants organization as me and Mays," McCovey told Chris Haft of MLB.com in 2014. "We got all the publicity, but we all appreciated Jimmy. He looked up to guys like myself and Mays, but we looked up to him as much as he did us."

Davenport was an All-Star and a Gold Glove winner during the Giants' World Series season of 1962.

One of the original San Francisco Giants, he was one of three rookies to crack the Opening Day lineup when the team played its first game upon arrival from New York. Davenport also had the distinction of taking the Giants' first West Coast at-bat, striking out against Don Drysdale of the Los Angeles Dodgers in the bottom of the first inning at Seals Stadium on April 15, 1958.

Things got better from there. Davenport went on to lead the NL in sacrifice hits in '58 and was named to the all-rookie team by the *Sporting News*.

He'd joined the Giants during spring training that season because of his obvious cool at the hot corner. Coaches got one look at Davenport's reliable

Davenport also had the distinction of taking the Giants' first West Coast at-bat.

glove work and paved the way for their third baseman of the future. He got the job ahead of incumbent Ray Jablonski, even though Jablonski was coming off a season in which he batted .289 with 57 RBI and a .346 on-base percentage.

"I was fortunate in that I could catch the ball, but I couldn't hit [as well as] Ray at that time," Davenport told author Steve Bitker in his book, *The Original San Francisco Giants*. "We got to be very good friends after a while, before he was traded at the end of that season.

"I was fortunate because we had so many good hitters around me, so that I didn't have to be a home run hitter to make the club.... No knock on Ray, but he was not a real good fielder."

As it turned out, Davenport could hit a little bit, too. On September 12, 1958, he went 7 for 10 in a doubleheader sweep of the Philadelphia Phillies. The rookie's day included a home run in each game and seven runs scored.

James Houston Davenport, born August 17, 1933, in Siuria, Alabama, grew up dreaming of being a professional football player. Davenport's powerful, accurate arm in the diamond was actually honed from years of tight spirals.

In his plans, his first stop was supposed to be playing college football for the Alabama Crimson Tide—until he learned that 'Bama would not sign married athletes. He'd married Betty when he was a junior in high school. So Davenport headed instead for Mississippi Southern on a football scholarship.

His career as a quarterback there included back-to-back upset wins over the same Alabama team that had turned him away for being hitched. It made for a lovely belated wedding present.

Davenport played well enough at Southern Miss to earn a spot in the school's athletic Hall of Fame. He was inducted in 2006, the same year as soccer star Mia Hamm.

By the time Davenport's college career was winding down, he recognized he wasn't a good enough passer to play in the NFL. So he signed with the New York Giants—the baseball version—as an amateur free agent in 1955.

Davenport went on to lead National League third basemen in fielding percentage three consecutive times, starting in 1959. When he won his Gold Glove in '62, he interrupted an 11-year string in which either Ken Boyer or Ron Santo won the award.

Davenport was the only Giants infielder to win a Gold Glove until first baseman Will Clark and third baseman Matt Williams each won one in 1991.

"The first thing you think about Jim as a player is that glove at third base," McCovey told MLB.com. "He wasn't flashy like Brooks Robinson, but he could really pick it over there. He was the best I've ever seen."

GIANTS GOLD GLOVE WINNERS

1957: OF Willie Mays
1958: OF Willie Mays
1959: OF Willie Mays, OF Jackie Brandt
1960: OF Willie Mays
1961: OF Willie Mays
1962: 3B Jim Davenport, OF Willie Mays
1963: OF Willie Mays
1964: OF Willie Mays
1965: OF Willie Mays
1966: OF Willie Mays
1967: OF Willie Mays
1968: OF Willie Mays
1971: OF Bobby Bonds
1973: OF Bobby Bonds
1974: OF Bobby Bonds
1987: P Rick Reuschel
1991: 1B Will Clark, 3B Matt Williams
1993: OF Barry Bonds, C Kirt Manwaring, 2B Robby Thompson, 3B
    Matt Williams
1994: OF Barry Bonds, OF Darren Lewis, 3B Matt Williams
1996: OF Barry Bonds
1997: OF Barry Bonds, 1B J.T. Snow
1998: OF Barry Bonds, 1B J.T. Snow
1999: 1B J.T. Snow
2000: 1B J.T. Snow
2003: OF Jose Cruz, Jr.
2005: C Mike Matheny, SS Omar Vizquel
2006: SS Omar Vizquel

Willie Mays was voted to the All-Time Gold Glove Team, announced by Rawlings in 2007

Davenport once played a record 97 consecutive errorless games at third base, a string that ran from July 26, 1966, to April 28, 1968. That mark stood until 2000, when John Wehner of the Pittsburgh Pirates made it 99 games.

"Jim was a human vacuum at third base, and a hell of a major league prospect," Cepeda told *Baseball Digest*. "A great teammate. I liked him right away."

That '62 season would also be Davenport's best with the bat—by far. He batted .297 with 14 home runs and 58 RBI.

Davenport was the only Giants infielder to win a Gold Glove until first baseman Will Clark and third baseman Matt Williams each won one in 1991.

Davenport might have done even better, had a fastball from Drysdale not broken his hand in mid-August. He missed about two weeks, which might explain why he once said: "The trick against Drysdale is to hit him before he hits you."

Davenport capped his best season by nudging San Francisco into the World Series. In the finale of a three-game NL playoff against the Dodgers, he drew a bases-loaded walk off Stan Williams to force home Felipe Alou with the go-ahead run in the ninth inning. The Giants held on to win 6–4, capturing their first NL pennant.

"We had the type of club that year where we were always going to catch up," Davenport told Bitker. "I don't care how many runs we were behind, we had the type of club that could put some quick numbers on the board, with McCovey, Cepeda, Mays, and the Alous.

"We just felt lucky going into the ninth inning that we were not beat. Luckily, Stan Williams walked me on a 3-and-1 pitch to bring home the winning runs. We got to be good friends after that, and now when I see Stan, he says, 'I should be wearing that World Series ring.'"

Davenport spent his entire 13-year big-league career with the Giants and later worked in capacities that included scout, coach, minor league instructor, big-league manager, and finally, a special assistant for player development. By the time of his death on February 18, 2016, he had spent 51 years in the organization.

He still ranks among San Francisco's all-time leaders in hits (eighth) and triples (tied with Will Clark for seventh). In 1982, he was voted by the fans as the third baseman on the Giants' 25th Anniversary Dream Team and to this day is regarded as one of the best defensive infielders in team history.

Davenport also has a claim to infamy in the organization, serving as manager for the 1985 team that lost 100 games for the only time in franchise history. The team was 56–88 at the time of his firing.

He had brief coaching stints over the years with the San Diego Padres, Philadelphia Phillies, and Detroit Tigers but returned to the Giants for good in 1993.

"They've been awfully good to me, no question about that," Davenport told MLB.com. "Everything I have, I owe to the Giants, that's for sure."

50

BRANDON CRAWFORD

There's a now-famous Brandon Crawford photo unearthed from deep in the *San Francisco Chronicle* archives.

It shows little Brandon, age five, looking forlorn and leaning against a railing at Candlestick Park. Next to him is a handmade orange sign that says, "Do what's right! Keep Giants in SF."

Taken in late September 1992, the photo hails from when the franchise seemed destined to relocate to Tampa, Florida. Brandon was a fan in the stands for what could have been the last home series in San Francisco, and a *Chronicle* photographer was on hand to document the gloom.

Click!

Flash forward nearly two decades and the kid stays in the picture. The Giants never left and, in a way, neither did Crawford. The Bay Area native grew up to be the team's dazzling defensive shortstop with a knack for the big hit.

"It truly is a dream come true," Crawford said in October of 2012. "When I was a little kid, this is what I dreamed about, going to the World Series with the Giants, playing shortstop, and it's all kind of just coming together. It's awesome."

It's a cute story. But things haven't always been picture perfect. Crawford took a while to develop.

As a rookie in 2011, the left-handed batter hit just .204 with a .288 on-base percentage. Those totals crept up to .248/.304 in his second season, but he still struck out 95 times in 435 at-bats.

Memorable as it was, it was hardly Crawford's biggest home run for the Giants. Heck, it wasn't even his biggest grand slam.

In the field, Crawford would make an eye-popping play one moment and an eye-gouging miscue the next. For three consecutive seasons starting in 2012, he ranked in the league's top three for errors.

Absurd as it seems in retrospect—now that he has blossomed as one of the league's best glovemen—there were times when Crawford had to assure fans that he could catch the ball.

"I know I'm a good defender," Crawford insisted after a two-error game on May 3, 2012, part of an early season slump. "It'll come back. All the errors have been a little different. There's not one key I've been focused on. I'm sure I'll get out of it."

And if he missed a ball, the Giants backed him up.

"You have a young player and there's going to be ups and downs," manager Bruce Bochy said then. "He's a gifted shortstop."

Eventually, Crawford caught on. The man raised as a Giants fan emerged as a key cog, offensively and defensively, for World Series–winning teams in 2012 and '14.

In 2015, he became the first Giants player to win the Gold Glove and Silver Slugger awards in the same season since Barry Bonds did it in 1997.

"This guy has a burning desire to be a great player," bench coach Ron Wotus said during the 2014 playoffs. "He works as hard as any infielder I've ever had in San Francisco. And we've had some great ones. Omar Vizquel, J.T. Snow come to mind. But Brandon never takes a day off on defense. Never."

Even in those tough early days, Crawford showed flashes of what was to come. In his major league debut, on May 27, 2011, the Bay Area native hit a grand slam in the seventh inning off the Brewers' Shaun Marcum in Milwaukee.

Only five previous players had hit a home run in their first big-league game (including Bobby Bonds of the Giants in 1968). Crawford had been called up from Class-A San Jose just two nights earlier. And here he was circling the bases on a night that would end with a postgame shaving-cream pie to the face.

Welcome to the big leagues, kid.

"It was all unreal," Crawford said that night. "Awesome. I mean, I still kind of have the jitters about it."

Oft-forgotten is that the homer had extra meaning for a team in crisis. It was two days after Buster Posey, the MVP catcher, went down in a heap after getting wiped out at the plate by hard-charging base runner Scott Cousins of the Florida Marlins.

Posey's season was over, and, as the Giants knew, their playoff chances probably were, too. On their morose team flight to Milwaukee, Bochy had gathered his players for a "soldier on" pep talk.

"We talked about a few things," Bochy said later that night. "The loss of Buster, how important it's going to be to move forward.

That's what Buster would want. We need to find out how good we can be without Buster. We have to answer that question."

Crawford's slam transformed a 3–1 deficit into a 5–3 lead, and the Giants held on for a 5–4 victory.

"That was a big moment for him, but a bigger moment for the team considering what we've gone through," winning pitcher Tim Lincecum said that night.

Memorable as it was, it was hardly Crawford's biggest home run for the Giants. Heck, it wasn't even his biggest grand slam.

The Giants' path to the 2014 World Series began with a treacherous journey to Pittsburgh for a one-game National League wild-card playoff. Playing on the road and facing red-hot Edinson Volquez—a 1.08 ERA in five September starts—San Francisco's playoff run could have lasted all of nine innings.

Instead, Crawford crushed a fourth-inning pitch into the right-field seats at PNC Park. That broke open a scoreless game and propelled the Giants toward an 8-0 victory.

"You're just looking for a timely hit," Bochy said, "and we couldn't have gotten a bigger one."

Crawford became the first shortstop to hit a postseason grand slam, as well as the first not to care about such trivia.

"It's obviously cool to do something like that, but you can't hit a grand slam without the guys in front of you getting on base," he said. "So it's kind of a team thing in that sense, and I'm just glad it helped us get a win. That's what matters, in the end."

It was the first postseason grand slam by a Giant since Posey hit one in the decisive Game 5 of the 2012 NLDS. Only three other players besides those Giants teammates have slammed in a do-or-die playoff game: Bill "Moose" Skowron (1956 World Series), Troy O'Leary (1999 ALDS), and Johnny Damon (2004 ALDS).

While his bat provides the footnotes, Crawford's glove provides the footage. A highlight reel of Crawford's best defensive plays could win both a Gold Glove and a Golden Globe.

"He's a wizard out there at shortstop," Giants starter Tim Hudson said after a 1–0, 12-inning victory on April 9, 2015. "He makes all the routine plays and makes all the tough plays seem routine. We expect that from him every day. We don't take it for granted. Especially for me, a guy who likes to keep the ball on the ground and pitch to contact, he's a breath of fresh air."

Crawford became the first shortstop to hit a postseason grand slam, as well as the first not to care about such trivia.

After a game against the Los Angeles Dodgers, pitcher Ryan Vogelsong was asked to explain his game plan.

"Getting ground balls to Crawford," he replied. "That was the plan."

Fielding prowess is difficult to quantify, although advanced metrics from FanGraphs.com, Baseball Prospectus, and Baseball Info Solutions are helping to sort through the haze. The quick version, for those not fluent in DRS (defensive runs saved) or dWAR (defensive wins above replacement), is that Crawford rated highly for several years. In 2015, he moved closer to the elite shortstops, working his way into the conversation with the astounding Andrelton Simmons of the Atlanta Braves.

Unofficially, Crawford also rates highly in the Repressed Smiles category. That's because he tries not to show even a hint of celebration after a nifty catch. He'll make a diving backhanded grab and act as if it was a harmless pop-up.

"That's kind of like pimping home runs for me, like how guys will stand there in the fifth inning and watch their two-run home run," Crawford told writer Alex Pavlovic of Comcast Sports Net Bay Area in 2014. "I don't do that. I try and act like you've been there before. Act like you've done it before.

"There are already so many ups and downs throughout the course of the season and the game that I don't want to get too fired up or down on myself. If I make a good play, that's great, but I still have to go hit, and it's not an easy thing to do if you're too emotional."

Crawford can act like he's been there because, of course, he has. He grew up less than an hour from San Francisco, attending Foothill High in Pleasanton. He even has playoff experience: Crawford was nine months old when his father, Mike, took him to the playoff series against St. Louis in 1987.

The Giants took the 6'2", 215-pound infielder out of UCLA in the fourth round of the 2008 draft. Eventually, everything fell into place.

Click!

"I got choked up," his mother, Lynn, told Ann Killion of the *San Francisco Chronicle*. "How many mothers get to see their child fulfill the dream they've had since they were little?"